Southern African Wildlife

A VISITOR'S GUIDE

Mike Unwin

edition
2

www.bradtguides.com

Bradt Travel Guides Ltd, UK
The Globe Pequot Press Inc, USA
Wild Dog Press, South Africa

Reprinted January 2014
Second edition published June 2011
First published May 2005

Bradt Travel Guides Ltd
IDC House, The Vale, Chalfont St Peter, Bucks SL9 9RZ, England
www.bradtguides.com
Published in the USA by The Globe Pequot Press Inc,
PO Box 480, Guilford, Connecticut 06437-0480

ISBN: 978 1 84162 347 4

British Library Cataloguing in Publication Data
A catalogue record for this book is available from the British Library

Photographs
Principal photographers: Philip Perry (PP), Mike Unwin (MU) and Ariadne Van Zandbergen (AZ)

Additional photographs: Hilary Bradt (HB); Kevin Carlson/Nature photographers (KC);
Richard Du Toit (RT); Nick Garbutt (NG); Kathy Gemmell (KG); Michael Gore/Nature
photographers (MG); Jack Jackson (JJ); Chris McIntyre (CM); Rod de Vletter (RdV)

With kind permission of Frank Lane Picture Agency (www.flpa.com): Stephen Belcher (SB/FLPA);
Neil Bowman (NB/FLPA); Jim Brandenburg (JB/FLPA); Jonathan Carlile (JC/FLPA); Nigel Cattlin
(NC/FLPA); Peter Davey (PD/FLPA); Nigel Dennis (ND/FLPA); Wendy Dennis (WD/FLPA);
Reinhard Dirscheri (RD/FLPA); Dickie Duckett (DD/FLPA); Richard Du Toit (RT/FLPA);
Gerry Ellis (GE/FLPA); Suzi Eszterhas (SE/FLPA); Tim Fitzharris (TF/FLPA); Michael & Patricia
Fogden (M&PF/FLPA); Bob Gibbons (BG/FLPA); Patricio Robles Gil (PRG/FLPA); Vincent Grafhorst
(VG/FLPA); Christian Heinrich (CH/FLPA); Marijn Heuts (MH/FLPA); John Holmes (JH/FLPA);
Mitsuaki Iwago (MI/FLPA); Gerard Lacz (GL/FLPA); Frans Lanting (FL/FLPA); Chris Mattison
(CM/FLPA); WT Miller (WM/FLPA); Hiroya Minakuchi (HM/FLPA); Mark Moffett (MM/FLPA);
Piotr Naskrecki (PN/FLPA); Philip Perry (PP/FLPA); L Lee Rue (LR/FLPA); Malcolm Schuyl (MS/
FLPA); Jurgen & Christine Sohns (J&CS/FLPA); Chris & Tilde Stuart (C&TS/FLPA); Martin Van
Lokven (MVL/FLPA); Ariadne Van Zandbergen (AZ/FLPA); Pete Walentin (PW/FLPA);
Winfried Wisniewski (WW/FLPA); Martin B Withers (MW/FLPA); Bernd Zoller (BZ/FLPA)

With kind permission of Struik Image Library (www.imagesofafrica.co.za): Shaen Adey (SA); Daryl and
Sharna Balfour (D&SB); Andrew Bannister (AB); Keith Begg (KB); Marius Burger (MB); Roger de
la Harpe (RH); Nigel Dennis (ND); Gerhard Dreyer (GD); Richard Du Toit (RT); Leonard Hoffman
(LH); Ian Michler (IM); Peter Pickford (PPk); Hein Von Horsten (HVH); Lanz Von Horsten (LVH)

Illustrations Mike Unwin
Maps Steve Munns

Designed and formated by Pepenbury Ltd
Production managed by Jellyfish Print Solutions; printed in India

CONTENTS

AUTHORS AND PHOTOGRAPHERS

Mike Unwin first came to Bradt's attention in 2000, when he won the annual Bradt/*BBC Wildlife* Travel Writing competition. He now writes regularly for numerous publications, including the *Independent, Wanderlust, BBC Wildlife* and *Travel Africa*, and is editor of *Travel Zambia* magazine. Among his many other books for both adults and children are *Swaziland: The Bradt Travel Guide, 100 Bizarre Animals* (both Bradt) and *The Atlas of Birds* (Bloomsbury). Now based in the UK, Mike spent seven years working in Southern Africa. But work – which included teaching in Zimbabwe and publishing in Swaziland – always came a poor second to wildlife: he led the Swaziland Bird Club, volunteered with the South African Frog Atlas project, painted dioramas for the Swaziland Museum of Natural History and generally pursued all manner of beasts into every corner of the region. Mike's photographs and illustrations appear in much of his work, including this book. One day he *will* see a pangolin.

Philip Perry (www.pperrywildlifephotos.org.sz) emigrated to Africa to pursue wildlife photography and, though he travels widely, Africa's unrivalled wildlife always draws him back. Winner of the *British Birds* 'Bird Photograph of the Year' in 1991, he has also photographed and co-authored numerous books for adults and children, including *Wild Swaziland*.

Ariadne Van Zandbergen (philari@hixnet.co.za) is a travel and wildlife photographer who specialises in Africa. Her work has appeared in numerous books and periodicals and from her home in Johannesburg she runs an extensive photo library dedicated to Africa.

ACKNOWLEDGEMENTS
Many people helped with this book. I am indebted to two in particular: Ara Monadjem, for expert advice and inspiration in the field; and Kathy Gemmell, for editorial expertise and for sharing everything. Any mistakes are mine, not theirs. In southern Africa, many friends have provided support and encouragement over the years. Special thanks go to Peter and Carole Murby, Francie and Shepherd Shonhiwa, Rex and Mardee Wilson, Luchi and Marjorie Balarin, Elias Ndwandwe, Paul Rhymer and Rod de Vletter. For help while writing this book, I'm also grateful to Marianne Taylor, Claudia dos Santos, Carmen Swanepoel and Chris McIntyre.

Many thanks to the Bradt team: Hilary Bradt, Tricia Hayne and Adrian Phillips for bringing the first edition to fruition; Maisie Fitzpatrick and Anna Moores for their help with this second edition. Thanks also to Mike Miles for sterling design work throughout.

Finally, thanks – as ever – to my wonderful family for getting me started.

Front cover, main image: giraffe (J&CS/FLPA)
Front cover, inset images (*left to right*): leopard (PP/FLPA); tree agama (WW/FLPA); red-headed weaver (FLPA)
Back cover: white-fronted bee-eater (MU)
Title page (*top to bottom*): rock monitor (MU); ground hornbill (MU); meerkat (RT)

This book is for Florence.

IMPRESSIONS

🐾 Leaving camp before dawn, you follow an old elephant trail deep into the bush, shouldering through the clutching thorns and dew-laden cobwebs. Night lingers in the soft mechanical 'prrrp' of a scops owl and the quavering fragility of a fiery-necked nightjar, but the pale eastern glow prompts a clamour of francolins and the eerie wail of returning jackals. First light, slanting across the trail, picks out the imprint of its nocturnal commuters: everywhere the neat cloven signature of impala – here overlaid with the firm stamp of zebra, there embroidered with a genet's tiny-pawed motif.

🐾 The first hippo breaks the surface just twenty metres away with a hydraulic hiss of escaping air. Another head bobs up. Then another. Pink goggle eyes peer suspiciously over bristling muzzles and ears twitch irritably as your paddle strikes the water – perhaps a little too urgently – and you pull towards the bank. Your canoe nudges into the lilies, disturbing a malachite kingfisher that whirs away in a flash of blue and orange. A startled water monitor scrambles down the bank into the safety of the dark water.

🐾 As you crest the ridge, a sharp whistle jerks your gaze up to a dolomite pinnacle where a klipspringer is poised tiptoe for flight. Another whistle follows from his mate below, and both antelope flip over the edge like abseilers. Easing the pack from your shoulders, you slump into the shade of a sugarbush – porcupine quills strewn like an offering around its base – and scan the valley with binoculars. A black eagle angles into the updraught, white rump flashing in the sunlight. Its rakish shadow sweeps the cliffs, scattering dassies from the ledges.

🐾 Sandgrouse clatter up from the water's edge and wheel away into the darkness, wings and ripples catching the last embers of the day. This morning, through the dust and glare, two hundred nodding zebra had filed out of the thorn scrub, the leaders forced belly-deep into the waterhole by the jostling ranks behind. Now evening assembles a new cast. The first player enters stage right: a black rhino, huffing from the shadows, calf at her heels. At the moan of a distant lion she pauses, radar ears rotating and nostrils scouring the breeze. Then, with a stamp and a snort, she steps up to drink.

🐾 The turtle's tracks plough a broad furrow up the beach, as though some pocket landing craft has emerged from the ocean. Somewhere up towards the dunes, beyond your torch beam, she is ponderously excavating sand. It's past midnight, and the Southern Cross has slipped below the horizon. She's swum thousands of kilometres to be here; you've tramped an hour along the shore. Shortly, once the plum-soft eggs start falling, your guide will take you for a closer look. But for now you squat on the warm sand and watch the ghost crabs scuttle across the gleaming moonlight behind each retreating wave. From the dark forest behind comes the unearthly scream of a bushbaby.

INTRODUCTION

WHAT'S NEW?

Eight years have passed since this book was first published. In that short time the wildlife of southern Africa has seen various changes. Conservation has had its successes, such as the return of bateleurs and vultures to South Africa's Kalahari farmland. Yet old enemies, such as rhino poaching, have reared their ugly heads, while more insidious threats, such as climate change, loom ever larger. Politics has also brought contrasting fortunes: the status of Zimbabwe's wildlife remains uncertain as that country continues to struggle, yet Mozambique has seen the rebirth of some wonderful wildlife areas as it continues to rebuild.

What hasn't changed, however, is that there are still few destinations to rival southern Africa for sheer abundance, variety and visibility of wildlife. This second edition includes fully updated information on places, population statistics and species names. An injection of exciting new images also means that it illustrates even more species than before.

HOW TO USE THIS BOOK

Travel guides will help you plan a wildlife trip to southern Africa and field guides to identify what you see there. This book is neither of those things. Rather, it aims to bridge the gap between the two by offering an overview of the region's wildlife from the visitor's perspective.

Southern Africa is defined here as the seven countries south of the Zambezi and Kunene Rivers: namely Botswana, Lesotho, Namibia, South Africa, Swaziland, Zimbabwe and the southern half of Mozambique. The wildlife of Zambia and Malawi is similar in many respects, however, and this guide would certainly not be redundant in those countries.

Separate chapters tackle most major taxonomic groupings: *Mammals*, *Birds*, *Reptiles and amphibians* and *Invertebrates*. The exceptions are freshwater fishes and underwater marine life – both covered only in passing, as these are specialist fields generally of more interest to anglers and divers respectively. Taxonomic order is treated flexibly: for example, hyraxes (Hyracoidea) are placed near rodents, with which they are often confused, rather than elephants, to which they are – believe it or not – more closely related. A guide of this size cannot encompass everything, so the selection of species reflects what the average visitor is most likely to encounter and be able to identify. Thus, for example, each antelope species gets individual treatment, while invertebrates are described at a more generic level. The text does not focus only on identification – that's what field guides are for – but aims to give some insight into the animals' lives.

Other chapters put the wildlife in context: *Habitats* describes and locates the region's major habitat types (biomes), including their flora; *Tracks and signs* investigates the evidence that animals leave behind; *Making the most of it* offers practical advice on how to go about finding and enjoying the wildlife; and Where to go describes the basic geography and key wildlife areas of each country. *Further information*, meanwhile, suggests good sources for planning and enjoying your visit.

WHAT'S IN A NAME?

Beware: species names can vary between regions and change over time, often causing confusing discrepancies. Birds, especially, can be a minefield: today's dusky indigobird, for instance, was yesterday's black widowfinch. If in doubt, check the scientific name. A basic grasp of taxonomic terminology helps you to understand how scientific names work – as in the following examples.

	Lion	**Puff adder**
Kingdom	Animalia (animals)	Animalia (animals)
Phylum	Chordata (vertebrates)	Chordata (vertebrates)
Class	Mammalia (mammals)	Reptilia (reptiles)
Order	Carnivora (carnivores)	Squamata (lizards and snakes)
Family	Felidae (cats)	Viperidae (vipers)
Genus	*Panthera* (big cats)	*Bitis* (African adders)
Species	*Panthera leo* (lion)	*Bitis arietans* (puff adder)

A species name is always an italicised binomial (two-part name), with the first word denoting the genus. Sometimes a trinomial (three-part name) is used to denote a race – for example, *Equus zebra hartmannae* is the Hartmann's race of mountain zebra (species *Equus zebra*). Because of the difficulty of identifying invertebrates, this book refers to many only by their family (eg: Scarabaeinae – dung beetles) or order (eg: Odonata – dragonflies). The word 'species' is sometimes abbreviated to 'sp' ('spp' in the plural).

Wild dog, Cape hunting dog or African painted wolf? Whichever name you prefer, this fascinating and endangered predator will always be *Lycaon pictus* to scientists. (AZ)

LEARNING THE LINGO

Any visitor in search of southern Africa's wildlife will encounter a range of unfamiliar local terminology. Afrikaans, in particular, has had a major influence across the region and many animals, such as klipspringer ('rock jumper') and boomslang ('tree snake'), are known universally by their Afrikaans name. The following are a few more common and useful Afrikaans terms:

donga   ditch or dry river bed
fynbos   (pronounced 'fainboss') Cape coastal heathland
kloof   deep valley or ravine
kopje   (pronounced – and sometimes spelt – 'koppie') rocky outcrop
veld   (pronounced 'felt') grassland or savannah – also *bushveld, highveld, thornveld* etc.
vlei   (pronounced 'flay') low-lying marshy area
spoor   animal tracks or signs

Some common animal names, for example nyala, are also derived from Bantu languages, and a flick through the phone book reveals the cultural significance of wildlife: *Indlovu* (elephant), *Inyati* (buffalo), *Impofu* (eland), *Ingwenya* (crocodile) and *Imvubu* (hippo) are all common surnames in SiZulu-, SiSwati- or SiNdebele-speaking regions. Many African names are highly descriptive; for example *Inhleka bafazi*, meaning 'cackling women', is the Zulu term for the red-billed woodhoopoe and is a perfect (albeit sexist) evocation of the call of this garrulous bird.

The world of southern African wildlife is also steeped in the language of safari – derived from the activities of the early 'white hunters' and still redolent of an era of colonial plunder. *Safari* itself is an East African (kiSwahili) word for 'journey', today applied to almost any eco-tourism activity. 'Big game' tends to describe the larger mammals once most sought after by hunters, from antelope to zebra, and 'big game park' refers to areas where these animals are now protected. 'Big five' is an unavoidable term applied exclusively to the lion, leopard, buffalo, rhino and elephant – those animals which were once, reputedly, the hunter's most dangerous adversaries and so today retain a kudos that pulls in the punters. (New private reserves are always anxious to re-establish these species on their property in order to boast the 'big five' in their promotional blurb.) Those turned off by hunting hyperbole may find the 'little five' – antlion, leopard tortoise, buffalo weaver, rhinoceros beetle and elephant shrew – a more appealing concept.

THE SOUTHERN AFRICAN ENVIRONMENT
LAND

The 3.5 million km² of southern Africa are dominated by a great interior plateau, averaging 1,000–2,000m above sea level. In the west, this plateau sags into the vast depression of the Kalahari basin, where an unbroken mantle of sand represents the windblown detritus of millions of years of erosion across the uplands. To the east, it falls away on to the humid, subtropical coastal plain. The plateau is bordered by an escarpment, which, at its most dramatic, forms the imposing wall of the Drakensberg in eastern South Africa, reaching 3,482m at Thabana-Ntlenyana in Lesotho.

A rainy season storm breaks over Etosha Pan, Namibia. (PP)

Elsewhere the escarpment is broken into a series of isolated ranges, from the Eastern Highlands of Zimbabwe to the Cape fold mountains and Namibia's Naukluft massif. Most of the region's major rivers, including the 2,740km-long Zambezi, drain the plateau eastwards into the Indian Ocean, cutting broad swathes across the Mozambique floodplain. One major exception is the Orange, which channels the waters of the Drakensberg westwards to the Atlantic. The drainage of the Kalahari basin has been severely disrupted by past tectonic upheavals, and today the Okavango River, which once flowed east into the Limpopo or Zambezi catchment systems (according to which geologist you believe), peters out in the ancient sands, never to reach the sea.

CLIMATE

Southern Africa is a warm and largely dry land, though there is much local variation. In most regions, the seasons can be simply divided into the summer 'rainy' season, from November through to March, and the winter 'dry' season, for the rest of the year, with a brief spring-like transition in September/October but not much in the way of autumn. The climate is strongly influenced by two contrasting oceans: the Atlantic washes the west coast with the cold Antarctic waters of the Benguela Current, while the Indian Ocean brings the warm equatorial waters of the Agulhas Current to the east coast. Most rainfall is borne on anti-clockwise winds from the warm Indian Ocean. It falls heavily during summer in eastern districts and on the escarpment (over 1,000mm a year), leaving little to water the arid central and western districts, where large areas receive less than 150mm a year. An exception to this pattern is the southwestern Cape, which receives its rainfall in winter from the Atlantic. Summer is warm everywhere, with temperatures in low-lying areas such as the Kalahari and Zambezi Valley frequently exceeding 40°C and sweltering humidity along the Mozambique and KwaZulu-Natal coasts. Dry winter days generally peak at a pleasant 20°C, but can be cold at high altitudes, with snow falling in the Drakensberg and Cape ranges. In arid and desert regions winter days are warm, but night-time temperatures plunge below zero.

WILDLIFE

The richness of sub-Saharan Africa's wildlife can be attributed to it having avoided the succession of alternating ice-ages and interglacial periods that wrought havoc on prehistoric life over much of the rest of the world. Instead, milder variations of climate encouraged diversity rather than extinction, and southern Africa became a hotbed of evolution. Remnants of the first mammal-like reptiles, dating back 280 million years, have been dug from the fossil beds of the Karoo, while one of the earliest hominids, *Australopithecus*, was first discovered in South Africa in 1925, prompting ongoing investigations into our own ancestry.

Today, southern Africa is best known for its large mammals, and the prolonged dry conditions of the last few million years have fuelled their diversity by shrinking the tropical forests to open up a mosaic of savannah and other habitats. However, large mammals are merely the most conspicuous members of an all-star cast, which includes a cornucopia of smaller life forms. Much of this fauna is shared with other parts of sub-Saharan Africa where similar habitats occur – thus the visitor to Masai Mara in Kenya will find many of the same species as in South Africa's Kruger Park. Endemic species – those unique to southern Africa – tend to occur in more isolated habitats and include such regional specialities as the girdled lizards of the Karoo and the sugarbirds of the Cape fynbos.

Top Restios are among the endemic flora of the Cape. (GD)

Above Visitors from distant shores, such as this European roller, swell the ranks of southern Africa's resident wildlife. (MU)

THE HUMAN FACTOR

One species forged in Africa's great evolutionary furnace has had a devastating effect on thousands of others, and, having modified much of the mother continent for its own ends, is fast ruining it for everything else. For millennia, people lived cheek by jowl with other animals, competing for resources in a sustainable way. But in the last few centuries, with the advent of commercial agriculture and industrialisation, these resources have been plundered on a massive scale, driving many animals into pockets and margins of subsistence or – in the case of the bluebuck (see page 80) – oblivion.

Humans are hunters: Stone Age rock art all over southern Africa tells us this much. However, with European technology came slaughter on an unprecedented scale. At first it was sport: the early pioneers heading north from the Cape left the

6

bush strewn with carcasses. Then it was trade – particularly ivory, indelibly tainted with the blood not only of elephants, but of slavery. Finally animals just got in the way: either – like buffalo – they spread cattle diseases, or – like lions – they had the temerity to eat the livestock that supplanted their natural prey.

Even more devastating than hunting the animals themselves has been the expropriation of their land. Fences, cattle, wheat fields and forestry plantations soon replaced guns as the most potent weapons of destruction, and many precious habitats, especially fynbos, forest and highveld grassland, have since been reduced to fragments, their wildlife scattered and dwindling. Part of this insidious process has been the introduction of exotic species, from the blue-gum to the Indian myna, which flourish at the expense of indigenous flora and fauna. Of course, this tale of doom and gloom simply reflects a depressing pattern around the globe. However, in much of the world the damage took place so long ago that we take its effects for granted, whereas in Africa, the process – being relatively recent – is more visible, and its alternatives that much more demanding of our attention.

CONSERVATION

The foundations of southern Africa's conservation movement were laid in 1897 in South Africa, with the creation of the Hluhluwe Reserve in today's KwaZulu-Natal (see page 271). Today a vast patchwork of national parks and game reserves extends right across the subcontinent. However, the nature of conservation has changed radically over the last hundred years. The first parks were influenced by hopelessly inappropriate European models, with the aim being to establish a healthy population of 'game species', often at the expense of anything else. It seems incredible that, a mere 50 years ago, wild dogs were eradicated as 'vermin' by wardens of reserves such as Hwange, keen to build up their antelope stocks, while today, in the very same reserves, conservationists are engaged in a last-ditch struggle to save the few remaining packs of this now critically endangered animal.

Today's understanding of the ecological 'big picture' has brought a movement away from the management of land for individual species towards the preservation of biodiversity across entire habitats. Unfortunately pressures on land are such that habitats can seldom be left to go their own way, and conservation today often requires intervention. Scientists have been able to restore biodiversity to many areas by careful habitat management and the reintroduction of once indigenous wildlife. The recovery of the white rhino, from a beleaguered handful in KwaZulu-Natal to a regional population of over 18,000, is an impressive example of what can be achieved. Much of this reconstruction work takes place on private land, and a proliferation of private reserves and game farms across the region has provided a massive boost to conservation. Harsh lessons have been learnt along the way – teenage gangs of orphaned elephants translocated from the Kruger have, without adult supervision, run amok in smaller reserves – but today some private reserves offer wilderness and wildlife to rival the best of the national parks. The ambitious Transfrontier Conservation Areas (TFCAs), or 'Peace Parks', aim to re-establish ancient migration routes by linking conservation zones across national boundaries. They include the Great Limpopo

Transfrontier Park, opened in December 2002, which protects 35,000km² of land across the borders of Mozambique, South Africa and Zimbabwe. TFCAs present massive logistical challenges, with great disparities of funding and infrastructure existing between neighbouring countries, and at present most exist only on paper. Nonetheless, the huge Kgalagadi Transfrontier Park, which straddles the borders of South Africa and Botswana, already provides an excellent model.

The most damaging legacy of the early days has been a widespread alienation of local communities from the conservation movement. The first parks were often created with a colonial disregard for the wishes and rights of the people who already lived there, many of whom were forcibly evicted from land set aside for wildlife. The

Rhino skulls, their horns crudely hacked away, bear gruesome testimony to the bloody work of poachers. (MU)

ensuing resentment found expression in the wholesale poaching of the 1970s and '80s, when impoverished peoples sought to scrape a living from a rampant illegal wildlife trade that targeted valuable species such as black rhino and elephant for lucrative foreign markets. Conservationists now understand that their real battle is for the trust and support of local people, and that unless local communities can realise tangible benefits from conservation, then any initiative is doomed to failure. Today, a number of schemes enable rural communities to manage their own land for conservation in return for revenue derived from ecotourism – including commercial hunting. Although this may sound distasteful to Western ears, it recognises the African reality that successful conservation must be integrated with sustainable development and wildlife has to pay its way. Today, southern Africa is learning to appreciate the importance of preserving its natural environment for generations to come. However, land and resources are under more pressure than ever. At the start of the 21st century, with much of the region facing serious food shortages and the population set to double within 25 years, it could do with all the international support it can get.

As a responsible visitor to southern Africa, you are a vital cog in the machinery of conservation. If you are troubled by enjoying your leisure in a part of the world wracked with poverty, consider that the problems won't disappear if you simply stay at home. On a local level, ecotourism provides employment and a real incentive to look after the natural environment. On a national level, it generates vital revenue – especially much-needed foreign currency – for struggling economies, and so contributes to the advances in education, healthcare and agriculture that are all essential for effective conservation. On a personal level, your interest may promote awareness and foster interest in others, which can only be a good thing. Southern Africa offers the world's best wildlife experiences. Enjoy it.

HABITATS

Kalahari sunrise (PP)

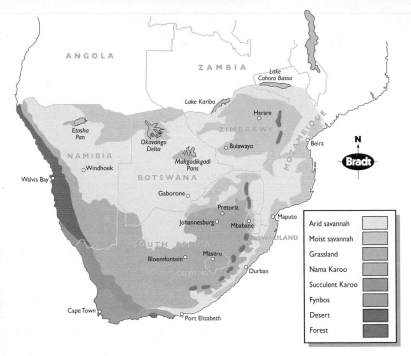

Arid savannah
Moist savannah
Grassland
Nama Karoo
Succulent Karoo
Fynbos
Desert
Forest

The word 'habitat' is very versatile. It can refer to a single location, such as a pond, or paint a broad-brush picture of a landscape type, such as desert. In this book, it is used to describe any area where you are consistently most likely to see a particular kind of animal. A basic understanding of habitats lets you know what to expect, wherever you are, and increases your chances of finding and identifying animals. It also enhances your overall wildlife experience by explaining why animals live where they do, and how different animals co-exist.

All habitats fall within broad ecological zones, called biomes, that extend over large natural areas. A biome is defined by its principal vegetation type, such as forest, which in turn reflects the influences of elevation, topography, climate and soil type. Where different habitats within a biome they form mixed habitat zones, called ecotones. Southern Africa is divided into seven principal biomes: savannah woodland, grassland, nama Karoo, succulent Karoo, fynbos, desert and forest (see map above). Each one is described separately in this chapter, along with waterways, coasts and the man-made habitats that impinge upon them all.

SAVANNAH WOODLAND, OR BUSHVELD

In a southern African context, savannah woodland is the correct ecological term for what is often described as bushveld, or often just simply 'bush'. For many people, savannah evokes East Africa's vast open grasslands, so the South African term 'bushveld', which combines the English word 'bush' with the Afrikaans word for 'field', is probably a more helpful term for this habitat, which comprises equal proportions of grass and tree cover. Technically speaking, woodland is defined as any continuous growth of trees where the crowns are not touching. Whatever you call it, this habitat covers much of the northern half of the region. It is where most of the large mammals are found and consequently where the best-known reserves are situated, including Kruger, Etosha, Hwange, Moremi and Chobe. Two principal types are recognised according to their climate, elevation and plant composition: arid 'sweet' bushveld and moist 'sour' bushveld.

Fire is critically important to the health of all bushveld. Annual dry-season burns, often started by lightning strikes, race across the parched land, leaving ash and charcoal in their wake. Though these fires may appear devastating, in fact they enrich and maintain the habitat by burning off old inhibiting growth, returning nutrients to the soil and controlling the encroachment of trees. Most fire burns just above ground level, so grasses, which have their buds at the base of the plant, survive the flames

Fever trees are among the tallest and most conspicuous of the acacia family. They thrive in low-lying bushveld, close to water. (ND)

and sprout as soon as the rains fall upon the newly enriched soil. Most mature bushveld trees are fire-resistant, since the vital growth layer – the cambium – lies beneath the tough outer trunk.

Looking for a home where the buffalo roam? The bushveld offers just the right combination of grazing and cover for these heavyweight herbivores. (MU)

ARID SAVANNAH, OR LOWVELD

Arid savannah, sometimes known as 'lowveld', is low-altitude bushveld characterised by rich, heavy soils and low annual rainfall (250–650mm). It extends from northeast South Africa and southern Mozambique, over the low-lying areas of northern and southern Zimbabwe, across most of Botswana – taking in the Kalahari 'desert' – and across central and northeast Namibia. Arid savannah supports a greater density of large mammals than any other habitat, and the nibbling herds play a major role in shaping and maintaining the landscape. Different soils give rise to distinct tree and plant communities, each of which supports its own fauna. Impala, blue wildebeest and giraffe are all typical lowveld mammals, while shrikes, rollers and hornbills are among the best-known birds.

'Thornveld' is the name given to arid savannah dominated by acacias. These resilient trees have loose, fissured bark, tiny compound leaves to reduce heat loss and wicked paired thorns that restrict the browsing of herbivores to a sustainable level. There are many species, all of which produce nutritious seed pods that feed a variety of browsers and foragers. The widespread umbrella thorn (*Acacia tortilis*) is the best known, with a flat-topped silhouette that has become emblematic of Africa. The larger, more robust knobthorn (*Acacia nigrescens*) has a spiny trunk when young, and often grows in association with the marula to form a sub-habitat known as knobhorn/marula savannah (eg: in the central Kruger). The fever tree (*Acacia xanthophloea*) has a distinctive powdery yellowish bark. It grows near water, and owes its name to the mistaken belief of early pioneers that it harboured a fly that spread malaria.

Bushveld browsers find nutritious nibbles among the trees, from the seed pods of the scented thorn (*top* MU) to the butterfly-shaped leaves of the mopane (*above* MU).

'Mopaneveld' is the name given to large tracts of open woodland, mostly in low-lying northern areas, where the deciduous mopane tree (*Colophospermum mopane*) holds sway. This tree, which grows in shrub form on some soils, has distinctive butterfly-shaped leaves that carpet the ground with an autumnal layer of reds and golds in the dry season. Though mopaneveld appears superficially to be an unpromising landscape, it is actually very rich in wildlife, supporting many large browsers – including elephants – and a wealth of smaller creatures, from tree squirrels to mopane snakes.

An acacia's battery of thorns offers little defence against giraffes, which crane into the canopy to get at the goodies other browsers can't reach. (MU)

Besides acacias and mopanes, many other bushveld trees will catch your attention. The marula (*Sclerocarya birrea*), which often grows in association with the knobthorn, is prized by man and beast for its yellow, plum-like fruits – harvested to make a seasonal, traditional liquor. The statuesque anna tree (*Faidherbia albida*), also known as winterthorn due to its late flowering, produces curling pods that are a treat for elephants, who hoover them up like popcorn. The rain tree (*Lonchocarpus capassa*), with its deep tap roots, shows a good growth of greenery during even the driest times and gets its name from the continuous pattering of droplets excreted by sap-sucking insects that live on its large, round leaves. The lala palm (*Hyphaene coriacea*) grows beside water courses in low-lying, sub-tropical areas. Its name derives from the Zulu for sleep; perhaps because of the potent palm wine produced from its sap, or perhaps because its large fanned fronds are traditionally woven into sleeping mats. The leadwood (*Combretum imberbe*) grows very slowly and, as the name

A baobab may exceed 20m in circumference and live for over 4,000 years. African legend holds that this enormous tree was hurled from the heavens by the monkey god and landed upside down in the soil, leaving its roots clutching at the air. (ND)

Flowers, such as the wild hibiscus (*left*, MU) and impala lily (*right*, MU), add a splash of colour to the bushveld at ground level.

suggests, has very dense wood that weighs up to 1,200kg per cubic metre. Dead leadwoods, casualties of lightning or elephants, remain standing for years. Growing bigger and older still is the grotesque baobab (*Adansonia digitata*), whose swollen trunk and twisted branches strike an unmistakable silhouette in arid northern regions. Despite their size, baobabs can be toppled by elephants, who gouge deeply into their fibrous trunks in search of hidden moisture.

Beneath and between the trees grows an equally impressive diversity of grasses. These range from 'sweet' grasses, such as Guinea grass (*Panicum maximus*) and red grass (*Themeda triandra*), that provide excellent grazing in low-lying areas, to the much less palatable thatching grasses, such as *Hyperthelia* and *Hyparrhenia* species, which prefer disturbed or moist environments and are usually a good indication of past fires. In summer, after the rains, the ground is adorned with wild flowers, from the humble blooms of the wild hibiscus (*Hibiscus calyphyllus*) to the blushing pink of the impala lily (*Adenium obesum*).

Scattered across arid savannah regions are bare patches of ground, often with a whitish tinge to the soil. These are known as sodic sites, and reveal a concentration of alkaline salts in the soil. This soil forms a hard impermeable layer that discourages plant growth and traps rainwater. Animals are drawn to lick the salt deposits, and to drink from the shallow temporary pans. In time, a steady passage of drinkers and wallowers enlarges the pan, excavates and removes the mud, seals the bottom and creates a proper seasonal waterhole. Elephants often play a critical role in this process.

Kalahari

The Kalahari (or Kgalagadi, to use its uncorrupted African name), has long been described as a desert, although arguably it receives too much rainfall to qualify. This vast area of arid savannah carpets the largest single unbroken mantle of sand

The gemsbok occurs in small herds throughout the Kalahari. It is perfectly adapted to the arid environment, obtaining valuable minerals from the dry riverbeds (*above*, AZ) and precious moisture from the fruit of the tsama melon (*right*, AZ).

anywhere on Earth, blown by ancient winds across the calcareous bedrock of what was once a huge inland lake. These sands once stretched to the Equator, linking the Kalahari to the Sahara. Today they cover much of Botswana and extend east into Zimbabwe, south into South Africa, and west into Namibia. The Kalahari landscape is characterised by thinly grassed plains and a scattered growth of thorn trees. Towards the south, a series of low red dunes snake across the land. Unlike those of the true Namib Desert, these are immobile 'fossil' dunes. Further north and east, the woodland is more dense and varied. Temperatures in the Kalahari can exceed 40°C and rainfall averages only 250mm a year, most of which falls in a handful of heavy summer storms. Though watercourses may be bone dry for most of the year, the alluvial soil along their banks supports a rich growth of permanent vegetation. Alkaline depressions, such as those at Makgadikgadi Pans (see page 256), briefly become enormous shallow lakes after the rains, attracting breeding colonies of waterbirds, including flamingos, to their invertebrate-rich waters.

Kalahari rains spark a prolific burst of growth: lush green bushman grass (*Stipagrostis* spp) sprouts from the sand, little *duiweltjie* flowers decorate the dunes and gnarled blackthorns burst into scented puffball blossoms. The camelthorn (*Acacia erioloba*) often appears to be in a state of lifeless disintegration, but this most distinctive Kalahari tree has a remarkable capacity to survive drought and provides a haven of food, shelter and shade for a host of creatures. The shepherd's tree (*Boscia albitrunca*) is a smaller, versatile species with a distinctive whitish trunk, so named because sheep and goats are partial to its leaves. At ground level, the tsama melon (*Citrullus lanatus*) sends its runners over the dunes to produce succulent round fruit, each 90% water, which provide vital moisture for many animals, from gerbils and porcupines to gemsbok and brown hyenas.

Life in the Kalahari is one of feast and famine, and the fauna has evolved to make the best of the seasonal fluctuations in food and water. Larger herbivores, such as springbok, are nomadic and trek long distances in search of the rains and new growth. Others, like gemsbok, have a specialised physiology that allows them to survive extreme drought and heat. Many smaller animals, from scorpions to barking geckos, are nocturnal and use burrows to shelter from the heat of the day. Underground, mole rats store bulbs as insurance against the dry months, while on the surface, ground squirrels use their tail as a sunshade and find relief in shallow trenches of cooler sand. The Kalahari has never offered much to man, and it is only the nomadic San people who have learned to survive its extremes. Today, much of it remains true wilderness, and offers an unspoilt wildlife experience quite unlike any other in the region.

MOIST SAVANNAH

In savannah regions with an annual rainfall of 500–1,100mm, the woodland is more dense, and consists predominantly of broad-leaved deciduous trees such as *Brachystegia*. This habitat is also known as *miombo* woodland, or 'sourveld', on account of the coarse, unpalatable grasses, such as russet grass (*loudetia* spp), that grow on its relatively infertile soils. It does not support the same number of large ungulates (hoofed mammals) as arid savannah, but sustains low-density grazers such as sable and reedbuck. Moist savannah covers the central Zimbabwe highveld and is also found across northern Botswana and Namibia and South Africa's Northern Province. Typical trees include the msasa (*Brachystegia spiciformis*), which is common across much of Zimbabwe, and the kiaat (*Pterocarpus angolensis*), or African teak, which, like many similar hardwoods, is much in demand from the timber and curio trades. The red bushwillow (*Combretum apiculatum*) prefers rocky hillsides and, like all members of the large combretum family, has papery, winged seed pods. The silver cluster-leaf (*Terminalia sericea*) has bunches of leaves covered with distinct, silvery hairs.

ON THE ROCKS

Savannah woodland is often punctuated by outcrops of rock, sometimes eroded into intriguing shapes and improbable arrangements of standing stones. These are known locally as kopjes. Each one is a little elevated ecosystem, with niches for a range of specialised plants and animals. Euphorbia species, such as the candelabra tree (*Euphorbia cooperi*), protect their fleshy limbs with sharp spines, and their milky sap is toxic to most browsers. The large-leaved rock fig (*Ficus abutilifolia*) manages without topsoil by extending sinuous roots over the rock surface and into its crevices. These sheltered plant communities are largely protected from the fires that often race through on the ground below. Kopjes provide homes and refuges for many animals, from dassies and plated lizards to leopards and pythons.

The moist grasslands of South Africa's eastern escarpment (*above, MU*) provide habitat for ground-nesting birds such as the yellow-throated longclaw (*inset, ND*), which feed on the rich invertebrate life among the grasses.

GRASSLAND

True southern African grassland, like the great American prairies, is a country of big skies and empty, undulating plains, exposed to the violent battering of summer storms and charred by winter fires that advance in glowing lines along the horizon. Grass, in a variety of forms and families, is the dominant vegetation type. There are few indigenous trees or woody plants, and anthills often provide the only points of elevation. Grassland flourishes naturally at altitudes of over 1,000 metres. This habitat is known locally as 'highveld', and covers a large tract of South Africa's central and eastern plateaux, including Lesotho and parts of western Swaziland. Rain falls in summer and can average from below 500mm to well over 1,000mm per year, depending on topography. The hills are drained by numerous streams, and waterlogged low-lying areas form extensive vleis, or marshes, which in turn feed further streams. The cold, dry winters are characterised by the twin ravages of fires and frost, which are the critical factors in determining the extent and nature of plant growth.

LIFE ON THE GREEN

The grassland biome harbours a great number of southern African endemics – especially birds and plants. The grasses themselves vary from mostly short 'sour' types at higher altitudes, to taller, more palatable ones lower down, such as *Andropogoneae* species. Among them grow a variety of wild flowers, such as the towering Agapanthus, with its pale blue panicles. Rocky slopes sprout a richer growth of vegetation, including aloes, sugarbushes (*Protea* spp) and cabbage trees (*Cussonia* spp), while the winter flowers of the bottlebrush (*Greyia* spp) add a splash of scarlet to valleys and ravines. Animal life happens at ground level: grazers such as blesbok and oribi crop the sward; burrowers such as aardvarks and sungazers (see page 198) find refuge in the soil; kestrels and buzzards scan the tussocks for rodents; widowbirds cruise back and forth over the vleis; and grass snakes hunt the marshy ground for frogs. At the base of this food pyramid are termites, which swarm over the land, nibbling, transporting and recycling its nutrients, and crowding the landscape with the monuments of their industry.

AN ALTERED LAND

Before people and farming, South Africa's grasslands supported enormous herds of antelope such as blesbok and black wildebeest. Sadly, these grazers have long since been replaced by domestic livestock, and today little of the original habitat remains in its natural state. In many areas, overgrazing has caused devastating soil erosion and forests of invasive exotic plants, such as wattle and blue gum, have sprung up where no forest should be, exhausting the ground water and overwhelming indigenous vegetation. Unspoilt grassland, where most elements of the natural ecosystem remain intact, now exists only inside a few carefully managed reserves, such as South Africa's Golden Gate Highlands (see page 270) or Swaziland's Malolotja (see page 272). However, in many places, larger mammals have been successfully reintroduced to their former ranges. For botanists, any grassland holds spring delights, and for birders there is always something interesting, including specials such as blue swallow or ground woodpecker.

HIGHER UP

At higher altitudes, such as in the Drakensberg Mountains, grasses are shorter and trees even fewer on the ground. This habitat is known as 'montane' or alpine grassland, and it occurs at lower altitudes the further south you go. Winters can be very severe and the vegetation often has to withstand a covering of snow. Wildlife is limited to those hardier species that can cope with the cold and the meagre diet, and some species migrate downhill in winter. Typical montane mammals are grey rhebok and mountain reedbuck, while interesting birds include rockjumpers, bald ibis and the spectacular lammergeier. What the mountains lack in wildlife diversity, they make up for in scenery, and this habitat offers some healthy challenges for the well-prepared hiker.

Green, rolling hills and tumbling streams: the very un-African allure of the Drakensberg. (AZ)

Ferns flourish in the dank leaf litter of Knysna's ancient forest floor. Little of this primeval habitat remains in southern Africa. (GD)

FOREST

Forest, as opposed to woodland, comprises a dense growth of large, evergreen trees with a closed canopy above them, and only grows in areas of high rainfall. Indigenous forest is in short supply in southern Africa. It is divided into two main types – Afro-montane forest and lowland forest – which together occupy less than 1% of the region's total surface area. This dearth of forest stems partly from a predominantly arid climate, but it also reflects centuries of deforestation by man, for timber and for land. Today, though there are vast tracts of sterile conifer and gum plantations, all that remains of the indigenous forests are a few scattered fragments along the eastern escarpment and the coast and some grand furniture in the more opulent houses of the Cape.

AFRO-MONTANE FORESTS

Afro-montane forest occurs in patches in the Eastern Highlands of Zimbabwe, the Drakensberg escarpment and the southern Cape coast. It tends to grow on steep, south-facing slopes, with a tree canopy 10–25 metres above an open understorey, and ranges from high altitude (eg: Zimbabwe's Vumba) to low altitude (eg: Knysna in the Cape). Escarpment forest is often shrouded in fog, forming a moist, dripping habitat known as mistbelt forest.

Deep inside the forest it is dark, dank and dominated by the imposing trunks of evergreens, including ironwood (*Homalium dentatum*), stinkwood (*Ocotea bullata*) and the mighty yellowwood (*Podocarpus falcatus*), which towers above the forest, reaching heights of up to 40 metres and extending over 30 metres across the canopy. Conditions on the escarpment bring rain all year round and the limbs of the trees are swathed in moss and epiphytes. Tree ferns and ancient cycads grow beside streams, lichen and fungi flourish and the rich leaf litter crawls with an army of invertebrates. There is little other vegetation, except where enough light penetrates to allow shrubs and climbers a footing, and few larger mammals, though you might spot the droppings of a blue duiker, or hear the blood-curdling call of the tree hyrax by night. Bird life concentrates in the sunlit glades and forest edges, where drongos and flycatchers join mixed feeding parties, and rarities such as the Knysna woodpecker (*Campethera notata*) and orange thrush (*Zoothera gurneyi*) await the diligent birder.

The dazzling colours of Livingstone's turaco can be hard to make out in the dappled light of the forest canopy. (AZ)

COASTAL AND LOWLAND FOREST

Coastal forest extends from the sand dunes of KwaZulu-Natal northwards along the Mozambique coast, and merges into lowland forest further inland. Like montane forest, it is characterised by high rainfall and a continuous canopy, but its sandy soils support a denser understorey of shrubs and lianas. The canopy is also higher, with an average height of 20–35m. Typical trees include the flat-crown (*Albizia adianthifolia*), with its papery pods and great spreading canopy, while creepers such as the thorny rope (*Dalbergia armata*), with its torture-chamber spines, snake through the tangled branches. Sandy clearings support woodland trees such as marula, lala palm and green monkey orange (*Strychnos spinosa*).

Coastal forest provides a pocket of distribution for a number of animals more commonly associated with tropical Africa, such as the suni, green mamba and African broadbill. An early morning walk in this rich habitat can be a very fruitful wildlife experience: fresh earth on the trail may reveal the overnight grubbings of a bush pig, while a patter of hooves in the undergrowth betrays a red duiker, whose twitching tail retreats into a thicket; samango monkeys crash through the canopy above – either they've spotted you, or there's a crowned eagle about – and their alarm barks disturb a Livingstone's lourie, who disappears among the branches in a flash of scarlet. A gold-banded forester butterfly swoops across a sunlit glade, narrowly avoiding the fluttering sortie of a squaretailed drongo; the air hums with insects and the relentless chink chink of a distant tinker barbet punctuates the muffled surf beyond the trees.

DESERT

The Namib is southern Africa's only true desert and, at over 80 million years old, may be the oldest on Earth. It stretches for over 1,800km along the Namibian coast, from the Orange to the Kunene, and extends up to 150km inland, sandwiched between the sea and the escarpment. Like all true deserts, the Namib receives an average of less than 100mm rainfall a year, often much less, and large areas may receive no rain at all for years on end. Its forbidding landscapes are divided between a shifting dune 'sea' along the coast, and inland plains of gravel and calcrete. Granite inselbergs punch up through the stony wastes, and rocky canyons are incised into the plain, evidence of an age when the rivers flowed. With no permanent water and temperatures that soar by day and plummet by night, life has a tenuous foothold in this hostile land. Nonetheless the Namib supports an amazing diversity of highly specialised fauna and flora.

It is hard to believe that life can retain any foothold in the baking sands of the Namib Desert (*right*, MU). But nature has evolved remarkable ways to combat the extreme conditions: the ancient *Welwitschia mirabilis* plant (*below*, CM) can survive years without water; Peringuey's adder (*bottom*, LH) buries itself beneath the dune surface to escape the heat and ambush its prey.

LIFE FROM THE SEA

The towering sand dunes of the coastal Namib are among the tallest in the world. They form a series of ridges, up to 30km long and over 250m high, that are forever shifting with the action of the winds. Here life appears no more likely than on the moon. Yet it is made possible by fog – a thick blanket of it – produced as the cold Antarctic waters of the Benguela Current meet the warm continental landmass. The fog rolls inland at night, over sand and gravel, for up to 25km, bringing moisture to a myriad tiny plants and animals, from delicate lichens that coat the stony flats, to tenebrionid beetles (see page 216), which allow droplets of fog to condense on their tiny, inverted bodies.

Sustained by the fog and a meagre residue from brief seasonal rains, the gravel plains support a scattering of perennial vegetation. This includes a few coarse grasses, succulents such as *Euphorbia damarana*, and, in the rockier areas, dwarf trees such as the squat *Commiphora wildii*. Most remarkable of the desert plants is the ancient cone-bearing *Welwitschia mirabilis*, endemic to Namibia, which has been carbon-dated and revealed to be over 1,000 years old in some cases. This bizarre, dead-looking plant has a gnarled, rock-hard stem and two leathery leaves that sprawl across the ground like a stricken octopus, tattered and shredded with age. Where ancient riverbeds, such as the Kuiseb and Swakop, penetrate the desert, the hidden water table sustains stoical trees, including camelthorns and tamarisks, creating improbable wedges of lush greenery between the barren canyon walls.

The desert is full of surprises. Fragments of dead animal and plant matter, buried in the dunes, are combed from the sand by wind, providing food for a thriving community of invertebrates, reptiles and birds. Dune ants monopolise the few tough grasses, milking the sugary juices from sap-sucking bugs; spoor spiders (*Seothyra* spp) and Peringuey's adders bury themselves in the dune face to ambush their prey; the shovel-snouted lizard balances on two legs to protect its feet from the scorching surface. The gravel plains support gerbils, geckos, chameleons, chats and larks, while nocturnal predators such as Cape foxes, striped polecats and barn owls hunt the kopjes and gulleys. And it's not only the small fry that find a living: hardy gemsbok penetrate deep into the desert along watercourses to forage among the dunes, surviving on camelthorn pods and the succulent flesh of the desert melon.

HOLDING OUT FOR RAIN

When good rains fall inland, flash floods churn down the canyons, leaving behind them a string of fast-evaporating pools – oases for thirsty animals and breeding frogs. Above the canyon walls, the desert floor bursts into life, as long-dormant seeds raise a lush carpet of green grass and herbage. This profusion of growth draws wandering springbok and Hartmann's mountain zebra, and means times of plenty for predators such as brown hyena and lappet-faced vulture. The tree-lined canyon walls teem with birdlife, as chats, titbabblers and flycatchers, among others, compete for breeding territory while the going is good. In the remote northern Kaokoveld (see page 264) even elephants are drawn into the desert, tramping river valleys, such as the Huab, and following ancient routes across the sand to brief seasonal oases.

Winter rainfall carpets the Succulent Karoo with flowers (*above*, GD), luring legions of nectar-hungry insects that, in turn, feed the armadillo girdled lizard (*right*, LH). This bizarre-looking reptile confounds would-be attackers by rolling itself into an unswallowable bracelet of spiny scales.

THE ARID ZONE

The arid zone, or semi-desert, covers most of southwest South Africa, where it is known as the Karoo, and extends up into northern Namibia. This is a land of stony plains, rugged hills and sparse vegetation, divided by botanists into two distinct biomes: the Succulent Karoo is a narrow strip along the sandy coastal plain of Namaqualand; the much larger Nama Karoo dominates the central Cape and extends north into the Namibian interior. The key to the whole area lies in its geology, and the rocks and fossils of the Karoo have taught us much about the shaping of Africa as we see it today. About 250 million years ago, as southern Africa emerged from an ice age, numerous rivers flowed from the retreating ice sheets into this great natural basin, creating vast low-lying swamps and depositing layers of sand, silt and mud to form the sedimentary sandstone and shales known today as the 'Karoo system'. About 50 million years later, as the super-continent of Gondwana began to break up, seismic forces raised and ruptured this basin, creating rifts and faults and spewing out a thick layer of volcanic lava, seen today as the resistant dolerite ridges that crown every flat-topped hill. Today the marshlands are long gone, and the whole region rarely receives more than 250mm of rainfall annually. The rainfall decreases steadily towards the west, where it falls only in winter. The climate is harsh, with winter frosts (and even snow in the southern mountains) and very hot summers.

BLOOMING AND SEEDING

Despite the barren appearance of its landscape, the Karoo boasts a rich diversity of flora. The Succulent Karoo is dominated by (surprise, surprise!) succulents, such as euphorbias and misembryanthemums, all characterised by their adaptations for surviving drought, including fleshy water-retaining stems, fine waxy leaves to reduce water loss, and thorns to deter browsers. In early spring, after the meagre winter rains, the Succulent Karoo bursts into flower and the ground is carpeted with a spectacular display of annuals. This blaze of colour seduces an army of pollinating insects, with each plant hosting its own particular species. In a month the blooms are over, and the plants quickly set seed to take advantage of the dry winds that disperse them across the land.

The Nama Karoo has fewer succulents and is characterised by dwarf woody shrubs. Heading eastwards you will find a progressively greater diversity and abundance of grasses and a scattering of trees, such as the sweet thorn (*Acacia karoo*), which cluster along watercourses. Grass sprouts with the first rains, sets seed quickly and then withers – the seeds lying dormant until the next season's rains.

BEYOND THE VANISHED HERDS

Sadly, the Karoo no longer has much in the way of large mammals. Early pioneers found lions roaming the hills and migrating herds of springbok millions strong, but hunters quickly put paid to all this excitement, and the ensuing years brought unchecked slaughter (spelling doom for the quagga, a now extinct race of the zebra), followed by devastating overgrazing by livestock. Today, reintroduction programmes have restored mountain zebra, springbok and other grazers to a few protected pockets, while the wilder thickets and gulleys still provide homes for versatile and tenacious species such as kudu, klipsringer, caracal, aardwolf and black-backed jackal. However, the Karoo has much to offer besides large mammals: holes and burrows provide shelter for scorpions, geckos, ground squirrels and meerkats; cape cobras and pale chanting goshawks scour the scrub for reptiles and rodents while black eagles scan the kopjes for dassies; larks, chats and korhaans pick over the stony ground for a rich variety of insects, including endemic tenebrionid beetles and impossibly camouflaged toad grasshoppers.

DAMARALAND

In Namibia, a northern extension of the Karoo biome leads to the scenic grandeur of Damaraland (see page 264) where a different cross-section of arid-zone species is found. Commiphoras and quiver trees (*Aloe dichotoma*) cling to the boulder-strewn hillsides, while savannah woodland species such as mopane and anna trees line the dry riverbeds. Local wildlife specialities include the herero chat (*Namibornis herero*), Damara dik-dik and brown hyena. The former glories of Damaraland's wildlife are recorded in the region's abundant rock art, in which kudu, eland, elephant, lion, rhino and giraffe are traced with tender precision across slabs of dolomite. In today's more arid era, a few black rhino and elephant still wander the desolate wilderness of the Kaokoveld to the north, following the river courses deep into the interior.

King proteas thrive on the fynbos-covered lower slopes of Table Mountain. Like all fynbos flora, their magnificent blooms are dependent upon a regular cycle of fires that enriches the soil with precious nutrients. (ND)

FYNBOS

Fynbos, pronounced 'fain-boss', describes the belt of scrubby heathland that carpets the hillsides of South Africa's southwestern Cape. The word itself, meaning 'fine bush' in Afrikaans, refers to the fine-leaved, shrubby species that make up much of the vegetation. Superficially this land has a Mediterranean feel, with its mosaic of tough low bushes on poor, rocky soil and a climate of warm, dry summers and cool, rainy winters. Fynbos is found from coastline to mountain top. It reaches north to the Cederberg and east to Port Elizabeth, but is found nowhere more than 200km from the sea.

BOTANICAL BONANZA

The magnificent king protea (*Protea cynaroides*), South Africa's national flower, is emblematic of the extraordinary floral riches of the fynbos. The Cape is one of the world's great botanical hotspots, and is classified as the sixth (and smallest) of the world's floral kingdoms. Its 8,600 plant species within only 90,000km^2 represent the highest concentration of plant species on Earth, 68% of which are endemic. The explanation for this lies in prehistoric climate changes which left the Cape ecologically isolated, enabling certain plant genera to evolve an unparalleled diversity. Today, the erica group alone boasts over 530 species (compared with, for example, six in the UK).

Fynbos is subdivided according to the relative prevalence of its main plant families. 'Restioid' fynbos is dominated by the rush-like restios (see page 6), with their fire-resistant buds, which ecologically replace grasses. 'Proteoid' fynbos is characterised by taller protea bushes, with their tough leaves and intricate flowers, and related plants such as the garish pincushion (*Leucospermum*). 'Ericoid' fynbos is dominated by heathers, just like European heathland, and grows mostly on acidic soils in high-rainfall areas. Amongst a superabundance of other flowers are tiny lobelias and pelargoniums, and a fine selection of geophytes, or bulbous plants, such as lilies, irises and orchids. The whole bewildering array ensures a floral kaleidoscope, with each season adding a new splash to the palette.

Fire occurs here in regular cycles, ideally at 10–12-year intervals. Though these burns can appear devastating, they are vital to the health of the fynbos: the seeds of some plants actually require the heat of the fires to germinate, while nutrients locked up in woody growth are released to enrich the soil for all.

The Cape sugarbird uses its long, curved bill to probe a pincushion plant for its nectar. This species is endemic to the Cape and helps pollinate its food plants. (ND)

FYNBOS FAUNA

By contrast with the flora, fynbos fauna is relatively limited. The poor soils support few grasses, so there is a dearth of larger grazers and their predators. However the animals of the fynbos are integral to its ecology, and many endemic species have evolved, including the geometric tortoise (*Psammobates geometricus*), black-girdled lizard, Cape golden mole and Cape grysbok – the one antelope with a taste for the tough, indigestible leaves.

By feeding on nectar, many creatures, including insects, birds and mice, play a vital role in the pollination of the fynbos, and some enjoy specific relationships with particular flowers: the Cape sugarbird is drawn to proteas; the orange-breasted sunbird visits only certain ericas; and the mountain beauty butterfly (*Aeropetes tulbaghia*) has a taste for red-flowered geophytes.

FYNBOS UNDER THREAT

The precious fynbos is now a critically endangered habitat. Its already restricted area is being eroded and fragmented by the human demand for land. Though the tough vegetation can withstand fires and frosts, it can't survive being ploughed up for vineyards, nor does it flourish on the insidious creep of pollution from mushrooming urban development. Another significant threat comes from the steady advance of invasive alien plants, such as the Australian black wattle (*Acacia mearnsii*) and Port Jackson willow (*Acacia saligna*). Today, you can best experience the delights of the fynbos in protected areas, such as the Cape of Good Hope Nature Reserve. Don't leave it too late.

WETLANDS AND WATERWAYS

Southern Africa is essentially a dry land, so fresh water often provides a lifeline for wildlife in otherwise barren terrain. Inland waters, including pans, waterholes, lakes, rivers and marshes, lay a patchwork of secondary habitats over existing biomes. Each is a distinct ecological landscape with its own flora and fauna, and some of the richest wildlife in the region is found beside water, from the great dry-season elephant herds of the Chobe, to the summer-night frog chorus of St Lucia.

DESERT DELTA

Botswana's Okavango Delta is the world's largest inland delta, covering over 15,000km^2 during peak floods, and one of the world's natural wonders. It is formed where the Okavango River meets the Kalahari and divides into a myriad channels and waterways before the sands swallow it up. Here, the arid woodland habitat is fragmented into islands, some large, others tiny, separated from each other by shallow, meandering channels lined with dense beds of reed and papyrus and fringed with lush riverine vegetation. Larger islands support typical woodland flora and fauna, while aquatic species, from crocodile and hippo to sitatunga and Pel's fishing owl, frequent the waterways. The Okavango has a magnetic influence on the wildlife of the region, drawing great seasonal herds of herbivores, including buffalo and elephant, to enjoy its clear waters and plentiful food. In the north, the Linyanti Swamps of the eastern Caprivi Strip extend this habitat still further.

A mighty river for a mighty thirst. During the dry season, the Zambezi lures some of Africa's largest and noisiest elephant herds out of the bush. (MU)

RIVERS AND STREAMS

Southern Africa's rivers drain from the highlands and extend ribbons of life across the arid interior. Up in the hills, fast-flowing streams support fish, frogs and crabs, which in turn feed hunters such as the giant kingfisher and spotted-necked otter. Down in the lowlands, rivers slow down and spread out, and here they become the focus of many of the region's most important wildlife areas. Along the meandering floodplain of the Zambezi, pods of hippos slumber beneath the gaze of the fish eagle, carmine bee-eaters throng their sandbank colonies and, in peak season, good grazing draws the herds down from the escarpment to create one of the greatest concentrations of large mammals in Africa.

Riverine forest

In arid woodland areas, rivers – whether dry or flowing – can be spotted from a distance by the greenery along their length. Rich alluvial soils and a ready water supply allow a variety of trees to flourish, forming a dense micro-habitat known as riverine (or riparian) forest. This supports a rich fauna, particularly fruit-eaters such as louries, fruit-bats and monkeys, and cover-hugging browsers such as bushbuck. Typical riverine trees have a dense crown, and include the Natal mahogany (*Trichilia emetica*), jackal-berry (*Diospyros mespiliformis*) and sausage tree (*Kigelia africana*) which has enormous sausage-shaped fruit and attractive blood-red flowers pollinated by fruit-bats. The impressive sycamore fig (*Ficus sycomorus*) is the giant of the riverine forest, with a huge buttressed trunk and a rich crop of figs clustered along its branches throughout the year. Like all fig trees, its fruits are pollinated by a species of wasp, which lays its eggs inside.

Sycamore fig trees dominate the dense riverine forest that extends a meandering lifeline through the parched bushveld (*far left*, MU). Other riverine species include the sausage tree, whose immense swollen fruit (*left*, MU) can weigh over 10kg.

28

LAKES, DAMS, PANS AND WATERHOLES

Natural lakes are in short supply in southern Africa, but man-made dams provide water for wildlife in many regions. These range from small farm dams, which attract weaver colonies and egret roosts to their overhanging trees, to the enormous Lake Kariba, the world's second largest man-made lake,

Blue wildebeest trek vast distances to slake their thirst. (PP)

which has flooded the Zambezi Valley over an area of more than 5,000km^2. Kariba's margins have no natural riparian vegetation, but the semi-aquatic grasses attract herds of grazers, while the drowned trees and bare shorelines provide an ideal habitat for wading birds. Kariba also has abundant crocodiles, which thrive on fish such as Kariba bream.

Natural lakes vary in ecology according to their size, shoreline and water quality. Limestone-bedded pans on the South African highveld are rich in aquatic invertebrates, and can hold great concentrations of waterbirds. Salt pans, such as Makgadikgadi in Botswana and Etosha in Namibia, provide little fringing or surface vegetation for breeding birds, but their algae-rich soup is ideal for filter-feeders such as flamingos, which sometimes breed in large numbers. The St Lucia lake system of northern KwaZulu-Natal is one of the region's most important wetlands. Its nutrient-rich waters feed a wealth of fish and other aquatic life, while the dense *Phragmites* reedbeds form an ideal breeding habitat for frogs and smaller birds such as bishops, crakes and warblers. Hippos plough access channels through the reeds and fertilise the waterways with their dung.

Painted reed frog

Waterholes are integral to the ecology of woodland habitats and often provide a convenient focal point for watching wildlife. In parks without permanent rivers, such as Hwange or Etosha, they draw a continual stream of drinkers, creating a radiating network of game trails. Natural waterholes are created by the flow of rainwater into depressions and are enlarged and consolidated by the actions of large mammals such as elephants (see page 59). They are seasonal in nature, often withering to baked mud in the dry season, before bursting into life with the rains to support a community of small creatures, from frogs and terrapins to dragonflies and sandpipers. In many parks, artificial waterholes have been created to provide more water for animals and better viewing for visitors. This can be a mixed blessing, since the animals may not disperse to natural water sources, and the surrounding area becomes so degraded that the herds run out of food. In severe droughts, animals die from starvation before thirst. Many authorities are now reconsidering this strategy, in order to try and rebalance the ecological equation.

FRESHWATER FISHES

Southern Africa's 250 or so species of freshwater fish range from the huge – up to 55kg – vundu (*Heterobranchus longifilis*) of the Zambezi to the tiny Clanwilliam redfin (*Barbus calidus*) of Cape mountain streams. They include the bottom-dwelling barbels and catfish (Clariidae), the minnows and yellowfish (Cyprinidae), the cichlids and tilapias (Cichlidae), and the eels (Anguillidae), which breed at sea and migrate back upriver to mature. Notable species include the tigerfish (*Hydrocynus vittatus*), much prized by anglers; the

Sharptooth catfish (*Clarius gariepinus*), South Africa (WD/FLPA)

brown squeaker (*Synodontis zambezensis*), which wields poisonous dorsal spines and squeaks when captured; and the lungfish (*Protopterus annectens*), whose air-breathing lung enables it to survive droughts in a cocoon of mucus beneath the mud. Exotic species introduced for food or sport include trout, carp and the tiny kapenta (*Limnothrissa miodon*), which sustains a whole fishing industry on Lake Kariba.

THE COAST

Southern Africa has over 5,500km of coastline, stretching from the Zambezi River delta in the northeast, around the Cape of Good Hope, to the Kunene River mouth in the northwest. The east coast is washed by the Indian Ocean, which brings the warm Agulhas Current down from the equator, while the Atlantic pounds the west coast, bringing the cold Benguela Current up from the Antarctic. In each case, a rich ecosystem flourishes where the land meets the sea.

A DESERT SHORE

Along the Atlantic coast, much of the hot, dry interior is barren and desolate, but the icy, nutrient-rich waters teem with marine invertebrates and fish, which in turn support breeding colonies of seals and seabirds. Namibia's Skeleton Coast derives its forbidding name from a history of shipwrecks, whose hapless survivors found only a scorching desert awaiting them on land. At the old whaling station of Cape Cross, a huge fur seal colony numbers over 150,000 individuals in the breeding season and lures enterprising scavengers such as jackals and brown hyenas from the desert. Further south, sheltered lagoons provide food and shelter for flamingos, pelicans, waders and grebes, while beyond the breakers, skeins of cormorants and other seabirds ply the rich fishing waters alongside the endemic Heaviside's dolphin (see page 116). South of the Orange River, the land supports more life, extending a fringe of coastal fynbos down to the shore. Seabirds avoid land predators by nesting on rocky outcrops and islands, and at Lambert's Bay thousands of Cape gannets jostle for position, while kelp gulls, cormorants and jackass penguins all find their own niches among the boulders. In sheltered bays, such as Langebaan Lagoon, huge flocks of migrant waders visit the tidal mudflats to stock up on marine invertebrates before their long onward journey.

ROUNDING THE CAPE

Off the Cape of Good Hope, snaking forests of kelp drift in the shallows and wash up along the beaches. Kelp is the world's largest algae, reaching lengths of up to 12 metres, and is built to withstand the heavy seas of Africa's stormiest coast. Low tide exposes a jumble of weed and shrinking pools, where foragers such as the black oystercatcher glean tasty molluscs and crustaceans. Even baboons venture on to the shore to prize limpets from the rocks. Out at sea, trawlers ply the fishing lanes, towing a wake of pelagic birds (see page 120), including some which breed in the Antarctic and seldom come within sight of land. East of the Cape, the sheltered bays provide some respite from the pounding Atlantic and it is here that southern right whales (see page 115) arrive every spring to breed and calve close inshore, sometimes heaving their huge bodies clear of the water in spectacular exuberance. Meanwhile, offshore seal colonies have to run the gauntlet of cruising great white sharks, the biggest and most impressive of all southern Africa's predators.

Eastwards, along the Garden Route, dense forests overhang a shoreline sculpted by the waves into jagged headlands and crescent bays. Low tide exposes rockpools, each of which supports an ecosystem in miniature. Life occurs in different bands up the shore, according to the reach of the sea: the lower zone is dominated by beds of brown mussels, while, higher up, limpets graze algae from the rocks and whelks scavenge among the weeds. In larger pools, sea anemones snare their prey with sticky tendrils, while starfish, rock cod and octopus hunt smaller fish and molluscs. At the top of the beach, freshwater streams tumble out of the forest, bringing down land predators, such as Cape clawless otter, to forage along the shore.

THE SARDINE RUN

Between May and July, southern African pilchards (*Sardinops sagax*) spawn en masse in the cool waters off the Cape and move northeast around the coast in their billions. Shoals can measure 7km long by 1.5 km wide, and from the air resemble oil slicks. Thousands of predators – notably dolphins, sharks, seals, bluefish and gannets – gather for the bonanza, breaking up the shoals into smaller 'bait balls' as it heads north. This phenomenon, known as the 'sardine run', depends upon a cold current and does not happen unless the water temperature falls below 21°C.

The sheltered bays of the Cape coast provide calving grounds for southern right whales. (HVH)

Lambert's Bay, on the Western Cape coast, is seabird city: thousands of gannets, gulls and cormorants make a living commuting back and forth from the teeming waves. (AZ)

TROPICAL WATERS

Heading up the east coast into the waters of KwaZulu-Natal, the influence of the warm Agulhas Current brings a distinctly tropical feel to the coastline. Mangroves growing along estuary shores provide a breeding ground for many reef fish. These trees are uniquely adapted to the brackish tidal conditions, their breathing roots protruding like periscopes from the intertidal mud (*Avicennia marina*) or raised on branching stilts (*Rhizophora mucronata*). Beneath them, fiddler crabs wave their outsized pincers in curious territorial combat and mudskippers – a fish which has evolved to breathe out of water – skitter across the mud on limb-like pectoral fins.

Although this coast lacks the great seabird colonies of the southwest, the fringing dune forest (see page 20) supports a number of species better associated with tropical Africa, including the palmnut vulture (*Gypohierax angolensis*), which feeds on the fruit of oil palms. On the beach, white-fronted plovers forage among the driftwood, pale ghost crabs scuttle into holes at your approach and, on moonless summer nights, sea turtles (see page 188) haul themselves out of the surf to lay their eggs. Further north, in sheltered inlets off Mozambique, a few endangered dugongs (see page 118) still graze the seagrass beds, just below the surface.

Offshore, the Maputaland and Mozambique coasts are lined with Africa's most southerly reefs, which provide a haven for reef fish, corals and invertebrates. These include such exquisite dainties as the emperor fish and clown fish and larger predators such as groupers and moray eels. Beyond the reef drop-off, big pelagic fish such as sharks, barracuda and tuna hunt the blue depths and the enormous whale shark, the world's biggest fish, cruises the surface filtering plankton.

THE HUMAN LANDSCAPE

The imprint of man is virtually inescapable in southern Africa. The indigenous people of the subcontinent – the KhoiSan – respected their environment and harvested its precious resources sustainably. With the first European pioneers began a process of plunder that changed the face of the region with shocking speed. Within a few hundred years, great tracts of pristine land were lost forever to farming and development. Today's so-called 'wilderness' is often not what it seems: the Karoo is overgrazed; cattle fences bisect the Kalahari; forestry plantations drain the grasslands; mining roads penetrate the Namib; and even the mighty Zambezi has been dammed into submission. But nature is tenacious, and even the most desecrated environment has wildlife to offer.

DOWN ON THE FARM

Today's sugar estates, wheat fields and gum plantations are poor substitutes for the rich habitats they replaced, but there are some compensations. Arable land is a good habitat for birds, especially ground feeders such as cranes, and supports small predators such as yellow mongoose and Cape fox. Cane fields attract rodents, which feed a healthy population of snakes, while orchards draw fruit eaters like fruit-bats and mouse-birds. Forestry plantations offer shelter to raptors such as black sparrowhawk (*Accipiter melanoleucus*), farm dams are always worth a scan for waterbirds, and – for the birder with a strong nose – the ripe, nutritious soup of sewage farms and settling ponds is a magnet for ducks, waders and flamingos. Although livestock farming is bad news for wildlife, leaving large areas irretrievably overgrazed, a few animals positively prefer disturbed ground – including aardvarks, who enjoy the easier digging – while others, such as fence-leaping kudu, will thrive on rough ranch land if left alone. Today many livestock farmers are turning to game

Panoramic farmland on the edge of the Karoo. But sheep and wheat leave no space for springbok. (LVH)

farming, which can prove profitable as well as environmentally friendly. Fields of grazing blesbok beside the motorway into Johannesburg, or giraffe loping across the ranches of Matabeleland, are not truly wild, but have been reintroduced by the farmer on to land managed for wildlife. When one piece of the ecological jigsaw is restored, others soon start falling into place.

ON THE ROAD

Keep your eyes open while driving. Not only to stay alive, but also because you might glimpse animals that are otherwise hard to see. This is particularly true of small predators at night, when headlights may produce a surprise marsh mongoose, striped polecat or even, if you're very lucky, a caracal. Tar roads after summer rains attract frogs, which in turn lure snakes. Unfortunately, certain animals – including puff adder, spotted eagle owl and bat-eared fox – are frequent road casualties. But at least this proves they're around. In open country, power lines

Tropical house gecko: the original lounge lizard

and telegraph poles provide good vantage points for birds. Each habitat has its own high-wire specialists, ranging from lilac-breasted roller in the lowveld, to eastern red-footed kestrel in the highveld, pale chanting goshawk in the Karoo, long-crested eagle on the east coast and black-shouldered kite just about anywhere. In fact, birders could chalk up half the region's raptors without ever leaving the highway.

Greater double-collared sunbird on hotel aloe (MU)

IN TOWN

If you're visiting southern Africa for the first time, don't assume that your wildlife experience begins with the big game park. The action starts the moment you arrive, with Abdim's storks on the runway or a slender mongoose dashing in front of your airport taxi. City streets are not very promising at ground level, but keep an eye on the skies, where aerial hunters such as little swifts and lesser kestrels cruise the free space and formations of ibises and egrets commute back to the suburbs. Large parks are oases for wildlife of all kinds, and botanical gardens – such as Kirstenbosch in Cape Town – attract numerous butterflies and sunbirds to their banks of flowers. Certain bird species, including red-throated wryneck (*Jynx ruficollis*), are more easily seen in a city park than anywhere else. Even your hotel can offer a safari in miniature: by day striped skinks stake out the patio, preying mantises and chameleons stalk the flowerbeds, and hoopoes probe the lawn; night brings the hoot of a spotted eagle owl, bats dipping over the pool, toads croaking from the lily pond and geckos ambushing moths under the terrace lights. Who needs lions and elephants?

MAMMALS

Black rhino at an Etosha waterhole (PP)

Southern Africa is home to 343 mammal species from a world total of about 5,500. They range from the world's largest land mammal, the six-tonne African elephant, to one of the world's smallest, the 3g least dwarf shrew (and probably also include the world's most medium-sized). Among the region's highlights are the vast bulk – so to speak – of the world's black and white rhinos, major populations of cheetah and wild dog, and regional endemics such as bontebok, mountain zebra and the rare riverine rabbit. The taxonomy of mammals is continually being reassessed, but it is generally accepted that 15 orders are represented in southern Africa. Of these, the bats (Chiroptera), rodents (Rodentia) and insectivores (Insectivora) contain by far the most species but, being mostly small and nocturnal, they are the least-known and hardest to identify. Higher on the agenda of most visitors are the 'charismatic megafauna', such as big cats, elephant, giraffe, rhino and zebra, for which the region's national parks are famous.

The fossil record reveals an even greater diversity of mammals in the past, including giant hyenas, sabre-toothed cats and short-necked giraffes, and the remains of *Australopithecus* and other early hominids suggest that our own species had an evolutionary cradle in the subcontinent. However, humans have since proved unwilling to share space and resources with other large mammals, and over the last few hundred years we have had a devastating impact on the region's mammal life, including hunting to extinction both the quagga (*Equus quagga*) and bluebuck (*Hippotragus leucocephalus*). Today others, such as the black rhino, are far from safe, and the revenue from ecotourism plays a vital role in funding their protection.

CARNIVORES

Southern Africa is richly endowed with carnivores (order, Carnivora), with 39 species divided into six separate families, ranging from the 220kg lion to the 220g striped weasel. Carnivores are hunters, with sharp carnassial teeth for shearing meat and binocular vision for capturing prey. Unfortunately, this has led them into perpetual conflict with humans, who, under the pretext of 'vermin' control, have declared war on most of them. Large species, such as lion, leopard and spotted hyena, have been eliminated across much of their range, while many smaller species, including bat-eared fox and aardwolf, are wrongly persecuted as stock-killers or fall victim to traps and poisons intended for larger predators. Not all carnivores eat exclusively meat: for instance, the honey badger and African civet are both omnivores that include fruit in their diet, and the aardwolf eats only termites.

CATS

Big cats (Felidae) are the number one safari attraction for most visitors, and with their stealth, beauty and grace, they have an undeniable glamour. Farmers, however, are less impressed, and the reputation of cats as livestock predators has long been their undoing, leaving most species largely confined to conservation areas. Of the seven species found in southern Africa, the lion and leopard are the only true 'big cats' (*Panthera*). The others, by virtue of their size and some fine anatomical distinctions, are classified as 'small cats' (*Felis*), while the anomalous cheetah (*Acinonyx*) falls somewhere in between.

Lion *Panthera leo*

The lion is Africa's largest cat and undisputed number one land predator. The massive male stands up to 1.2m at the shoulder and weighs 175–240kg. He is easily distinguished from the smaller female (110–150kg) by his heavy mane, which varies from blonde to almost black. Both sexes have a tawny to greyish-brown coat, which is faintly spotted in cubs.

Lions inhabit woodland and arid savannah across the region, but have been eradicated from much of their former range. Though the first European settlers encountered lions in the Cape, in South Africa today they are largely restricted to the Kruger and Kalahari, with a few small reintroduced populations elsewhere. Otherwise, northern Botswana (Chobe and Moremi), the Zambezi Valley (from Hwange to Mana Pools) and northern Namibia (Etosha) are the remaining strongholds. Lions wandering outside protected areas are heavily persecuted, while trophy hunting has severely unbalanced some populations. Although man-eating individuals are occasionally reported, lions generally give people a wide berth.

The preferred prey of lions is medium-large herbivores such as wildebeest but, when hunting cooperatively, they can overcome animals as big as buffalo or giraffe. Different prides specialise in particular prey and pass on the techniques to their young. One pride studied in Botswana habitually chased baboons up trees until the panicking primates leapt to their fates, while another picked off lost elephant calves from the migrating herds. Choice of prey varies according to habitat. In the Kalahari, where large mammals are seasonally scarce, lions are adept at capturing tricky smaller prey, such as potentially lethal porcupines.

An adult male lion is nearly 50% bigger than a female and easily distinguished by his luxuriant mane. (MU)

For its first few vulnerable months, a lion cub's spots serve as valuable camouflage. (MU)

Lions stalk their quarry by sight, using the utmost stealth and patience, before launching an explosive charge over the last 10–20 metres. The final approach is gripping: a lioness flattens herself to the ground only metres from her prey, every muscle tensed and tail twitching furiously, waiting for the prey to take just those few small steps into range. She knows that timing is critical, and that, given a head start, it would outpace her over distance. The victim is bowled over with a leap to the shoulders or hindquarters and then killed by asphyxiation, jaws clamped over the muzzle or windpipe.

Hunting large animals is risky – one kick from a zebra can blind a lion or break its jaw, while buffalo, giraffe and sable have all been known to kill lions – so dangerous prey is first immobilised by repeated attacks from behind. The death of a buffalo can be a long and grisly business. Although lionesses do most of the hunting, males are capable hunters when alone and will also help the pride to bring down larger prey. Contrary to popular myth, lions do not employ coordinated hunting strategies, but hunting in a group can confuse prey, and if one individual gets lucky, the whole pride will benefit. A kill may be dragged into cover before being eaten, particularly if hyenas are about. Lions bolt down huge quantities at a sitting, gorging themselves until they can hardly move, and may not leave a large carcass for several days.

FAMILY CATS

Lions are unique among cats for their highly social behaviour. An average pride numbers 10–15 individuals, exceptionally up to 30, comprising mostly females and same-aged cubs together with one or two adult males. Young males are driven out of the pride after about 15 months. These itinerant individuals form loose coalitions, hunting together and sometimes joining forces to take over a new pride by ousting the resident male. Despite its apparent somnolence, pride life can be brutal. To establish their authority, newly arrived males will sometimes kill cubs in order to bring the females back into oestrus and mate with them. Small wonder then that a lioness leaves the pride to have her cubs, keeping them hidden until such time as she deems it safe to introduce them to the fray. An average of three cubs is born after a gestation period of 110 days. Life is hazardous for youngsters in their early months, particularly at feeding times, when no quarter is given over the bloody squabble for a kill.

By day, lions may appear to do little more than lie around in a heap (*top*, AZ). Once darkness falls, however, they are cats on a mission (*below*, FL/FLPA) and may travel many kilometres in search of prey.

Finding lions isn't always easy. Southern Africa's bushveld is more challenging for the spotter than East Africa's open savannah, and a whole pride may remain completely hidden only metres from the road. In reserves, a gaggle of vehicles often signals that lions have been spotted, but the reward for joining the throng may be little more than a glimpse of a twitching tail. Lions do very little for much of the time, and are particularly inert during the heat of the day. Like most cats, they are primarily nocturnal, so the best time to find them active is at dusk or dawn. Hunts often take place shortly after sunrise, so get up and out early. Night drives also offer a chance to observe lions on the hunt and, in the Kruger Park, lions often follow paved roads at night, enjoying the residual heat from the tarmac. Even if they remain unseen, lions seldom go unheard. The territorial roar of a male is audible for up to eight kilometres on a still night, with one individual often being answered by a rival. The roar is a thunderous sequence of deep, rasping moans that gradually subsides into grunts. Heard close-up from beneath flimsy canvas, it will make your hair stand on end.

Leopard *Panthera pardus*

The combination of its grace, power and elusiveness gives the leopard a special allure. This enigmatic cat has long enjoyed a mythical status in African folklore for its reputed savagery and cunning. An adult stands up to 80cm at the shoulder and weighs anything from 40 to 90kg (about half the size of a lioness), though a distinct race in the Cape is much smaller. The male is much larger than the female, with a heavier head and prominent jowls. Though often confused with the cheetah (see page 42), which shares its general size and patterning, a leopard lacks the cheetah's striking 'tear' marks on the face, and the spots on its body form distinctive rosettes. A leopard is also more powerfully built, with a larger head and sturdier limbs than its delicate-looking relative, and tends to slink closer to the ground, holding the prominent white tip of its long tail in a distinct curl (often the first giveaway of an otherwise perfectly camouflaged animal).

Leopards are the most successful of the world's big cats, ranging from the deserts of Sinai to the snows of northern China. In southern Africa they occur across much of Zimbabwe, Botswana and Namibia, in and out of reserves. In South Africa, there are still good numbers in the north and northeast, with isolated populations in the Cape and Drakensberg and wandering the borders of Swaziland and Lesotho. Leopards tolerate a wide range of habitats, being completely absent only from pure desert, and can survive surprisingly close to people (leopards have been killed on the main Johannesburg to Pretoria highway). However, these solitary, nocturnal and cover-loving cats have guarded their secrets well; only comparatively recently have scientists gained any real insight into their private life.

The behaviour and diet of leopards depend upon their environment. In areas of plentiful prey, leopard density is high and an individual's territory may be no more

A leopard is the consummate predator: stealth, power and purpose – all in a stylish package. (PP)

than 10km². In leaner areas, a territory may span 20 times this. Leopards are opportunist hunters. Though small to medium-sized antelope constitute their typical prey, anything from frogs to baby giraffe may make the menu. They even show a taste for smaller predators, including stray dogs, and will snatch an unwary baboon if they get the chance.

Leopards hunt by stealth and use any available cover to creep as close as possible before the final charge. Larger prey is usually strangled, while a bite to the skull does for smaller prey, but the chase is quickly abandoned if the

A leopard may protect its kill from other predators by hauling it into a tree. (WW/FPLA).

first attempt fails. Being solitary hunters, leopards will generally not risk injury by defending a kill against lions or hyenas.

Adult leopards are solitary except during courtship. Mating is brief and secretive, by comparison with the noisy, public couplings of lions. The female gives birth to an average litter of three cubs – which she hides from danger – including male leopards – in a nook or crevice. Cubs stay with their mother for up to 18 months, during which time they hone their hunting skills through play and on live prey that the mother brings back for this purpose. Adults mark their territorial boundaries using scratching posts and urine sprays. Leopards are generally silent animals, but call with a deep, rhythmic grunting – like the sound of a heavy saw. Though extremely shy of people and not dangerous under normal circumstances, an angry leopard is not to be trifled with.

ALWAYS SPOTTED; SELDOM SEEN

For visitors, a leopard sighting is a lucky and usually fleeting moment (except in some private reserves where experienced rangers know individual cats well enough to find them on demand). Early morning and dusk are the best times of day to look. Most fruitful, where possible, is a night drive. Since leopards are highly territorial, a pattern of recent sightings in one area may indicate a resident individual. By day, scrutinise the thick cover along watercourses: a leopard may be sprawled in a sandy riverbed or draped across an overhanging branch. Spotting a kill may lead to the killer itself, possibly in a neighbouring tree. Rocky outcrops are favourite haunts, and the alarm calls of other animals – shrieking baboons or snorting impala – sometimes give a leopard away. Once disturbed, it will usually disappear, but stick around – the curious cat will not have gone far and may reappear for another look. If this happens, stay quiet and still. A leopard is sensitive to noise and movement in a vehicle, and, at the slightest cough or twitch of a zoom lens, it may vanish behind the merest sprig of a bush or melt, improbably, into a knee-high tussock.

Cheetah *Acinonyx jubatus*

Out on a limb, literally, from all other cats, the cheetah is built entirely for speed, and is – in short bursts – the world's fastest mammal. Similar in size to a leopard, it differs by having smaller, solid spots and distinct black 'tear' markings on the face, while its build resembles more that of a greyhound than a cat, with a small head, narrow waist, deep chest and long slender limbs. Other unusual features include non-retractable claws (visible in its tracks) that function like a runner's spikes and a wickedly sharp dewclaw, set high up on each foot, to deliver the slashing blow that fells its prey. Males and females are similar, but the cubs are born with a silvery mane that camouflages them in the long grass. A rare genetic variant known as the 'king cheetah', with spots elongated into stripes, has been recorded from parts of Zimbabwe and the Kruger. Cheetahs do not roar, but make various high-pitched, chirping sounds, as well as hissing and purring.

Cheetah at full tilt. (SB/FLPA)

THE CHASE

Cheetahs prey mostly on small to medium-sized antelope, including impala, springbok and steenbok, and will also take hares and large ground birds such as kori bustards. They prefer fairly open country with good visibility, and will climb a fallen tree or termite mound to scan for prey. A hunting cheetah approaches slowly to narrow the distance until, triggered by the flight of its quarry, it launches the attack, accelerating quickly from an initial jog into a bounding sprint. At speeds of up to 100km/h, the flexible spine catapults its legs forwards in five-metre bounds, while the long counterbalance tail swings back and forth as the cheetah twists and turns to track the desperate evasive jinking of its prey. This phenomenal speed can only be sustained for a short burst and, to save limbs from injury and its brain from overheating, a cheetah will pull up short if the quarry is not quickly overhauled. A successful chase ends with the cheetah toppling its prey with a blow from behind. Before the prey can recover, it is seized by the throat and strangled. Mindful of other thieving predators, the cheetah may drag its kill to cover, but generally starts feeding immediately.

The downside of the cheetah's specialisation is its vulnerability to more robust competitors, including lions, leopards, hyenas and even pushy vultures. Built only for speed, it is a one-trick pony, lacking the strength of other large predators and ever wary of injury. It has evolved to exploit the flight instinct of its prey, but can't handle anything that fights back. To minimise competition, cheetahs are among the few large predators that habitually hunt by day. Nonetheless, kills are frequently stolen, and the exhausted cats themselves are sometimes killed in the conflict. (There are even records of cheetahs killed and stashed in trees by leopards.)

Cheetahs have an unusual social system, in which the female remains solitary while groups of young males, often brothers, bond together into adulthood.

Male cheetahs are avid scent markers of their territorial boundaries, and the vicious skirmishes between rivals sometimes prove fatal. Out in the open, the cubs are vulnerable to predators, and to offset the high mortality rate, large litters of three to six are born. At seven months, youngsters make their first tentative efforts to hunt, and their mother brings back live prey for them to hone their skills.

The cheetah is sparsely distributed throughout southern Africa, confined mainly to reserves, though some still survive on ranchland in Zimbabwe and, in particular, Namibia. Once bred for hunting in Arabia, today this cat is internationally

A cheetah cub's silver mane is a camouflage feature that is lost by adulthood. (AZ)

endangered, with fewer than 10,000 individuals remaining in the wild. Its future is further jeopardised by a lack of genetic diversity due to near extinction in the last ice age. Nonetheless, the visitor may get lucky in larger parks such as Etosha, Hwange, Moremi, Kruger or Kgalagadi. Cheetahs' diurnal lifestyle and liking of elevated vantage points makes spotting easier. Vehicles should always allow them space, since disrupting a kill could be the difference between life and death for this most fragile of predators.

A termite mound makes an ideal vantage point for spotting prey in the flat terrain of the Okavango Delta. This half-grown cub will learn by watching its mother. (M)

Caracal *Felis caracal*

The caracal is the largest of four smaller cat species also found in southern Africa. This beautiful animal stands around 45cm at the shoulder and weighs up to 18kg. Also known as the African lynx, or *rooikat* in Afrikaans, it has a lynx-like short tail and tufted ears, and a distinctive angled profile that slopes down from rump to shoulder. The uniform rich tawny coat is emblazoned with expressive dark markings around the eyes and muzzle. A caracal's powerful build enables it to take prey as large as small antelope, and its real party trick is a prodigious leap – propelled by powerful hind legs – to bring down birds in flight. It is widespread across the region and still thrives in many farming areas, despite a long history of persecution. Unfortunately the caracal does take the odd sheep or goat, but by keeping down the numbers of dassies (see page 106), which can outgraze livestock in rocky areas, it actually does farmers a service.

A typical cat, the caracal is solitary, nocturnal, and seldom seen. The best chance of a sighting is in the smaller Cape reserves of South Africa, such as the West Coast, Mountain Zebra, and Karoo National Parks (see pages 269-70). But equally, keep an eye out on any road at night.

Serval *Felis serval*

The elegant serval is roughly the same size as a caracal, but more delicately built (rather like a cheetah compared to a caracal's leopard). It has a yellowish fawn coat, strongly spotted and barred, with long slender limbs and enormous, constantly mobile ears. Servals prefer moist grassland areas and are absent from the arid south and west. Their ideal habitat is one that teems with rodents, since the serval is a mouser *extraordinaire*, pinpointing the slightest rustle of a vlei rat with a swivel of its radar ears, and pouncing with arcing, four-footed leaps through the long grass. The litter of two to three cubs is born in high summer to coincide with the peak rodent population.

Don't be fooled by these bright, sunlit images: southern Africa's smaller cats are nocturnal and rarely seen at all, let alone by day. The caracal (*above*, JB/FLPA) is the largest and most elusive and occurs throughout the region. The serval (*opposite above*, RH) is a long-legged stalker of grasslands in the north and east. The widespread African wildcat (*opposite below*, PP) is the bush-wise ancestor of the domestic house-cat.

Servals are threatened throughout the region by habitat loss, but are still widespread in Zimbabwe. Other good spots include the KwaZulu-Natal Midlands and the Okavango Delta. Since servals are nocturnal, they are most often seen after dark, although these elusive cats can be spotted on early mornings or late afternoons, particularly during overcast weather. The plaintive, high-pitched 'how-how-how' call carries some distance on still nights.

African wild cat *Felis sylvestris*

This most widespread of African felines is the ancestor of our domestic moggie, first tamed by the Ancient Egyptians over 5,000 years ago. Weighing 2.5–6kg and standing up to 35cm at the shoulder, it has a sandy to greyish coat, patterned with faint stripes, and is distinguished from its domestic cousins by a longer-legged build and markedly rufous ears. The wildcat is found in all habitats except thick forest

and pure desert. It hunts alone for rodents and birds, though is itself often a target for larger predators, including pythons and birds of prey. Shy and nocturnal, wildcats hole up in burrows by day and are seen most often at night – though in some remote areas, notably the Kalahari, daylight sightings are not unusual. As hunter and hunted, a wildcat moves with characteristic caution, trotting quickly between patches of cover and frequently stopping to scan its surroundings. Ironically, interbreeding with its domestic descendants now threatens its survival as a distinct species.

Black-footed cat *Felis nigripes*

If wildcats are hard to see, then the little-known black-footed, or small-spotted, cat is effectively off the agenda for the average visitor (although there are occasional night-drive sightings in South Africa's Addo Elephant National Park). This diminutive hunter, weighing only 1–2kg, has a heavily spotted, pale coat and distinctive black feet. It is restricted to the arid southwest, from the Karoo to western Botswana and central Namibia, where it hunts rodents, reptiles and insects, resting by day in the burrows of other animals. Known to farmers as the 'anthill tiger', the black-footed cat is reputedly very aggressive – a practical necessity for such a vulnerable little creature.

It's share and share alike at a wild dog kill, with adults making room for pups. A large carcass is consumed in minutes, leaving precious little for scavengers. (PP)

DOGS

Dogs (Canidae) evolved for chasing prey in open grasslands, and although evolution has since taken many of them in other directions, the basic anatomy of lithe build, long muzzle, bushy tail and non-retractile claws is derived from this lifestyle and true of all dogs today. Southern Africa has five species, ranging from the pack-hunting wild dog to the insectivorous bat-eared fox. All are social creatures to some extent, and show sophisticated organisation, communication and breeding behaviour.

Wild dog *Lycaon pictus*

The African wild dog, once known as the Cape hunting dog, and sometimes referred to today as the African painted wolf, is one of Africa's most endangered mammals. For years this fascinating carnivore was labelled a wanton killer and eliminated as vermin – even in parks such as Kruger and Hwange. Today this ignorance has largely been defeated and wild dogs are winning back friends among tourists and conservationists alike. Unfortunately, the damage has been done, and today fewer than 4,000 remain.

The wild dog is a slim, long-legged animal, standing about 75cm at the shoulder and weighing 20–30kg. Taller than a jackal and slimmer than a hyena, its combination of Mickey Mouse ears and white-tipped tail is unmistakable (see page 3). The bizarrely mottled coat, like a tie-dyed rug, is uniquely patterned in each dog, enabling researchers to distinguish and study individuals. The wild dog's preferred habitat is open bush country with good visibility, and in prey-rich areas such as the Okavango, packs may number over 30. Today they occur in northwest Zimbabwe, across northern Botswana and into northern Namibia, with the Kruger Park holding South Africa's only viable population. Kruger, Hwange and, in particular, Okavango/Moremi can all produce good sightings. However, the wild dog is a great nomad and may wander miles from its usual range, posing a major problem for conservationists trying to protect it.

Wild dogs are highly efficient predators. Hunting in packs by day, they have a higher success rate than any other of Africa's large carnivores. The preferred prey is medium-sized antelope, such as impala, or the young of larger species such as kudu. With impressive speed and stamina, wild dogs pursue their quarry over a distance, singling out an individual and worrying at it until, often by sheer weight of numbers, they bring it down. Though grisly to watch, the end is mercifully quick. Pack life is complex and endlessly entertaining, with the ritualised politics of adults and the constant chittering of excitable pups. A pack centres around one dominant breeding pair and occupies a temporary den for breeding. Litters are unusually large, up to ten or more, and females cooperate in raising the pups. Kills are shared amicably, and when one is made some distance from the den, adults return with meat to regurgitate to the pups. Their cooperative behaviour gives wild dogs an edge over competitors and they will readily put hyenas or leopards to flight. Only lions are a serious threat: attacks from these big cats take a significant toll on wild dogs, which prefer to avoid areas of high lion density.

Black-backed Jackal *Canis mesomelas*
The black-backed jackal is the commoner of two species of jackal in southern Africa. This slim, medium-sized canine stands 40cm at the shoulder and weighs 7–10kg. The sandy to reddish coat has a dark 'saddle' across the back, liberally flecked with white, and the tail is dark-tipped. Black-backed jackals are widespread and highly

Always with an eye for the main chance, the black-backed jackal is one of Africa's most successful predators. (AZ)

versatile, found anywhere from the Drakensberg grasslands to the Skeleton Coast. Their catholic diet ranges from fruit and insects to birds and young antelope, and they are adept at scavenging from beneath the noses of larger predators such as lions and hyenas. Jackals are notorious among farmers for their canny ability to evade any trap. In fact, despite persecution, they thrive on farmland, and top the food chain in areas where larger predators have been eradicated.

Black-backed jackals can be active by night or day. They are often seen lying up near waterholes in the early morning, or trotting back along the road after a night's hunting. Towards late afternoon and evening, particularly in the breeding season, they announce themselves with a drawn-out wailing, one individual answering another until an unearthly chorus builds up: Africa's answer to the wolf. They also utter a repeated yapping when tailing a predator – a call that sometimes betrays an irritated lion or leopard. A litter of one to six pups is born in early spring, and the young stay with adults for over a year. Jackals pair for life and scattered family groups stay loosely in touch, sometimes coming together at times of plenty. Communication involves a complex language of calls, scent marking and posturing.

Side-striped jackal *Canis adustus*

Side-striped jackal

The side-striped jackal is fractionally larger than the black-backed and is overall greyer in appearance, with a white-tipped tail, more pointed ears and a pale stripe along each flank. It inhabits higher rainfall areas to the north and east of the region, being common in Zimbabwe but absent from the arid western tracts of South Africa, Botswana and Namibia. Hwange, Chobe and Moremi are all good places for sightings. This jackal is more nocturnal and less vocal than its cousin and generally keeps to itself. Its diet includes large quantities of fruit and rodents, for which it wanders up to 15km each night, according to seasonal supply. The litter of four to six pups is usually born in a burrow excavated by another animal.

Bat-eared fox *Otocyon megalotis*

No bigger than a domestic cat, the bat-eared fox seems little more than an animated ball of grizzled fluff with huge ears and a bushy tail. Closer inspection also reveals long dark legs and a dark face mask. This unusual canine feeds almost entirely upon termites. It inhabits arid western regions, being particularly common in the Kalahari, where small family groups, each comprising a breeding pair with offspring, forage together, regularly cocking ears to the ground for the rustle of termites. Being on the menu for many larger predators, bat-eared foxes are equally vigilant for danger and quick to dash for cover. Back at the burrow, they groom each other constantly and communicate with a semaphore of ear and tail signals. The litter of four to six cubs, born in an underground den, is guarded by the male while the female is out foraging. Bat-eared foxes may be encountered at night anywhere within their range, but can also be seen by day during winter. Sadly, this species is a common road casualty in the Cape, and entire families are sometimes wiped out beneath the wheels of a large truck.

Cape fox *Vulpes chama*

The Cape fox is fractionally smaller than the bat-eared, and lacks the face mask and oversized ears, having instead an attractive tawny and silver coat and a dark, bushy tail. This species is endemic to southern Africa, and widespread in open country across the southern and western regions. It thrives in the wheatfields and fynbos of the Cape, feeding on insects, reptiles and rodents, but in some areas it has earned a reputation as the killer of new-born lambs (a rare occurrence) and it is depressing to find a row of these exquisite creatures strung up along the fence of a Free State sheep farm. To see one alive, try the Kgalagadi Transfrontier Park. In late spring you can watch pups at play around the den.

Bat-eared foxes (*right*) are sociable little canines with prodigious powers of hearing. (PP)

Limestone outcrops flank the dry river valleys of the Kgalagadi Transfrontier Park, providing perfect denning sites for the secretive Cape fox (*below*). (PP)

HYENAS
Spotted hyena *Crocuta crocuta*

Hyenas (Hyaenidae) have always had a bad press. Whether as accessories to witchcraft in African folklore, or as the cowardly bad guys of Disney's *Lion King*, these much-maligned animals still inspire revulsion amongst many people. This is a great pity, since hyenas are truly fascinating creatures.

The spotted hyena is the largest of the family, standing up to 85cm at the shoulder, with the larger female reaching 70kg. It is easily recognised by its

A hyena's power is concentrated at the front end. (FL/FLPA)

rounded ears, sloping gait and front-heavy profile, with the long neck and powerful shoulders supporting massive, bone-crunching jaws. This versatile, sociable predator is both an accomplished scavenger and an efficient hunter, using teamwork to overcome prey as large as kudu and, in sufficient numbers, even driving lions off their kill. Communication is vital to success: individual hyenas foraging alone keep in contact with whooping calls – a spine-chilling backdrop to the African night – and gatherings around a kill generate a chorus of ghoulish cackling.

Hyena clans are matriarchal and, as a bizarre by-product of its high testosterone levels, the female hyena has a false male organ – an erectile 'pseudopenis' – which inspired an ancient belief that these animals were hermaphrodites. They mark territory with 'pastings' of a pungent secretion from the anal gland and often use communal latrines – conspicuous by their litter of white, bone-filled droppings (known to rangers as 'bush meringues'). A litter of one or two cubs is born in an underground den, sometimes located in a drainage culvert, where available, and youngsters are often seen lazing around the entrance during the early morning or late afternoon.

Spotted hyenas prefer open bush country. Although eradicated from most of South Africa, they are widespread elsewhere and in some reserves remain relatively common, often visiting camps to scavenge from bins and stake out barbecues. In fenced camps, try searching with your torch along the perimeter wire after dark. In unfenced camps, such as those in Chobe or Mana Pools, don't leave out anything overnight – walking boots and even frying pans have been lost to these opportunist jaws – and never sleep outside your tent.

Brown hyena
Parahyaena brunnea

The brown hyena is endemic to southern Africa, and more widespread than is often realised. It has a similar build to the spotted, but is smaller (around 45kg), and easily distinguished by its pointed ears and long mane of dark hair across the back and shoulders. Brown hyenas are nocturnal, and more reclusive and solitary than their spotted

The brown hyena covers great distances in its largely solitary foraging. (ND)

cousins. Although tolerant of a variety of habitats, they tend to avoid areas where the spotted is numerous, and today are best known from the dry scrublands of the Kalahari. Here they chiefly scavenge, but also supplement their diet with tsama melons (see page 16), and plunder ostrich nests for their eggs. On Namibia's Skeleton Coast, the brown hyena has learnt to survive on seashore pickings, and has acquired the Afrikaans name *strandwolf* (beach dog). Other good places to look for this elusive animal are the Kgalagadi Transfrontier Park and Pilanesberg National Park (see page 268). They also occur surprisingly close to habitation, including in the Magaliesberg Hills northwest of Pretoria.

Aardwolf *Proteles cristatus*

Weighing only 6–11kg, the aardwolf is much the smallest member of the hyena family, although its long erectile mane can give a deceptive appearance of size. It has a dark muzzle and pointed ears and its fawn coat is thinly patterned with stripes. Aardwolfs are widespread, though seldom seen. They inhabit open country, from arid scrub to moister, high-altitude grasslands. Although maligned as lamb-killers by farmers, little could be further from the truth, since the aardwolf feeds almost exclusively on termites. In fact it doesn't have the teeth to deal with meat at all – the long canines are purely for self-defence – and a much more

The aardwolf's predatory features belie its humble diet of ants. (ND)

important tool is its tongue, with which it can lick up over 100 million termites a year. Aardwolfs den in the old burrows of other animals, particularly aardvarks. Although largely nocturnal, they may be spotted out and about on an overcast day. Night drives in the Cape and Karoo parks often produce a sighting, and Malolotja in Swaziland's highveld (see page 272) is an excellent spot.

BADGERS, POLECATS, WEASELS AND OTTERS

Five species of mustelid occur in southern Africa. This family of small to medium-sized carnivores all have sinuous bodies and short legs and are relentlessly energetic in their pursuit of food. They vary widely in lifestyle and diet: otters pursue fish and crabs underwater; weasels wriggle down holes after rodents; honey badgers snap up and dig out just about anything that takes their fancy.

Honey badger *Mellivora capensis*

The honey badger's fearsome reputation belies its modest size. Weighing only 8–14kg, its notorious aggression means that larger animals, even lions and leopards, treat it with great respect. Lurid bush tales describe badgers attacking buffalo, shredding pythons and demolishing steel traps. Despite a whiff of hyperbole in some such stories, this is nonetheless an impressive little animal. Its characteristic jog-trot through the bush, nose to the ground and short tail held erect, suggests an animal with little to fear, and one theory holds that its conspicuous silver mantle serves, like a wasp's stripes, to warn off would-be aggressors.

The honey badger is stockily built, with a short tail, broad head, powerful forelimbs and long claws for digging. It wanders great distances in search of food, and its diet includes insects, fruits, reptiles and small mammals. Honey is a particular delicacy, for which the badger will raid bees' nests, its tough coat protecting it from stings. Unfortunately this habit has led it into trouble with bee-keepers, especially in the Cape, where many honey badgers are trapped and poisoned every year – although simply raising beehives on solid metal poles can solve this problem.

Honey badgers enjoy intriguing cooperative relationships with other animals and birds, including the greater honeyguide, which leads the way to bees' nests (see page 166) and the pale chanting goshawk (see page 151), which accompanies a foraging badger to pounce on whatever it flushes out. Though widespread across the region, and found in most habitats except pure desert and intensive farmland, they are nocturnal and not easily seen. The easiest sightings are at camps, such as Hwange's Sinematella, where habituated individuals scavenge with alarming boldness.

Two honey badgers stand their ground against a pack of wild dogs. (SE/FLPA)

Polecat and weasel

The striped polecat (*Ictonyx striatus*) is another small carnivore with a warning worth heeding. Weighing about a kilogram, and no more than 60cm long, it has a striking black-and-white striped coat and bushy white tail, which – like a skunk – it waves in warning before spraying a foul-smelling liquid from its anal gland. Striped polecats are widespread across most habitats, but seldom seen, other than as roadkills, because of their solitary, nocturnal habits. The voracious little African weasel (*Poecilogale albinucha*) superficially resembles the striped polecat, with its black-and-white stripes, but is less than half the size (300g) and sleeker in appearance.

Striped polecat

Otters

There are two species of otter in southern Africa. The Cape clawless otter (*Aonyx capensis*) is the larger and better-known. Weighing up to 18kg and averaging around 130cm in length, it has a typical otter build, with the streamlined body, short legs and sturdy tail of an animal more at home in water than out of it. A typical sighting is little more than a retreating glimpse of whiskery muzzle or glistening back, but when left alone, the Cape clawless otter is an entertaining animal, particularly a female cavorting in the water with her cubs.

Otters use their dextrous toes to locate, catch and dismantle their food – mostly crabs, fish and molluscs – and their unwebbed front paws leave finger-like tracks, almost like a monkey's. These tracks, and the white droppings of crushed crab-shell, are often found beside water. The Cape clawless otter is reasonably widespread in rivers and wetlands to the east and north of the region, and a boat trip in Botswana's Chobe or Okavango may strike lucky. It may also be seen in the intertidal zone along much of South Africa's coast, although hikers on the famous Otter Trail should be prepared for disappointment.

The Cape clawless otter consumes its catch on land. (RH)

Weighing only 3–5kg, the spotted-necked otter (*Lutra maculicollis*) is less than half the size of the Cape clawless otter, and has dark blotchy markings on its pale throat and chest. It is more easily confused with the water mongoose (see page 57), but the latter is less aquatic, darker and bushier than both otters. The spotted-necked otter is a diurnal and sociable species that feeds mainly on fish, preferring faster-flowing, clearer waters than its more common cousin. It has a fragmented distribution in the southeast and far north of the region, with prime areas including the KwaZulu-Natal Midlands of South Africa and the Caprivi Strip of Northern Botswana and Namibia.

Genets are equally at home on the ground or in the trees. The large-spotted (*above*, ND) can usually be distinguished from the small-spotted (*right*, ND) by its black, rather than white, tail tip. Both species are common camp visitors in the right habitats.

CIVET AND GENETS

Although civets and genets are often referred to as a cats, they actually belong to a completely separate family – the Viverridae. The African civet (*Civettictis civetta*) weighs up to 16kg and stands about 40cm at the shoulder – the size of a smallish dog. Its greyish coat is blotched and spotted with black, and it has a banded tail and black face mask. Civets are widespread in the north and northeast, preferring thick cover near water. They are omnivorous, eating fruit, mammals, reptiles and invertebrates, and relish noxious creatures that other predators avoid, such as millipedes and toads. Their surprisingly large scats, identifiable by the crushed remains of millipedes, are deposited on territorial middens (see page 226). Civets are solitary and nocturnal, and walk with a characteristic stiff gait, head held low and back arched. They sometimes scavenge around camps after dark, where they may be quietly observed at close quarters.

African civet

Genets are much smaller than civets, with short legs and long, banded tails. There are two species in the region: the common or small-spotted genet (*Genetta genetta*) prefers drier country to the south and west; the large-spotted genet (*Genetta tigrina*) prefers higher rainfall areas to the east and north. Where their ranges overlap, for example in the Kruger, they can be told apart by their markings: the small-spotted has smaller spots, black legs and a white-tipped tail; the large-spotted has larger rusty-brown spots and a black-tipped tail. Each is about a metre long, and weighs 1.5–2.5kg. Genets are excellent climbers and often lie up in trees by day. Nocturnal and largely solitary, they forage in the branches and on the ground for insects and small mammals, and sometimes take roosting birds. You may spot them on night drives, or scavenging around camp after dark. With their long tails and lithe bodies, they appear almost to flow across the ground and along branches.

MONGOOSES

Southern Africa has 14 species of mongoose (Herpestidae). This diverse family of small carnivores includes several species with highly sophisticated social systems. The suricate (*Suricata suricatta*), better known in the UK as the meerkat, was catapulted on to the animal celebrity A-List following a popular 1990s TV documentary, *Meerkats United*. This unlikely superstar is a medium-sized mongoose with a big head, short tail and faint body stripes. It is found in the arid parts of South Africa, Botswana and Namibia, where it lives in underground colonies of ten or so adults (with their young) and forages by day for grubs, scorpions and other invertebrates. Foraging suricates are vulnerable to attack from above by birds of prey, so sentries take turns to keep a lookout from a high vantage point while the others dig. If danger is sighted, the sentry whistles an alarm and the whole group dives for cover. A threat at ground level, such as a jackal, is repelled by the group advancing in one bristling phalanx. This spirit of cooperation also helps in rearing the young, which are

An enterprising meerkat sentry will often clamber to the top of a bush for a better view of its surroundings. At the changing of the guard another takes its place, though getting down isn't always as easy as getting up. (RT)

A miscellany of mongooses.
From top to bottom: banded
mongoose (AZ); dwarf mongoose (MU);
yellow mongoose (AZ); slender
mongoose (MU)

suckled by all the females in a colony. Suricates are well-known from the Kalahari, but can be encountered anywhere in the right habitat. Their antics are undeniably entertaining, with noses alternately buried in the ground or pointed to the sky.

In the woodland savannah of Zimbabwe, northern Botswana and northeast South Africa, the suricate is replaced by two other sociable mongoose species. The banded mongoose (*Mungos mungo*) is medium-sized and greyish brown, with a pattern of dark bands along its back. It is often found close to water, where troops of up to 40 may be seen by day – often foraging tamely around camps and lodges (the waterfronts at Victoria Falls and Chobe are prime spots). Like suricates, banded mongooses show great cooperation in defence, and have even been seen to pursue a martial eagle up a tree to rescue one of their troop. They feed by rummaging amongst leaf litter for invertebrates, often alongside other foragers such as vervet monkeys or guinea fowl.

At only 350grams, the dwarf mongoose (*Helogale parvula*) is much the smallest of the family. But what it lacks in size, it makes up for in character. Dark chestnut brown and little bigger than a hamster, this diminutive mongoose lives in colonies in termitaria or old hollow logs. A foraging troop does not venture far from home, and is often located by the high-pitched, bird-like contact calls. When disturbed, the troop dashes for cover, but if you stay still, a succession of beady-eyed faces will pop back up from their holes until, mongoose by mongoose, the whole colony cautiously re-emerges.

Solitary mongooses

A smallish mongoose seen alone by day in the northern half of the region is likely to be a slender mongoose (*Galerella sanguinea*). This rapacious little animal captures rodents, lizards and sometimes – like Kipling's *Rikki Tikki Tavi* – snakes. It is brownish in colour, as slim as its name suggests and has the diagnostic habit of arching its long black-tipped tail over its head as it dashes for cover. Two separate colour forms found in Namibia – a dark brown and a reddish one – have recently been recognised as distinct species. Slender mongooses inhabit open woodland, where they make their home in hollow trees or termitaria. They also do well in suburbia.

The yellow mongoose (*Cynictis penicillata*) is also usually seen alone by day, although this species actually lives in loose colonies, often sharing burrow systems with suricates or ground squirrels. It is similar in size to the slender mongoose, with a foxier face and a bushier, white-tipped tail, always held horizontally. The typical race has a yellowish fawn coat, although a greyer race is found in northern Botswana. This mongoose inhabits the more arid western half of the region, where it thrives in the wheat fields of the Cape and is a confiding camp visitor in the Kgalagadi Transfrontier Park.

The small grey mongoose (*Galerella pulverulenta*) is, reassuringly, small and grey. This largely solitary and diurnal species is found in the southwestern third of the region where it is a prolific predator of rodents in a variety of habitats, including along the seashore and around farm buildings. It hunts along regular pathways through low cover, always holding its bushy tail low.

Larger mongooses

There are six other mongoose species in the region, most of which are nocturnal and less often seen. The cat-sized white-tailed mongoose (*Ichneumia albicauda*) is the largest, weighing up to 5kg, and is reasonably common in moist woodland to the north and east. Caught in the spotlight, it strikes a distinctive profile as it zig-zags back and forth, foraging for small animals, with hindquarters raised and head held low. This mongoose has a greyish coat, black legs and a diagnostic thick white plume of tail. It is often seen on night drives in the southern Kruger and KwaZulu-Natal parks.

The water mongoose (*Atilax paludinosus*) is another larger, solitary species, weighing up to 4kg. As the name suggests, it lives close to water, where it hunts for frogs and crabs and is often mistaken for an otter (see page 53), though it has a shaggier, dark brown coat and a more pointed face. Water mongooses swim well and leave distinctive splayed tracks in riverside mud. They occur in suitable habitats to the east of the region, including seashores, and also penetrate the drier interior along rivers.

The large grey, or Egyptian mongoose (*Herpestes ichneumon*) is up to a metre long, with a tapering black-tipped tail. It hunts alone, often by day, in riverine habitat to the north of the region and along the southern and eastern coasts.

The white-tailed mongoose is strictly nocturnal. (PP/FLPA)

AFRICAN ELEPHANT

The African elephant (*Loxodonta africana*) is the world's biggest land animal and looms large in the history and culture of the continent. A mature bull can weigh a massive six tonnes and stand four metres at the shoulder, while the smaller cow, at 2.8–3.5 tonnes and just over three metres, is not exactly little either.

Almost every part of this extraordinary animal is unique. The trunk functions as both the world's longest nose, able to sniff out food or danger from kilometres away, and as a fifth limb, nimble enough to pluck a seed pod and strong enough to tear down the whole branch. The tusks are outsized incisor teeth that have evolved into lethal weapons and also serve as tools for heavy-duty labour such as digging up roots and splitting open tree trunks. The huge ears not only provide acute hearing but also help keep the elephant cool by circulating its entire blood supply through a fine network of blood vessels at the surface. Even an elephant's skin is unlike any other animal's: its great wrinkled expanse is riddled with cracks and fissures where trapped mud stays moist and evaporates slowly, providing constant cooling. The whole immense bulk is supported by massive, column-like legs which give a running elephant a peculiar, shuffling gait – though it can cover ground with deceptive and alarming speed. Most disconcertingly, the spongy soles on its huge, round feet enable an elephant to tread almost silently over a crunchy carpet of leaves.

SHAPING THE LAND

Elephants have a greater impact on their own landscape than any other mammal except man. By destroying trees, they open up woodland into grassland and change a whole area's ecology. During droughts, big herds wreak havoc, leaving an apparently apocalyptic landscape of smashed and splintered trees. However, while seemingly laying waste to their environment, elephants also enrich and fertilise it: fallen trees offer browse for other herbivores and a micro-habitat for many smaller animals; marula seeds and palm nuts pass through elephants intact and are fertilised en route to germinate wherever they fall; fresh droppings provide rich pickings for foragers such as francolins and baboons, before being broken down by dung beetles and dispersed to enrich the soil (see page 216). By using the same regular wallows, elephants also create important seasonal waterholes into which their well-worn trails funnel any rainwater run-off, and the wells that they dig in dry riverbeds are used by many other animals – when they can get a look in.

Elephants eat anything vegetable and they eat a lot of it: over 150kg a day in the case of a large bull. To fuel their great bulk, over half their time is spent feeding, by both day and night. Not much escapes a hungry elephant: roots and tubers are excavated with tusks or feet and shaken free of soil; grass is torn up with the trunk; leaves are pulled down from branches six metres up; big trees are shaken like saplings to scatter their prized seed pods or simply pushed over to get at their goodies; bark is ripped off like potato peel and the juicy inner pulp gouged out by tusks. This mountain of food needs washing down, and elephants gather daily to drink – an adult downing up to 200 litres in a single session. They also bathe, wallow

Elephants tend to be right- or left-tusked, the favoured tusk usually appearing more worn or damaged than the other. Bulls have larger tusks than cows, though size varies from one region to another (there are few big tuskers in the calcium-poor soils of Hwange, for example, but the Kruger produces some monsters). Bulls, like the one pictured here, usually feed alone and can be distinguished from cows by their more hollow temples and rounded forehead. (AZ)

and frolic with great exuberance and are strong swimmers, readily crossing rivers as broad as the Zambezi, with trunks raised aloft like snorkels. Elephants have even been recorded swimming over 25km across Lake Kariba, following ancient drowned migration trails.

Nothing quite like it for cooling the blood. A mud wallow at South Africa's Addo Elephant National Park (see page 270) affords welcome relief from the hot, dry bush. It also makes a perfect playground, where youngsters can hone their social skills under strict adult supervision. Addo's elephants represent a remarkable conservation story: today's population of over 450 is descended from only 11 individuals, the sole survivors of relentless persecution by farmers and ivory hunters in the early 20th century. (PP)

Elephant society is matriarchal. A breeding herd is led by a dominant female, together with her offspring and related cows with their youngsters. Adult bulls join the herd when the cows are ready to breed but otherwise hang out in smaller bachelor groups. Sometimes herds of several hundred may gather, but family groups never lose their individual identities. There is no breeding season. After a gestation period of 22 months, a single calf is born, weighing about 120kg. It is pink, hairy and pretty much helpless, maturing at about the same rate as we do. Calves require patient tuition from their mother and elder siblings in everything from basic trunk skills to finding food and water, and other females within the herd may share parental duties. The old matriarch is a repository of wisdom and experience, leading the herd to food and water along trails trodden by generations and steering them away from danger.

Herds communicate with trumpets and gurgles, and their deep 'tummy rumble' (actually produced in the throat) uses low-frequency infra-sound to keep in contact over many kilometres. Elephants are extremely tactile animals, and use their trunks to signal greeting, affection or concern. They will go to great lengths to rescue a trapped calf or support an injured companion and even appear to grieve for their dead, sometimes lingering around the body for days and defending it from scavengers.

Elephant bulls become sexually active at about 15 years, although most don't get to mate until around 30 years. When searching for females on heat, males go into *musth* – a kind of supercharged state of arousal, indicated by glandular secretions from the sides of the head as well as the huge, mobile and dribbling penis. During this time, young bulls swagger around aggressively and will challenge older ones for access to the females. Confrontations are usually settled by a ritualised display of size and status, but the occasional titanic battles may prove fatal for one combatant. Elephants can also be very stroppy towards other animals. They hate lions, which do occasionally pose a threat to calves, but may also chase away other animals from a waterhole for no apparent reason.

Elephants' most important daily requirements are food, water and shade. They once occupied most habitats across the region, but today are largely confined to savannah woodland towards the north. A loosely contiguous population, numbering over 150,000, stretches down the Zambezi Valley, through Hwange and Chobe, into the Okavango. Numbers fluctuate seasonally, but the peak dry season gathering along Chobe's waterfront is probably the biggest anywhere in Africa. There are also good numbers in northern Namibia, the Limpopo Valley, the Zimbabwe Lowveld and the Kruger Park. South Africa has several small relic or reintroduced populations, and a few wary elephants survived the wholesale wartime poaching in southern Mozambique. Most unusual are the 'desert elephants' of northern Namibia's Kaokoveld, which trek huge distances across the barren wastes in search of food and water.

Elephants can be everywhere or nowhere: in the dry season, they can dominate the landscape; in the rainy season the bush seems to swallow them up. Look for signs of recent activity, such as newly broken branches, steaming dung or fresh tracks. Stop and listen: feeding elephants are often betrayed by low rumblings or the crack and crash of tumbling foliage. Always respect an elephant's space. It is one of the only animals that, if pressed too hard, may attack a vehicle. Most aggression is bluff, but don't take any risks (see page 238). An unhappy or irritated elephant will turn to face the intruder with ears spread and head held high, followed by a shake of the ears and a trumpeted warning. If you meet a herd feeding at leisure, pull over and turn off your engine. They will soon relax and you can then enjoy them in peace and quiet. If a big bull decides to block the road, just be patient – he'll eventually get bored and wander off. In some areas, such as Savute and Mana Pools, old bulls are regular camp visitors and will wander among the tents or chalets. Don't worry: they know you are there. Keep quiet and still, and you will enjoy the thrill of a really close encounter with the biggest of beasts.

PROTECTING ELEPHANTS

The dilemmas of elephant conservation are well known. Hundreds of years of slaughter for ivory peaked in the 1970s and 80s when poaching ran rampant across the continent, culminating in the 1989 international banning of the ivory trade. Several southern African countries opposed this ban, arguing that elephants had to pay their way, and pointing out that successfully protected elephant populations in the region had reached unsustainable levels. Today the debate continues. Some parks still pursue a controversial habitat management policy of culling elephants, although others – such as the Kruger – are also exploring alternatives such as contraception. Populations remain healthy for now but, with regional instability and an ever-increasing demand for land, the situation may yet change.

HOOFED MAMMALS

Herbivores with hooves are known as ungulates. They are divided into two principal orders according to the number of toes on each foot: zebras (one toe) and rhinos (three toes) are odd-toed ungulates (Perrisodactyla); all the rest, including antelope, buffalo, pigs, giraffes and hippos, are even-toed ungulates (Artiodactyla), with either two or four toes on each foot. Africa has the world's greatest variety of ungulates, ranging in size from the 3kg blue duiker to the two-tonne white rhino. Some, such as zebras, are grazers; others, such as giraffe, are browsers; a few, such as bush pigs, will root out anything they can get their snouts into.

RHINOS

Rhinos are the tanks of the bush – massive walls of grey flesh, each surmounted by two bizzare and lethal horns (composed simply of compressed hair-like keratin fibres). Two species of these prehistoric-looking herbivores are found in the region, and both have been brought perilously close to extinction. Today southern Africa, and in particular South Africa, protects over 80% of Africa's remaining rhinos.

White rhinoceros *Ceratotherium simum*

After elephants, the white rhino is the world's biggest land mammal. A mature bull can weigh more than 2,300kg and stand 1.8m at the shoulder; the smaller cow weighs up to 1,600kg. Its alternative name, square-lipped rhino, is more helpful, since this animal is certainly not white: the word derives from the Afrikaans *weid*, meaning wide, which describes the broad shape of its muzzle. The white rhino is exclusively a grazer and crops grass with its tough lips like a giant lawnmower. The black rhino, by contrast, has a hooked upper lip for browsing. But you don't need to get this close to tell the two animals apart. The white rhino is much bigger, carries its huge head low to the ground, and has a distinct hump on the neck and a fin-like ridge on the spine.

The white rhino, pictured here, can be distinguished from the black by its massive head – usually held low to the ground – and its square, grass-cropping muzzle. Females have longer, slimmer horns than males, with the record length being 1.58m. (MU)

The white rhino, like the black, uses regular rubbing posts to relieve itself of troublesome skin parasites. In this case, a large rock hits the spot. (PP)

It is also a more sociable animal and generally held to be more even-tempered than its notoriously irascible relative. Personally, I wouldn't get too friendly with either of them.

White rhinos inhabit open bushveld, where they spend up to 50% of their time grazing, rotating their feeding areas to maintain a number of regular 'lawns'. They drink daily, usually in the evening, and cool off by day in mud wallows, which also helps to remove skin parasites. A regular wallow usually has a nearby favourite rubbing post; a low stump polished to a fine finish by generations of itchy rhinos. The male is highly territorial, and marks his boundaries along well-worn paths with urine spray and huge dung middens – up to 30 within a territory of 2–5km. Having deposited a fresh load, he scrapes into it with his back feet, picking up a scent to spread along the trail, and leaving distinctive drag marks. Conflicts between rivals sometimes turn into thunderous jousting battles, which can last for hours and may even cause fatal injuries.

Rhino courtship lasts 20 days and culminates in a strenuous half-hour of mating. There is no set breeding season, and after a 16-month gestation, the female gives birth to a single calf weighing about 45kg. Newborn calves have no horns and are vulnerable to attack by any lion or hyena that can get past the vigilant but cumbersome mother. It is not uncommon to see a rhino with a damaged or missing ear or tail from such attacks. In flight, a female white rhino shepherds her calf in front, whereas a black rhino calf trots along behind its mother. Calves remain with their mother for two to three years, and several half-grown calves may stay with an adult female. Where the ranges of females overlap, white rhinos may form groups of six or more.

The white rhino represents one of the world's great conservation success stories. Having been reduced to a single population of about 100 animals in KwaZulu-Natal at the turn of the century, careful protection and reintroduction have seen it recolonise many former haunts. Although its status in Zimbabwe, Botswana and Namibia remains precarious, this species now thrives in South Africa, which has a total population of over 16,000. Prime spots are Imfolozi or Hluhluwe (see page 271) and the Kruger. However, a dramatic resurgence of poaching since 2009 has become a serious cause for concern.

A black rhino often hides away in thorny thickets, where it uses its hooked upper lip for browsing on twigs and foliage. (MU)

Black rhinoceros *Diceros bicornis*

The black rhino (see page 35) is seriously endangered. Only around 4,000 are thought to remain, of which over 3,000 are in southern Africa. By contrast with the white rhino, this animal was common across Africa for much of the 20th century, and white hunters slaughtered thousands with impunity. But since the 1960s, its accelerated decline, mainly due to the lucrative eastern market for rhino horn, has been among the most catastrophic of any mammal. The 'rhino wars' of the '80s and '90s, which claimed the lives of many rangers and poachers, made international headlines, but still failed to save the beleaguered Zambezi Valley population. Although the situation has since stabilised and South Africa now has a slowly growing population, many black rhinos remain only in secure, fenced areas, which does not bode well for the free-ranging future of this animal.

Black rhinos are much smaller than white rhinos, weighing 'only' 900–1,200kg and standing about 1.6m at the shoulder. They are no more black than white rhinos are white, but diagnostic features include the hooked upper lip, smaller head – generally held up – and an altogether slighter build, with a distinct saddle to the back. After watching white rhinos, the first view of a black rhino suggests a dynamic and streamlined animal. Indeed, this massive creature is surprisingly agile and can reach an alarming 55km/h at full tilt. Black rhinos have a reputation for bad-tempered aggression. In fact, they are timid but curious. With acute smell and hearing, but poor eyesight, they are quick to perceive a threat but slow to identify it, so sometimes opt for a blind charge as the best form of defence. This can be a nerve-racking experience for the onlooker, and sometimes requires an awkward scramble up the nearest tree. An excited rhino emits an odd range of noises, including a shrill squealing and an intimidating steam-train-like puffing.

The preferred habitat of black rhinos is dense thicket, not far from water, where they browse on a variety of plants – including those toxic to other animals, such as tamboti (*Spirostachys africana*) and euphorbias. The tough, prehensile upper lip pulls twigs into the mouth, where they are neatly sheared off by the slanted cheek teeth. (Black rhino droppings are full of these small twigs, all clipped at the same 45° angle.) Like white rhinos, black rhino bulls maintain regular territorial dung middens. Confusingly, they sometimes deposit their coarser, woody droppings on top of a white rhino's finer, grassier mound. The breeding behaviour of black rhinos is also similar to white rhinos, with a single calf born after a gestation period of about 450 days.

Today black rhinos are best seen in the Zululand parks, or Etosha, where they visit floodlit waterholes at night. They are doing well in the Kruger, but are hard to see unless tracked on foot. Visitors to the remote stretches of Namibia's Kaokoveld may meet one of this region's unusual 'desert' rhinos. Elsewhere, a few private reserves in South Africa, Zimbabwe and Swaziland protect small, reintroduced populations. Black rhinos are much harder to find than white. They seldom venture into the open, and if disturbed are more inclined to retreat. By day they stick to cover, enjoying the cool breezes of a ridge top or lazing in a wallow deep in the bush, but they may be seen when they emerge at dusk to drink.

The essence of a black rhino is in its silhouette: streamlined and dynamic (for a rhino), with head held high. (MU)

HIPPOPOTAMUS

The hippo (*Hippopotamus amphibius*) is the fattest of Africa's giants. A mature bull can weigh more than 2,000kg; the female is about 25% smaller. The extraordinary shape reflects an amphibious lifestyle of lounging all day in water, where the bulk provides buoyancy, then feeding by night on land, where short sturdy legs carry it efficiently between grazing grounds. The cavernous mouth houses enormous teeth, with forward-pointing incisors and curved canines up to 50cm long. These are useless for feeding (a hippo eats only grass) but are lethal fighting weapons – indicating why the aggressive hippo has gained a reputation as the most dangerous mammal in Africa.

By immersing themselves in water, often on a submerged sandbank, hippos can keep cool and protect their vulnerable skin from the sun. They can stay underwater for up to six minutes, and the tiny eyes, ears and nostrils perched on top of the head enable them to breathe, see and hear whilst almost completely submerged. After dark, hippos emerge from the water to graze, consuming up to 40kg of grass a night, cropped close to the ground with horny lips to clear neat hippo 'lawns'. Good grazing is as important to a hippo as water, and it will travel up to 30km overland to find new grazing grounds. Despite their bulk, hippos can produce an alarming turn of speed when pressed. They follow regular paths, bulldozing tunnels through waterside vegetation, and create a distinctive parallel-tracked trail with their broadly spaced pairs of legs. Each print shows four toes; quite distinct from the three-toed print of the similar-sized rhino.

By day hippos are highly gregarious. A dominant bull defends a territorial pool or stretch of river, where he presides over a mixed pod of females and young. As rivers shrink, herds are forced together and the intense social pressures lead to much argy-bargy. Hippos are very noisy. Their characteristic call – a series of deep, resonant grunts culminating in a great whinny and snort – is as evocative of African rivers as the cry of the fish eagle. Territory is marked by the scattering of dung, both in the water and over trailside bushes. This is done with a rapid flicking of the tail, audible over the water like a burst of clapping. Conflicts between bulls are usually settled by ritual displays of size and rank, including protracted 'yawns' to display their armouries of teeth. However, the scarring across their backs testifies to some bloody battles. Fights may last for hours and cause chaos: the two combatants plough through the water, crashing over sandbanks and into other hippos and inflicting terrible wounds with their teeth. Deaths are not uncommon.

Hippos give birth to a single calf after a gestation period of 240 days. A newborn calf is vulnerable to attack by large crocodiles, or even to being crushed by other hippos, and at first suckles underwater, hidden by the mother. Adults are too big for any predator, although lions very occasionally kill a sick or injured individual. Hippos were once found in all the region's major rivers and wetlands, but hunting and habitat destruction have eradicated them from many areas. Today the greatest concentration is found along the Zambezi, from Victoria Falls right through to its delta in Mozambique. There are also good numbers in the Chobe, Okavango and Caprivi regions of northern Botswana and Namibia. In South Africa, the

A bull hippo's 'yawn', far from expressing lazy contentment, is actually a signal of territorial aggression that warns rivals to keep away (*left*, RT). Hippos are less friendly than they may appear: there is no real bonding between females in a pod, which leave the water at night to feed alone though they return each morning to their shared stretch of river (*below*, MU). Unlike other mammals, which store the sun's heat and dissipate it by night, hippos must immerse themselves in water during the day to keep their body temperature constant.

Kruger Park and Greater St Lucia Wetland Park (see page 271) both support large populations. Organised cruises are a good way to view hippos at close quarters, while for the more intrepid, a guided canoe trip on the Zambezi offers the ultimate hippo experience (see page 245). In the water, hippos – especially territorial males – should always be given a wide berth. On land, they may charge anything that blocks their route to water, so never put up your tent along a hippo trail and check with a torch before moving around at night. Hippos may also lie up on land on overcast days, and hikers along the St Lucia shorelines should be cautious.

WILD PIGS
Pigs (Suidae) may not be the most elegant of mammals. However, their toughness, intelligence and versatility has allowed them to exploit a wide range of habitats and they enjoy a more catholic diet than most herbivores, with fruit, roots and sometimes even meat on the menu. Two species occur in southern Africa.

Warthog *Phacochoerus africanus*
The warthog is a familiar character around camp, where it roots about quite undeterred by people – often snuffling around chalets or trimming the lawn. This popular porker has made a name for itself as the world's ugliest animal. A male stands up to 70cm high at the shoulder and weighs 60–100kg. The female is a little smaller. Its delicate hindquarters are dwarfed by an enormous head, adorned with bizarre warty protrusions and an impressive set of tusks (particularly in the male). Bushy whiskers sprout around the mouth and the eyes are set high up. Unlike the shaggy bushpig, a warthog is almost hairless, apart from a coarse mane along the neck and shoulders. Its grey-brown skin takes its colour from the mud in which it frequently wallows.

Warthogs feed by day, grazing on bended fore-knees and grubbing up roots with their rubbery snout. Sows live in small groups with their young, while males generally stay apart in separate bachelor gangs. Home is usually a disused aardvark

burrow, often dug out further by the warthog using its spade-like muzzle. Unusually, warthogs enter their burrow backwards. This enables them to use their tusks for defence, or bolt out and make a run for it. Warthogs also have the endearing habit of trotting with their tails held erect, like a line of moving radio antennae, enabling them to stick together in long grass. Females give birth to a litter of two to three piglets in summer, each weighing less than 1kg. Predators include lions and leopards, but this feisty pig can put up a spirited defence. Warthogs prefer arid savannah and are found in the northern half of the region, across much of Botswana, Zimbabwe, Namibia and northeastern South Africa.

Bushpig *Potamochoerus larvatus*

The bushpig is much less well-known than the warthog, being a secretive and nocturnal forest animal. However, it is actually surprisingly common in the right habitat and can wreak havoc in maize fields and cane plantations. An adult is similar in size to a warthog, weighing 60–100kg, sometimes more, but has a thick coat of red-brown hair topped with a whitish mane, a pale whiskered face and tasselled ears. Bushpigs lack the warthog's warts, and their sharp, protruding incisors are much shorter than a warthog's tusks. Piglets are striped for camouflage, like the young of many forest animals.

A group (or sounder) of bushpigs is led by a dominant boar along regular forest trails. Here they use their tough snouts to dig for roots and tubers, but will also scavenge and may even kill small animals. The sow has her litter in summer in a nest of dry grass, and defends herself and her young aggressively. The leopard is the bushpig's main predator, and the big cat's decline in many areas has allowed the pig to flourish. Bushpigs are never found far from water and often quite close to people. They occur in northern and eastern South Africa and in a separate population along the Cape coast, as well as across Zimbabwe, Mozambique and northern Botswana. Bushpigs are hard to see, but sometimes visit camps at night, particularly in KwaZulu-Natal.

Southern Africa's two pigs are very different creatures: the warthog (*far left*, PP) is a conspicuous daytime bushveld forager, whereas the bush pig (*left*, WD/FLPA) is a shy, nocturnal forest-dweller and much harder to see.

GIRAFFE

The giraffe (*Giraffa camelopardalis*) is the tallest animal in the world – by a neck – and has the biggest heart of any land mammal. Males may tower over 5m and weigh over 1,200kg; the smaller females reach 4.5m and weigh up to 850kg. The complex pattern of irregular dark blotches is unique to each individual and is excellent camouflage in the dappled light of the open woodland where they browse. Males tend to grow darker with age and females paler, but a surer way to sex giraffes is by their horns: males' are much thicker than females' and worn smooth by years of fighting.

HIGH SOCIETY

Giraffes spend 15–20 hours a day feeding. Their great height enables them to browse from the crowns of trees (see page 13), where, without competition, they can freely select their favourite species, such as knobthorn. The long, prehensile tongue deftly plucks leaves, flowers and pods from the battery of thorns and giraffes create a kind of bush topiary, pruning trees into tell-tale hourglass or conical shapes. Drinking is more of a challenge. A giraffe scans long and hard for danger before spreading its front legs and lowering its head awkwardly to water. Thirst quenched, it jerks up its head quickly to check that no predator has sneaked up in the meantime. An efficient digestive system enables the giraffe to extract every last drop of moisture from its food, and for such a huge animal it has tiny droppings – easily identifiable by the wide area over which they are scattered.

A giraffe gives birth to a single 100kg calf after a gestation period of 450 days. The calf can walk within an hour, and must follow its mother as she moves on quickly. Giraffes have large home ranges, but do not defend territories. They gather in loose groups of between four and 30, with individuals often wandering between groups. Bulls associate with cows only during courtship. They compete for mating rights by ritual 'necking': two males swing their heads at each other in what appears to be a leisurely manner, but is actually a series of sledgehammer blows that strike the opponent's flanks with resounding wallops. A giraffe's great height and excellent vision makes it the 'eyes of the bush' for many other animals, and a group of giraffes all staring intently in one direction is a sure sign of lions. Lions are indeed a serious enemy and quite capable of toppling an adult giraffe – often chasing it across uneven ground in the hope that it will lose its footing. Giraffes rely upon speed for escape and, although they appear to be moving in slow motion, that great loping stride can cover ground at 60km/h. Young giraffes are the most vulnerable, and mortality in the first year is high. However, adults can fight back fiercely, chopping down with their hooves to land pulverizing blows on an assailant.

Giraffes inhabit dry savannah woodland, including arid stretches of the Kalahari and Damaraland. Two separate populations occur in southern Africa: the eastern one stretches across the Kruger Park and into southern Zimbabwe and Mozambique; the western one from northwest Zimbabwe and across much

Being the world's tallest animal has its drawbacks, and giraffes are at their most vulnerable when levering themselves down to drink. Thankfully there's safety in numbers. (PP)

The pattern on Burchell's zebras varies from one region to another; those in Etosha, Namibia (*above*) have conspicuous shadow stripes on the body and largely unstriped legs. No two zebras anywhere share exactly the same pattern. (PP)

of Botswana into northern Namibia. Elsewhere in South Africa they have been reintroduced to various localities, including Zululand. There have never been giraffes in the ideal habitat of the lower Zambezi Valley, since they cannot negotiate the steep-sided escarpment. Giraffes can be numerous in prime country, and a good scan often reveals a long neck above the horizon. They are surprisingly tolerant of vehicles, but getting close to them on foot is a different matter.

ZEBRAS

The zebra is the quintessential African animal; the fat horse in stripy pyjamas at the end of every child's alphabet. Like all horses (Equidae), these odd-toed ungulates bear their weight on the middle digit of each foot, giving them a springy, energy-efficient gait and a distinctive horseshoe track. Zebras are exclusively grazers and are highly sociable. Two species occur in southern Africa.

Burchell's zebra *Equus burchellii*

Burchell's zebra, also known as the plains zebra, is the better-known species. Standing about 1.3m tall and weighing 290–340kg, this stocky animal always seems healthy, even when other animals wither beneath drought, though its plumpness can partly be explained by the fermenting action of bacteria in the gut. The pattern varies between regions and individuals, but the diagonal stripes across the rump and hindquarters are always the broadest, with pale 'shadow' stripes usually visible between them. Western animals, for example in Etosha, are paler and largely white below the knee. Different ideas have been advanced to explain a zebra's stripes. Camouflage in the long grass? Perhaps, but zebras can look very conspicuous against a dusty plain or lush green meadow. More convincing is the theory that the confusion of stripes baffles a charging predator trying to select a target from the herd.

Burchell's zebra often grazes alongside blue wildebeest, the two species complementing each other by feeding on different parts of the grass, and is quick to move on to the sweet new growth that follows a fire. It lives in small family groups, each comprising a stallion with mare and foals, while young males form separate bachelor herds. Each group obeys a strict pecking order as it files along well-trodden paths, heads nodding and fly-whisk tails swishing. The stallion generally brings up the rear, but will take the lead in more dangerous situations, such as when approaching a waterhole. Larger herds form during migration, sometimes numbering hundreds, or even thousands. Life in the herd is noisy and quarrelsome and rival males spar with snorts, bites and kicks. Zebras dominate waterholes aggressively – often at the expense of other species that struggle to find a drinking spot amidst the bustle of stripes and hooves. This feistiness also helps zebras in self-defence, and lions – their dominant predator – are careful to avoid the jaw-breaking kicks. Several different calls are used to communicate, the best-known being a far-carrying, hiccoughing 'kwa-ha-ha', heard by day and night when herds are on the move. A single foal, weighing 30–35kg, is born in summer after a gestation period of 360 days. It sticks close to its mother and can move with the herd within half an hour.

The preferred habitat of Burchell's zebra is arid savannah with access to water. It is found in the lowveld and Zambezi Valley of Zimbabwe, across the northern third of Botswana and in northern Namibia. In South Africa, it occurs naturally only in the Kruger Park, but has been reintroduced to the Zululand parks and many private reserves. The most rewarding viewing is at waterholes, where interactions between individuals and herds may be watched closely when they come to drink – usually in mid-morning. Lucky visitors may witness a mass migration, such as the spectacular annual gatherings in Botswana's Nxai Pan and Makgadikgadi Pans national parks.

Mountain zebra *Equus zebra*

Southern Africa is also home to two races of mountain zebra: Hartmann's mountain zebra (*E. z. hartmannae*) is found in central and southern Namibia, while Cape mountain zebra (*E. z. zebra*) inhabits the Cape and Karoo of South Africa. Both can be distinguished from their bushveld cousin by narrower striping along the flanks, without shadow stripes, and a grid-iron pattern across the top of the rump. Their legs are striped down to the hooves and, unlike Burchell's, the throat has a prominent dewlap. Hartmann's is the larger of the two races, standing up to 1.5m at the shoulder and weighing 250–350kg; the Cape stands up to 1.3m, weighing

Like all their kind, Cape mountain zebra stallions are fond of a scrap – especially when one tries to make off with another's mares. Rearing, biting, kicking, circling and neck-wrestling are all considered legitimate tactics. (PP)

250–60kg. Both are hardy animals of rugged terrain, where they supplement poor grazing with browsing and live in breeding herds of four or five animals, each comprising one stallion with his mares and foals. Although larger herds may gather, populations are restricted by drought and the availability of food. A stallion defends his herd fiercely against predators and the challenges of rival males.

Hartmann's mountain zebra occurs in discontinuous populations down the length of central Namibia, where it comes down from the escarpment to graze the adjacent lowlands during summer. It may be seen in western Etosha and the Kaokoveld, or in the Namib-Naukluft and Fish River Canyon parks, where its tracks and kidney-shaped droppings are a feature of mountain trails. These shy animals are well-camouflaged against scrub and scree, so scan hillsides with binoculars and listen out for a tell-tale clatter of hooves.

Fewer than 1,000 Cape mountain zebras remain. The only surviving natural population is in the Mountain Zebra National Park (see page 270), their final stronghold after near extermination in the 1930s, but introduced populations may also be seen in the Karoo National Park, De Hoop and other Cape reserves. Except for Hartmann's in western Etosha, neither race occurs alongside Burchell's zebra.

AFRICAN BUFFALO

The buffalo (*Syncerus caffer*) has always been a top contender for the ultimate safari accolade of 'most dangerous animal in Africa' and campfire tales recount its alleged ferocity, cunning and malevolence. Such tales generally hail from a bygone hunting era and today's visitor is unlikely to see anything very fearsome in this big black cow. A large bull may weigh over 800kg and stand over 1.4m at the shoulder, with cows being about 25% smaller. The coat is dull black in adults, worn to a patchy grey in old bulls, and reddish brown in calves. Both sexes have formidable curved horns: those of a bull are set in a massive horny 'boss' on the crown and may each measure over a metre along the curve. The powerful body, with its massive neck and shoulders, is supported by stocky legs set on broad cloven hooves. The large, fringed ears hang low, and the short tail sports a fly-whisk tassel.

Buffalo are highly gregarious, living in herds of a few hundred or sometimes even thousands of animals. Their prime country is wooded savannah with plentiful grass and available water. Although they have been accused of destructive overgrazing, herds tend to move on before they have exhausted a habitat. They also play an important ecological role by opening up areas of grassland for other species. Much feeding takes place at night. In the early morning or late afternoon herds visit water to drink, often wading in waist deep. Both males and females within a herd maintain

Dust hangs above a heard of buffalo on the move. (GE/FLPA)

Despite the male buffalo's intimidating appearance, females command more authority within the herd. (AB)

dominance hierarchies based on age. Old males eventually leave to form small bachelor groups, which stick close to water, wallowing in cooling mud or lying up in reed beds. These old timers are known as '*dagga* boys', from the Zulu word for mud, and are the grumpy individuals responsible for most hair-raising stories.

A single buffalo calf is born during summer after a gestation period of 11 months, and is well protected by the herd. The only enemies of adults are lions and, occasionally, large crocodiles. Lions are particularly partial to buffalo and may tail a large herd for some days looking for an opportunity. It takes several of the big cats to bring down a large adult, whose scything horns – even when toppled – can toss and kill a lion. A trapped buffalo's bellows of distress often bring its companions rushing back to turn the tables and rout the lions. Buffalo have even been seen to hunt down and kill a litter of lion cubs before the females could whisk them to safety.

Buffalo are now restricted to major conservation areas. In South Africa, this means the Kruger Park, plus Hluhluwe/Imfolozi and a few smaller restocked reserves. In Zimbabwe they are found along the Zambezi Valley and in the southeastern lowveld, while the region's biggest herds are in Zimbabwe's Hwange National Park and the Chobe and Moremi regions of neighbouring Botswana. Smaller numbers also survive in Namibia's Caprivi Strip and remote stretches of southern Mozambique. Finding buffalo is not always straightforward: a trampled mess of droppings and a lingering earthy scent may remain where a herd rumbled through during the night, but by morning the bush has often swallowed them up again. Big herds are not threatening to people, in or out of a vehicle. Although their first reaction may be to approach with heads raised, they are simply sniffing out your identity. Once this is confirmed, they usually thunder away in a cloud of dust, before stopping to stare back from a safe distance. Buffalo can readily be approached by canoe along the Zambezi, where they lift their head and stare in an uncomprehending way. On foot, however, a lone bull in thick bush is best avoided.

ANTELOPE

Antelope are cloven-hoofed ruminants that belong, with the buffalo, in the family Bovidae. Southern Africa has 33 different species, divided into several subfamilies – or tribes. All males have horns, though females of over half the species do not. Antelope show the most impressive diversity of any of Africa's large mammal families. They range from the huge one-tonne bull eland to the tiny 4kg blue duiker and have evolved a range of lifestyle to suit all habitats – from nomadic grazers, such as blue wildebeest, that roam the savannah in huge herds, to sedentary browsers, such as klipspringer, who occupy small territories in monogamous pairs. Many species have evolved complex territorial and breeding behaviour, involving scent-marking, dung middens and ritual fights or displays among competing males.

SPIRAL-HORNED ANTELOPE (SUBFAMILY STREPSICEROTINI)

These handsome, large to medium-sized antelope are closely related to the buffalo. There are five species in southern Africa, all of which are patterned to some degree with camouflage spots and stripes. None is territorial, and they all lack the special scent glands of other antelope. Instead, males use their impressive horns to battle out dominance hierarchies. Females lack horns (except for eland), and are strikingly different from males in size and appearance.

Eland *Taurotragus oryx*

The eland was both food and spiritual inspiration to the ancient peoples of southern Africa, and its angular contours remain etched across the walls of many a cave shelter. Today, those artists are gone and the eland too has declined, but places such as Elandsfontein and the common surname Mpofu (eland in Zulu) suggest how central to the region's culture this antelope once was. A bull eland is twice as big as any other antelope, weighing up to 900kg and standing 1.7m at the shoulder. With his massive square frame and prominent dewlap he resembles a prize bull and fears no predator except lions. The much slimmer female is about half the male's weight. Both sexes have straight horns with a single twist and are tawny in colour, becoming greyer with age. Despite their size, eland can jump a two-metre fence with ease.

Eland occupy a variety of open habitats, from montane grasslands to semi-desert. They are predominantly browsers, and can survive without water as long as they get enough moisture from their food. Herds are larger than those of other spiral-horned antelope, averaging 25–60 animals, though populations fluctuate seasonally – drought may drive large concentrations into one area, where they may not be seen again for years. Today eland are largely restricted to the north of the region, where the largest population is in Botswana. They are also found in Zimbabwe's Eastern Highlands and Zambezi Valley, northern Namibia and central Mozambique. In South Africa, they occur in many small, introduced populations across the country, but naturally only in the northern Kruger, the Drakensberg and the Kalahari. Wild eland are very shy and disappear at the sound of approaching vehicles more readily than most antelope. Listen for the clicking sound of their hooves, audible from a distance, as they approach a waterhole.

Eland (*top*, RT/FLPA) are the largest of the spiral-horned antelope and the only species in which both sexes carry horns. Greater kudu are more lightly built – especially the females (*above*, AZ) – although the bull (*right*, WW/FLPA) has the longest horns of any antelope.

Greater kudu *Tragelaphus strepsiceros*

The magnificent kudu makes a handsome emblem for South Africa's national parks. Bulls stand up to 1.5m at the shoulder and weigh over 250kg; smaller cows weigh up to 180kg. The spectacular spiral horns of the male, which develop over several years, are the longest of any antelope, the record standing at a whopping 181cm. Kudus are lightly built for their size, with long slim legs and necks. The grey-brown coat is chalked with flank stripes and face spots and trimmed with a mane along the neck and shoulders. Both sexes have big round ears and a bushy tail, and a shaggy fringe hangs from the throat of the male.

Kudu inhabit wooded savannah and rocky bush country, even in the arid Namib and Karoo. They browse during early morning and late afternoon on a wide variety of plants, including species toxic to other animals. Small groups number three to ten animals and males also form bachelor herds. Although rival bulls will lock horns over mating rights, they seldom use them in self-defence, relying on vigilance rather than aggression for their survival. When danger is spotted, kudu give a hoarse alarm bark, then flee with a distinctive rocking-horse running motion – the male laying back his horns to avoid obstructions. It is hard to approach this most alert of antelope on foot; however, lions and hyenas prey on adults, while the young are also vulnerable to leopards and wild dogs. Kudu are prodigious leapers and are hard to fence off roads or out of farms – hence the ubiquitous leaping kudu road sign. They are widespread across the northern half of the region, with separate populations in the Eastern Cape and Karoo, and can survive surprisingly close to people – though outside protected areas they are shy and largely nocturnal. Sightings are easiest in big bushveld reserves such as Kruger, Hwange, Chobe, Moremi and Etosha, all of which have healthy populations.

Bushbuck *Tragelaphus scriptus*

The bushbuck is the smallest of the spiral-horned antelope, the larger male standing 80cm at the shoulder and weighing up to 45kg. Its coat varies from a dark grey-brown in the south of its range to a rich chestnut further north (particularly in the Chobe race). Northern animals are also more heavily spotted on the flanks, although all bushbuck share the same white markings on the face, chest and throat and a dark stripe down the nose. Only males have the short, sharp horns, with which they can put up a courageous defence against enemies such as leopard.

The bushbuck's pattern of spots and stripes helps conceal it in dense riverine thickets. (MU)

Bushbuck stick to cover in wooded and riverine areas, and can be common in the right habitat, even adapting to farmland and plantations. They live alone or in pairs, and the single lamb is hidden by the mother for weeks, trusting to its camouflage when danger appears. As well as browsing, bushbuck often forage for pods and fruit beneath large trees, sometimes alongside monkeys or baboons. They may be seen in suitable habitat anywhere in the north and east of the region and along the Cape coastal belt, but are easily overlooked in the dappled forest undergrowth. Victoria Falls (see page 253), the St Lucia region and the rivers of the Kruger Park are all good localities for bushbuck, which can become very tame around lodges and campsites. Look out for their eye-shine in car headlights at night and listen for the sharp alarm bark.

Nyala *Tragelaphus angasii*

The distinctive nyala is halfway in size between a bushbuck and a kudu. The male stands up to 115cm tall and weighs up to 108kg. His shaggy charcoal-grey coat is set off by rufous knee-length 'stockings', a long white crest along the spine and powerful horns, twisted once and tipped with yellow. The female, by stark contrast, has a sleek chestnut coat (see page 271). Both sexes have bold stripes down the flanks,

At Mkuzi Game Reserve in KwaZulu-Natal, two male nyala contest mating rights through the curious contact-free ritual of 'lateral presentation'. Each contender circles the other in high-stepping slow motion, displaying his physique to best effect, until one eventually cracks and concedes defeat. (PP)

a bushy tail and a white chevron between the eyes. Young males resemble females, but acquire the male colouring as they mature. Where bushbuck and nyala occur together, such as in the northern Kruger, the females might be confused for one another by visitors, but nyala are larger, more boldly marked and more gregarious.

Nyala have a fragmented distribution. They occur in northeast South Africa and Zimbabwe's eastern lowveld and Lower Zambezi Valley, but are absent from Botswana and Namibia. Though not widespread, nyala can be locally common, especially in the Zululand parks, and have been successfully introduced to many game farms in South Africa. Prime nyala habitat comprises woodland and riverine thickets, where they browse in small mixed groups.

Sitatunga *Tragelaphus spekii*

The sitatunga is unique among antelope for its semi-aquatic lifestyle. Slightly smaller than a nyala, it stands up to 90cm at the shoulder, weighs up to 115kg and has twisted horns and a shaggy brown coat. Sitatunga live only in dense papyrus swamps, where they swim comfortably and wade neck-deep to browse on the shoots of young reeds, using their unusually long (up to 18cm), splayed hooves for support across the marshy terrain. In southern Africa they are confined to Botswana's Okavango Delta and the adjacent Linyanti and Caprivi regions. Exploring

Only a male sitatunga has horns. (JCS/FLPA)

these wetlands by dugout mekoro, you may surprise a sitatunga swimming across your path or, more likely, hear it crashing away through the papyrus.

HORSE-LIKE ANTELOPE (SUBFAMILY HIPPOTRAGINAE)

The Hippotraginae, or 'horse-like' antelope, are large, powerfully built grazers with striking facial markings and long horns in both sexes. Three species occur in the region: the sable and roan, both uncommon, inhabit savannah woodland in the north; the more numerous gemsbok is specially adapted to the arid west. A fourth species, the bluebuck (*Hippotragus leucophaeus*), was exterminated from the Cape in about 1800. All live in small family groups, each comprising a nursery herd of females and young led by a dominant cow and presided over by an adult bull who defends the territory and mates with the females. Young bulls retain their immature colouring as they mature to avoid conflict with older males. Females give birth to a single calf, which they move between hiding places over its first few weeks.

Sable antelope *Hippotragus niger*

The sable is an impressive animal. A mature bull stands 135cm at the shoulder and can weigh over 260kg. His jet-black upperparts contrast boldly with a white belly and badger-striped face, his powerful neck is trimmed with a stiff black mane and his head is crowned with formidable, heavily ridged horns that curve back towards the shoulder and can exceed 120cm in length. Females and immature males are smaller, with a reddish-brown coat and shorter horns. Sable inhabit savannah woodland where they both graze and browse, avoiding very open areas except when coming to drink – which they do regularly. Contests between rival males are usually settled by an intimidation display, in which the two animals stand nose to rump, flaunting their physiques, until one loses his nerve. Serious fights seldom occur, but in self-defence sable use their horns to deadly effect, going down on their knees and scything at an assailant. Lions, and even people, have been killed by sable.

Trophy hunting has eradicated sable from much of their former range. Today they are patchily distributed across the north of the region, being most common in Zimbabwe, where Hwange, the Matobo Hills, and Zambezi National Park are all prime spots. They also occur in northern Botswana (including Moremi and Chobe), northern Namibia (including Kaudom and Mahango) and northern South Africa (including the west of the Kruger Park). These shy antelope quickly retreat into cover when disturbed, usually presenting the photographer with more white rump than sweeping horns. They are most often encountered crossing the road, in which case it is best to stop and watch quietly rather than pressing forward and panicking them into flight.

Roan antelope *Hippotragus equinus*

The roan antelope has a superficially horse-like stature – hence its scientific name. A male stands over 140cm at the shoulder and can weigh nearly 300kg, making him the second largest antelope after the eland. The black-and-white face mask resembles a sable's, but the larger roan has a paler grey-brown coat and shorter horns (averaging 75cm in the male). Roan prefer moist woodland with tall grasses. They avoid areas dominated by bulk grazers such as zebra and will not share waterholes with other species. These factors, together with disease, have contributed to

Sable are shyer than most antelope, preferring to keep to cover, but will venture out into the open at selected feeding sites, such as newly burnt areas or moist vleis (*above*, AZ). Roan (*right*, MU) have paler coats and shorter horns. Both species are best seen at undisturbed waterholes around midday, when small family parties emerge to drink.

the roan's serious decline in the Kruger. Today it survives only in small populations in the north of the region, where its distribution is similar to the sable's, extending from the Zambezi Valley and lowveld of Zimbabwe, into northern Botswana, northern Namibia and far northern South Africa. Moremi is a good area to look out for this shy antelope. It is most often seen, like sable, emerging cautiously from woodland to drink, but quickly retreats to cover at any sign of disturbance.

Gemsbok will drink where water is available, but manage for much of the year with none at all. (PP)

Gemsbok *Oryx gazella*

The gemsbok, or oryx, is synonymous with the Kalahari (see page 15), and a herd of these magnificent antelope cresting a red sand dune is one of southern Africa's great wildlife spectacles. A bull stands 1.2m at the shoulder and weighs up to 240kg. Both sexes are powerfully built, with a deep chest and solid neck and shoulders. The sandy coat is adorned with bold black-and-white markings on face and legs, black striping along the flank, spine and throat, and a long, black horse-like tail. The straight, rapier-like horns can reach 120cm in length and are longer and narrower in the female. Calves are fawn in colour, without any body markings.

Gemsbok thrive in the arid west, from the barren Kalahari savannah to the stony wastes and sweeping dunes of the Namib, where their nomadic lifestyle does not allow them to be too strongly territorial. They are remarkably well adapted to their harsh environment: a low metabolism allows them to survive for much of the year without water, getting the moisture they need from their food, including desert melons that they dig up in times of drought; water loss through perspiration is minimised by allowing their body temperature to rise to an astonishing 45°C and then dissipating the stored heat at night; overheating is averted by a filigree of blood vessels in the nose, known as the carotid rete, through which all the blood that passes to the brain is circulated and cooled, and by seeking shade during the hottest part of the day.

Gemsbok are hunted by lions and spotted hyenas, but are capable of running their enemies through with their lethal horns. Solitary bulls can be aggressive and where they are habituated to people, such as at Sossusvlei in Namibia (see page 263), visitors should not get too close. Sossusvlei, with its panoramic dunes, offers undoubtedly the most dramatic gemsbok sightings. However, greater numbers can be seen in the Kgalagadi Transfrontier Park (formerly known, appropriately, as the Kalahari Gemsbok Park), the Makgadikgadi Pans and Etosha. Elsewhere, gemsbok are widespread across Botswana and Namibia, and they occasionally wander through into western Zimbabwe. In South Africa they have been reintroduced to many game farms in the northwest.

WILDEBEEST AND HARTEBEEST (SUBFAMILY ALCELAPHINI)

Hartebeest and wildebeest are large to medium-sized, gregarious grazing antelopes. There are seven species in the region, all of which have long faces, profiles that slope downward from shoulder to rump and short, twisted horns in both sexes. Breeding males are highly territorial, marking their patches with dung and scent and defending them from other males in vigorous struggles. Some species migrate long distances for food and water.

Blue wildebeest *Connochaetes taurinus*

The blue wildebeest is best known for its spectacular annual treks across Tanzania's Serengeti and as the hapless televised victim of countless lions and crocodiles. From a distance, it resembles a small, lightweight buffalo, with its dark coat, heavy forequarters and short, cow-like horns. A thick black mane and shaggy beard accentuate the ungainly, front-heavy appearance, and the long black face and small, high-set eyes create a lugubrious expression (see page 29). As if striving for some redeeming elegance, the delicate hindquarters are surmounted by an extravagant, black, horse-like tail. A male stands about 1.5m at the shoulder and weighs up to 250kg; the female is a little smaller. The brown to charcoal-grey coat has a few dark vertical stripes (hence the alternative name 'brindled gnu') but, despite a silvery sheen in certain lights, can hardly be described as 'blue'. By contrast with adults, calves are a rufous-fawn in colour.

A herd of blue wildebeest enjoys lush summer growth in the Kalahari. (VG/FLPA)

The black wildebeest is endemic to the highveld grasslands of South Africa, where numbers have recovered well from a historical low of little more than 500. Today, there are over 12,000, many on private game farms. (ND)

Blue wildebeest are short-grass grazers that inhabit open savannah and will tolerate arid country as long as there is water. They generally live in herds of up to 30 animals, but will migrate in their thousands in search of food and water, using a loping, energy-efficient gait to cover great distances with ease and keeping in contact with plaintive, nasal lowing. A male uses dung heaps and scent smearing to mark out a breeding territory into which he tries to corral passing females, each of whom may visit several territories for mating. Rival males spar on bended knee in fast and furious skirmishes. A single calf is born in early summer and can run with the herd within minutes of birth. This survival instinct helps them to escape the many predators who weed out the young or weak from a herd. Nonetheless, wildebeest form the staple diet of lions in many areas.

Blue wildebeest are often seen in the company of Burchell's zebra (see page 72), gathered in the midday shade of an acacia or trudging single file along well-worn trails. Mid-morning is the usual drinking time: the herd files into position around a waterhole and presses forward until a line of muzzles meets the surface. Wildebeest country is littered with clusters of sticky black droppings and areas of flattened grass where a herd has bedded down. Territorial males, reluctant to abandon their hard-fought positions, will allow a surprisingly close approach.

Southern Africa once boasted blue wildebeest herds to rival East Africa's, but hunting and cattle ranching have caused a steady decline. This highly nomadic species suffers when its movement is restricted, and an estimated 50,000 perished along the veterinary cordon fences of Botswana during the mid-1980s drought.

Today good numbers are still found in northern Botswana and the Kalahari, with sizeable separate populations in Kruger, Hwange and Etosha – though they do not naturally occur south of Zululand, nor in the Zambezi Valley.

Black wildebeest *Connochaetes gnou*

The black wildebeest, or white-tailed gnu, is much rarer than the blue wildebeest and endemic to South Africa. It was almost exterminated at the start of the 20th century, but has since recovered through careful conservation and reintroduction schemes. Today small herds graze the high grassland in many parts of central South Africa. The range and habitat of the black wildebeest do not overlap naturally with those of the blue and it is a strikingly different animal: dark chocolate brown (appearing black at a distance), with a stiff mane on the neck and shoulders, tufts of hair on the face and chest, back-curved horns like racing bike handlebars and a luxurious creamy plume of tail. It is also slightly smaller than the blue: a male weighs up to 180kg and stands up to 1.2m at the shoulder. Like blue wildebeest, males are intensely territorial and use vigorous displays to deter rivals and attract females, with much bucking, snorting and horning of the ground.

Red hartebeest *Alcelaphus buselaphus* and Lichtenstein's hartebeest *Sigmoceros lichtensteinii*

The red hartebeest stands about 1.25m at the shoulder, with the larger male weighing up to 150kg. It is rich golden brown in colour, with black legs, a black blaze down the nose, a pale rump and short twisted horns set high on the head. These hardy animals inhabit arid savannah, where they can survive without surface water and will trek long distances for fresh grazing. Herds generally number up to 20 animals, although hundreds may gather during a drought. Like all hartebeest, a territorial bull often stands on a conspicuous raised mound to flaunt his status. The single calf weighs about 15kg and, like wildebeest, is able to run with the herd from birth. The red hartebeest was once widespread in the region, but is now largely confined to central Botswana and Namibia, with Makgadikgadi Pans and Etosha being

The long narrow muzzle of the red hartebeest allows it to select nutritious grass leaves from among the withered growth of arid grasslands. (PP)

The sloping profile of the tsessebe (*above left*, AZ/FLPA) is typical of the alcelaphine antelope. The blesbok (*above right*, MU) is a more boldly marked member of the same family.

particularly good areas. In South Africa it occurs naturally only in the Kgalagadi Transfrontier Park, where wandering herds arrive after the summer rains, but has also been reintroduced to many game farms and private reserves.

The similar Lichtenstein's hartebeest (*Sigmoceros lichtensteinii*) is paler in colour, with a darker saddle on the lower back. Its short horns form a 'Z' shape when viewed from the side. This is one of the region's rarest large mammals, found only in a few fragmented populations in southeast Zimbabwe, Mozambique and the Kruger, where it was reintroduced during the 1980s. It prefers bushier habitat to the red hartebeest, where it will supplement its grazing with browse.

Tsessebe *Damaliscus lunatus*
The tsessebe has a reputation as the fastest of all antelope; its name means 'speed' in Tswana. Standing 1.2m at the shoulder and weighing up to 140kg, it is slightly smaller and darker than a red hartebeest, with a purplish sheen to the rump and shoulders, yellow-brown lower legs and a more open horn shape. Tsessebe frequent woodland savannah, generally in small groups and often with other grazers. A bull advertises and defends his patch with gusto. If posturing fails, fierce fights may develop between rival males, who wrestle with locked horns until, after a long chase, the loser is finally expelled. Calves are born during September/October and sub-adult males are driven from the herd by the dominant bull to form bachelor groups. Tsessebe are patchily distributed across the northern half of the region, including central Zimbabwe, northern Botswana and the Kruger. Elsewhere in Africa, several different races are recognised, including the East African topi.

Bontebok *Damaliscus dorcas dorcas* and blesbok *D. d. phillipsi*
These two similar antelope are both smaller than tsessebe, weighing about 62kg and 70kg respectively. Both have medium-length lyrate horns and a white blaze down the nose and forehead. The bontebok has black and brown upperparts flushed with a purplish gloss, which contrast smartly with the pure white belly, buttocks and lower legs. The less striking blesbok has a reddish brown body, less white on the legs and straw-coloured buttocks. Unlike the bontebok, the blesbok's blaze is broken

between the eyes. Identification is generally not a problem however, since these two antelope do not naturally occur together. The blesbok is found in the highveld and montane grasslands of central South Africa and Swaziland, where it thrives on game farms. The bontebok is much rarer, having been all but exterminated by the beginning of the 20th century, and today is carefully protected in a few southern Cape reserves, including De Hoop, the Cape of Good Hope and, of course, the Bontebok National Park. Both species are short-grass grazers, fond of new growth after a burn. On hot days, they have the peculiar habit of standing to face the sun with heads bowed. Whole herds adopt this stance together, as though in some ancient ceremony.

WATERBUCK, REEDBUCK AND THEIR ALLIES (SUBFAMILY REDUNCINI)
The reduncine antelope are grazers that inhabit wetlands or tall grasslands. They vary from the heavily built waterbuck of bushveld river valleys to the agile mountain reedbuck of montane hillsides. Only the males have horns which, in all but the grey rhebok, curve up and forwards. Most species live in pairs or small breeding herds.

Waterbuck *Kobus ellipsiprymnus*
The waterbuck is a large, thickset antelope with a shaggy grey-brown coat, unmarked except for a striking white ring around the rump (as though from a freshly painted toilet seat) and white marks around the eyes and mouth. The larger male stands up to 1.3m at the shoulder and can weigh over 250kg. His impressive curving horns can exceed 90cm in length. The smaller, hornless female has a donkey-like appearance.

As their name suggests, waterbuck are seldom found far from water. They inhabit floodplains and riverine bush to the north and east of the region, where small groups graze or browse in reed beds and adjacent woodland. Territorial bulls

A young male waterbuck engages his rival in a trial of strength, flashing a good view of his distinctive ringed posterior. Serious territorial combat takes place between adult males. (CH/FLPA)

preside over nursery herds of females and young, while young bulls form separate bachelor herds. A single calf is born in summer and spends its early weeks in hiding. Lions are alleged to find waterbuck unpalatable due to the strong, musky odour of their oily hair. Try telling this to the waterbuck, which frequently fall prey to the big cats. Waterbuck are found in northeastern South Africa and are abundant in the Kruger. They also occur in Zimbabwe's lowveld, the Chobe/Okavango region of Botswana and Namibia's Caprivi Strip, but are completely absent from the arid west (including the Kalahari and Etosha). On foot, waterbuck can be detected by the distinctive scent that lingers around their resting places.

The female waterbuck lacks the horns of the male. (MU)

Red lechwe *Kobus leche*

A classic image of the Okavango is herds of red lechwe bounding across a floodplain, throwing up sparkling plumes of spray. Although found nowhere else in the region, the red lechwe is abundant in these wetlands and along the adjacent Chobe. This medium-sized antelope is superficially similar to the smaller impala (see page 91), but at 100kg the male is nearly twice an impala's weight and is quickly identified by a characteristic high-rumped profile. Both sexes have a uniform chestnut coat (lacking an impala's graded tones), with white underparts and a black blaze down each foreleg. The male's sweeping horns may reach 90cm.

Red lechwe graze at the water's edge on semi-aquatic grasses. Although relatively slow on land, their long hooves and powerful hindquarters enable them to plough rapidly through water and they will plunge in to escape predators such as lions or wild dogs. Herds average around 30 animals, although much larger gatherings do occur. Territorial males shepherd harems of females and compete fiercely with rivals. Red lechwe always retreat towards water when approached, trotting away with a characteristic lowered head.

The powerful hindquarters of red lechwe – an adaptation for bounding over marshy ground – give them a distinctive high-rumped profile. (PP/FLPA)

Puku *Kobus vardonii*

Although the puku is common in Zambia, it only enters the southern African region on the Chobe floodplain. This medium-sized, stocky antelope is slightly smaller than the red lechwe, whose habitat it shares, with a male standing up to 80cm at the shoulder and weighing around 75kg. It also has a paler golden, unmarked coat, and shorter horns. Puku graze beside water in small groups of 5–30 animals and have a similar territorial system to lechwe. Rival males use their well-developed neck muscles to power fierce contests of pushing and butting.

Reedbuck *Redunca arundinum*

The common or southern reedbuck is another roughly impala-sized antelope. It stands 80–90cm at the shoulder and the larger male weighs 50–70kg. The coat is a uniform sandy brown, paler below, and the male's horns, up to 50cm in length, curve outwards and forwards. An obvious distinguishing mark is the bare glandular patch, the size of a coin, beneath each ear.

Research suggests that a female puku is more impressed by a male's looks – especially his bulging neck muscles – than by his lands. (MU)

Reedbuck are both grazers and browsers. They inhabit tall grass and reed beds in the north and east of the region, and are monogamous, generally living in pairs or small family groups. A mother hides her newborn lamb in the reeds and only introduces it to the male after three or four months. Reedbuck are distributed patchily in northeast South Africa, northern Botswana and Namibia, and across much of Zimbabwe. They are particularly numerous in the St Lucia wetlands of KwaZulu-Natal, where hikers along the eponymous Mziki Trail often flush them at close quarters. An alarmed reedbuck gives a piercing nasal whistle and bounds away with a rocking-horse canter, flashing the white underside of its tail.

The common reedbuck is generally seen in damp, long-grass habitats. (PW/FLPA)

Grey rhebok are hard to spot against a boulder-strewn hillside, until a sharp alarm whistle gives them away. (ND)

Mountain reedbuck *Redunca fulvorufula*

Weighing only 30kg, the mountain reedbuck is half the size of a common reedbuck. Like the reedbuck, it has a noticeable dark disc below each ear, but has shorter horns and a greyer coat, with pale underparts and a fawn neck. Mountain reedbuck inhabit hilly terrain, where they graze on rocky slopes in small family groups. An adult ram defends a small territory into which he attracts passing groups of females and young. This antelope is confined almost exclusively to eastern and central South Africa, with small populations in adjacent areas of Mozambique, Botswana and Swaziland. It is often encountered on hiking trails, attracting attention with a shrill alarm whistle before bounding away over the hillside.

Grey rhebok *Pelea capreolus*

The mountain reedbuck is often confused with the similar-sized but more lightly built grey rhebok, which is actually the sole member of a separate genus (*Pelea*). Seen well, the grey rhebok can be identified by its combination of long neck, long pointed ears, bulbous nose, woolly grey coat and thin horns (in the male) that point straight upwards from the crown. It occurs in small groups in the hills of central South Africa, Lesotho and western Swaziland, where it shares habitat with the mountain reedbuck, and also ventures on to the wheatlands of the southwestern Cape. Like mountain reedbuck, grey rhebok are best spotted on hiking trails, usually revealing their presence with a whistled alarm before bouncing away on stiff legs, flashing the white underside of the tail to alert the group.

IMPALA AND SPRINGBOK

These two medium-sized antelope are unrelated other than by popular perception. Each is the sole representative of a separate genus: the springbok (genus *Antidorcus*) is the only southern African gazelle (subfamily Antilopini), while the impala (genus *Aepyceros*), despite its gazelle-like build, is more closely related to the wildebeest (subfamily Alcelaphini, see page 83). Both can be very numerous and are usually the dominant herbivore species wherever they occur.

Impala *Aepyceros melampus*

The impala is so common in many reserves that it seldom gets the attention it deserves. This slim and elegant antelope stands about 90cm at the shoulder and weighs up to 50kg. The graceful, lyrate horns are only present in the male and can reach a length of 60cm. Its coat is graded from a reddish brown on

The impala's catholic feeding habits allow it to thrive where other antelope fail; today there are more in the region than ever. Only the males have horns (*right*, AZ), and they spend most of their time in bachelor herds away from the females and young (*below*, MU).

the back, through fawn flanks to a white belly and is adorned with delicate black markings, including a tufted scent gland above each rear hoof, vertical lines down the white buttocks and a broken blaze on the nose and forehead. A separate race with a boldly marked face, the black-faced impala (*A. m. petersi*), is found in northern Namibia.

Impala frequent woodland savannah with plentiful cover and permanent water, occurring in the north and east of the region but not in the hilly south or arid west. In the right habitat, they can be very numerous, and peak counts in the Kruger Park have topped 100,000 animals. Their success is due both to their versatile feeding habits, being both browsers and grazers, and their habit of lambing *en masse* at the start of summer, which gluts the market with young and ensures a high survival rate. Impala can also control their reproduction, suppressing fertility in times of drought and sometimes even producing a second lamb in April. Rams are aggressively territorial during the annual post-breeding rut, when the bush resounds day and night with the ugly roaring and snorting of rivals contesting claims and rounding up harems. At this time they can present a road hazard as they dash out in pursuit of each other. At other times males gather in bachelor herds, while females and young form larger mixed herds, sometimes hundreds strong. Territories are marked by glandular secretions and communal dung piles of black, currant-like droppings.

Impala are on the menu for most large predators, especially leopards, cheetahs and wild dogs. Nonetheless, they are not easy to catch, being fast, agile, and among the world's great jumpers. A fleeing group of impala breaks into soaring leaps, each flaunting its fitness to discourage pursuit. An approaching vehicle may sometimes alarm them into leaping clean across the road, each one springing from the very point where the last took off, to form a balletic arc of airborne animals.

Springbok *Antidorcas marsupialis*

Many visitors to the Kruger are disappointed not to find South Africa's national emblem leaping around its premier national park. In fact, the springbok is purely an animal of the arid west, where herds millions-strong once crossed the Karoo in some of the biggest animal migrations ever witnessed. Today, these mighty treks are long gone, but you can still see plenty of springbok by heading northwest into the Kalahari or onwards into Namibia. The Kgalagadi Transfrontier Park, Central

A group of springbok in the Kalahari keeps at a safe distance from a hunting lioness. (RT/FLPA)

Like Kalahari pogo-sticks, these pronking springbok are flaunting their fitness to predators and warning other herd members of danger. Nonetheless, predators, especially cheetah, are not always deterred. (PPk)

Kalahari, Makgadikgadi Pans, Nxai Pan and Etosha each support many thousand, while smaller numbers have been reintroduced to small reserves and game ranches across South Africa and Namibia.

Standing about 75cm at the shoulder and weighing around 40kg, the springbok is smaller than an impala and can be distinguished by the chocolate-brown stripe along each flank, separating the fawn upperparts from the white belly, and the bold black-and-white face markings. In profile, a springbok's rump stands higher than its shoulder, and both sexes carry short, lyre-shaped horns. In the few places – such as Etosha and Nxai Pan – where impala and springbok occur naturally together, impala prefer thicker bush, happy to leave the scorching plains to the tougher springbok.

Springbok inhabit arid savannah and semi-desert, where they graze, browse – being particularly fond of acacia flowers – and dig for succulent roots and tubers. They can do without surface water and have evolved to withstand the soaring temperatures of the semi-desert, positioning themselves when grazing to expose the smallest part of their body to the sun's rays, and reflecting direct solar radiation with their pale, shiny coat and white rump patch. Springbok live in small mixed groups, which join up to form larger – sometimes huge – herds during migration. Territorial males fight their patch and round up ewes during the rut, but at other times they gather in separate bachelor herds. Like impala, springbok are prodigious breeders: a ewe can conceive at only seven months and gives birth to a single lamb after 25 weeks. Also like impala, they can synchronise their reproduction so that a region's entire population drops its young over a few days during the December/January peak of summer growth, overwhelming predators to ensure a high survival rate of offspring.

Springbok have many predators, the cheetah being a notable specialist (see page 42). When fleeing, springbok break into a series of stiff-legged pogo jumps, arching their back and erecting a white crest of hair along the spine. This curious behaviour, known as pronking, emphasises a springbok's fitness and alertness in order to discourage a predator. Over-exuberant young springbok sometimes indulge in bouts of pronking without an enemy in sight.

Small antelope are at the bottom end of the ungulate scale. Each of these secretive and largely solitary creatures fills a different environmental niche: the common duiker (*top left*, PP) is a widespread skulker in scrub and thicket; the red duiker (*top right*, ND) forages on forest floors; the steenbok (*bottom left*, PP) frequents open grassland across the region; while Sharpe's grysbok (*bottom right*, PP) prefers rocky bushveld in the northeast.

DUIKERS AND OTHER SMALL ANTELOPE

Southern Africa is home to ten small antelope species – typically shy, delicate-looking, big-eyed creatures that dive for cover when disturbed. They comprise three species of duiker (subfamily Cephalophinae) and seven species of dwarf antelope (subfamily Neotragini). Being vulnerable to a wide range of predators, small antelope live in monogamous pairs rather than the larger, more visible family groups favoured by other species, and use scent glands to mark their territories. To fuel their high metabolism, most small antelope are 'concentrate selectors', foraging for nutritious morsels such as fruits, buds and flowers, rather than bulk grazing or browsing.

Common duiker *Sylvicapra grimmia*

The widespread common or grey duiker occurs in every habitat except desert, preferring areas of scrub and thicket where it browses singly or in pairs by day or night. Standing up to 50cm at the shoulder and weighing up to 18kg, it is the size of a small dog, with a more rounded back than the similar-sized steenbok. It has a uniform grey-brown coat, with a black streak down the nose, a hairy tuft on the crown and short straight horns in the male. This common species occurs in most parks and reserves and may be seen almost anywhere on the road at night. It tends to lie low to escape danger, but when flushed explodes from cover and flees in a series of bounding zig-zags.

Red duiker *Cephalophus natalensis* and blue duiker *Philantomba monticola*

The stocky red duiker inhabits pockets of indigenous forest in north and east South Africa and southern Mozambique, where pairs forage within small territories defined by dung heaps and scent markings. It is a little smaller than the grey duiker, with a rich chestnut coat, a tufted crest on the crown and short horns in both sexes. In the coastal dune forests around St Lucia, red duikers often associate with samango monkeys (see page 101), foraging on fruit dropped from the canopy. They can be hard to spot among the dappled shadows of the forest floor, but may approach quite close to a quiet observer.

Weighing only 4kg, the blue duiker is the region's smallest antelope. Hardly bigger than a hare, this secretive little creature has a blue-grey coat tinged with rufous, and tiny horns. It inhabits indigenous forest along South Africa's east coast, as far south as George, and also in the Eastern Highlands of Zimbabwe, where pairs forage on the forest floor, supplementing their diet with insects. This antelope is a favourite prey of the crowned eagle (see page 147). It is also a prized delicacy in the bushmeat trade, which today threatens its survival in many areas.

Steenbok *Raphicerus campestris*

The widespread steenbok is about the height of a common duiker, but is lighter in build, weighing no more than 11kg, with a more straight-backed profile. Its shiny rufous-fawn coat has pure white underparts and its face has a distinct Bambi appeal, with large, rounded ears, a black muzzle and big dark eyes accentuated by the pre-orbital scent-glands. The needle-like horns are found in the male only. Steenbok like open areas with nearby cover, where they browse selectively and dig for roots and tubers in the dry season, and also do well on overgrazed farmland. They are unusual among antelope in burying their droppings – a habit that may help to avoid detection by predators and also to reinforce territory. In many bushveld reserves the steenbok is the most commonly seen small antelope species, usually in pairs.

Grysboks

Grysboks resemble small, squat steenboks, with short faces and fur flecked with white. The Cape grysbok (*Raphicerus melanotis*) is the larger of the two, weighing about 10kg, and has a deeper rufous coat. It is endemic to the Cape coast of South Africa, where it inhabits fynbos and wooded gorges and also ventures on to farmland, making itself unpopular on vineyards by nibbling where it shouldn't.

The smaller (about 7kg) and paler Sharpe's grysbok (*Raphicerus sharpei*) is confined in South Africa to the northeast. It also occurs across much of Zimbabwe and southern Mozambique. Its preferred habitat is rocky bush, often at the base of hills. Grysbok browse and graze and are largely nocturnal, though they may be seen at dusk or dawn. Both species may be distinguished from steenbok by a more hunched posture, grizzled coat and lack of white underparts. When flushed, they scuttle away in a low run.

Oribi are usually seen in pairs. (AZ/FLPA)

Oribi *Ourebia ourebi*

An unusually tall steenbok seen in highveld grassland might well be the rare oribi, which stands up to 60cm at the shoulder and weighs about 14kg. This species is more yellow than a steenbok, with a longer neck, and flashes a conspicuous black tail tip in retreat. Today it is found only in isolated pockets of eastern South Africa, Swaziland, Mozambique, central Zimbabwe and northern Botswana, where it inhabits moist and montane grassland. The oribi is a grazer. Small groups sometimes gather to enjoy the new growth on burnt areas of land.

Suni *Neotragus moschatus*

The secretive little suni weighs no more than 5kg. It looks like a pocket-sized steenbok, with a rounded back and short thick horns. Though widespread in Mozambique, it is rare elsewhere, being found only in northern Maputaland, the northern tip of the Kruger and eastern Zimbabwe. Suni inhabit riverine thickets, where pairs follow regular pathways to browse on fresh leaves. They are largely nocturnal, freezing at any hint of danger, then zig-zagging away when flushed. Mkuzi and Ndumo (see page 271) are both suni hotspots, but you have to be lucky.

Klipspringer *Oreotragus oreotragus*

Klipspringer means 'rockjumper' in Afrikaans, and this unusual antelope is uniquely adapted for life among cliffs, gorges and granite kopjes. Standing up to 60cm at the shoulder and weighing around 12kg, it is roughly the size of a steenbok, but looks stockier due to the thick, coarse hair that cushions and insulates its body. A klipspringer has a grizzled coat, with prominent dark eyes and short horns in the male. Most unusual are its cylindrical, downward-pointing hooves, which give it a tip-toe walk and provide an amazing sure-footed agility on the rocks. Klipspringers form lifelong pairs, each marking out a small territory, where one browses while its mate acts as sentry. They are widespread in suitable habitat, and particularly common in the mountains of the western Cape, the Matobo Hills of Zimbabwe and along the Namibian escarpment. Here, they perch conspicuously on pinnacles and ridges, and when alarmed they give a piercing whistle – the ram's followed almost immediately by his mate's – before bounding away a short distance. Unfortunately, the soft fur of klipspringers was once much in demand for saddlebags and this charming animal has been eradicated from much of its former range, particularly in South Africa.

Damara dik-dik *Madoqua kirkii*

The Damara or Kirk's dik-dik is found only in northern Namibia, ·where it frequents bush thickets and rocky areas. This tiny, fragile-looking antelope weighs only about 5kg. It has short horns set in a crest of fur and its long, mobile snout contains a network of capillaries to cool blood circulating through the brain, helping it to survive very hot conditions. Dik-diks are browsers, sometimes standing on hindlegs for a better reach. Like klipspringers, they form lifelong pairs and mark their small territories with large dung piles. The restcamp at Waterberg Plateau (see page 265) and Dik-dik Drive near Etosha's Namutoni Camp are both excellent spots to see this antelope.

Few mammals are more sure-footed than the klipspringer (*top*, AZ), which often perches conspicuously high on rocky outcrops. Like the klipspringer, the Damara dik-dik (*above*, PP) marks its territory by smearing a tarry secretion on to twigs from the pre-orbital gland below its eye.

PRIMATES

Most primates, with their dextrous hands, agile limbs and fondness for fruit, evolved for a life in the trees, so, being somewhat short of forests, southern Africa cannot boast the wealth of species found further north in the continent. There are six species, discounting humans. These comprise three monkeys (Cercopithecidae), of which the chacma baboon and vervet monkey are widespread and common, and three bushbabies (Lorisidae), which may be seen by night in the right habitat.

MONKEYS
Chacma baboon *Papio hamadryas ursinus*
Apart from us, the chacma baboon is by far the largest primate in the region. It has coarse grey-brown fur, a long dog-like muzzle, deep-set eyes and a distinct kink in the tail, which it holds up in an inverted 'U' shape. Big adult males can weigh up to 40kg, twice the size of females, and with their powerful arms and massive canine teeth can look quite intimidating. Both sexes have a pad of grey skin on the buttocks, which swells to a raw red in females on heat. Babies are much darker, with a short muzzle and pink face. A slightly smaller and paler race, the yellow baboon (*P. h. cynocephalus*), replaces the chacma in central Mozambique.

To exploit the open habitats of southern Africa, baboons have evolved a diurnal, semi-terrestrial lifestyle, including a versatile diet and a highly hierarchical social structure, and studies of their complex society have shed some light on our own distant ancestors' first emergence from the trees. Like us, baboons rely on social skills for survival, thus much of their time is spent negotiating the delicate politics of the troop. Alliances are formed by currying favour, including strategic use of child-care and hours of devoted grooming, but squabbles erupt when rules are broken.

Troops range from fewer than 30 to more than 100 individuals, with each troop spanning the whole baboon social spectrum. Older males hold the ultimate authority, with which they direct the troop's movements and defend it from enemies. Sentries are kept posted, and their characteristic bark – *Wahoo!* – is a sure sign that you have been spotted. The troop cooperates to drive away a predator, even a leopard, with such occasions generating a squealing frenzy of excitement. Females come into oestrus on a 36-day cycle and may give birth at any time of year. Babies at first cling to their mother's chest, but later ride on her back. Though youngsters spend much of their time in boisterous play, they never stray far from their mothers.

Baboons are omnivores. They feed on anything from fruit and seed pods to birds' eggs and invertebrates, and will kill and eat animals as large as hares or newborn antelope. In rocky country, a foraging troop leaves its calling card by turning over every small stone in the vicinity in search of tasty titbits. At sunset the troop retires to spend the night in the safety of the treetops or an inaccessible cliff-face. Each new day is greeted with yells and shrieks as the baboons re-establish their ties and

An adult male baboon is a formidable animal, with canine teeth the size of a leopard's. He uses his strength and aggression to defend the troop and metes out stern punishment for any indiscipline among its younger members. (TF/FLPA)

Female baboons in a troop are all related to one another, unlike males, who leave the troop once they become sexually mature – after about six to eight years. Youngsters are nursed for about six months, and family bonds and social alliances are reinforced by constant grooming. (AZ)

return to the ground, thudding down from the branches like big hairy fruit. Baboons are hardy and resourceful and can adapt to almost any habitat, as long as they have daily drinking water and secure roosts. Despite having long been persecuted for their raids on crops, they still occur right across the region, only being completely absent from the central Kalahari and Namib. Their numbers are highest in reserves, where they have adapted to the presence of people and have learnt to exploit new opportunities such as dustbins or open car windows. Although baboons are fascinating and entertaining to watch, in popular tourist areas – such as Victoria Falls or Cape Point – they can become such a menace that some, sadly, have to be destroyed. For their own good, don't encourage them.

Vervet monkey *Chlorocebus aethiops*

The vervet monkey is much smaller and longer-tailed than a baboon. The larger male weighs up to 6kg and measures 100–120cm in length, over half of which is tail. Both sexes have grizzled greyish upperparts, pale underparts and a black face framed with white; sexually active males flaunt a conspicuous blue scrotum. The vervet inhabits mixed savannah and woodland edges, being equally at home on the ground or in trees. Troops of 20 or more establish a home range near abundant food and water, where they forage by day for a variety of plant and invertebrate food, using nimble fingers to pluck fruit, open seed pods and even catch flying insects.

A vervet monkey troop contains an even balance of males and females of all ages within a strict dominance hierarchy, and bonds are maintained by constant grooming and communication. A female may mate with several males within the troop, and her single baby, weighing 300–400g, can be born at any time of year. A young baby is highly dependent on its mother, and during its early months seldom loosens its tenacious grip on her fur. Facing predators from all directions, vervets have evolved a warning language to distinguish between different threats. An 'eagle bark', for example, gets the whole troop looking skywards and scrambling into a tree, whereas a 'snake chutter' has them up on their hind legs craning for a glimpse of python in the grass.

Vervet monkeys are found right across Zimbabwe and Mozambique, northern

Manual dexterity is a key vervet monkey attribute. Nimble fingers allow them to handle all kinds of tricky foods, leap with reckless agility between branches and groom each other's fur with tender precision. (MU)

Botswana and northern and eastern South Africa. Although they occur along the length of the Orange River, they are otherwise absent from the arid west. Like baboons, these resourceful animals have learnt to live near humans, even on the fringes of suburbia. They have become very tame around some camps and hotels, where they charm visitors with their antics but sneak through an open tent flap or kitchen window at the first opportunity. You have been warned.

Samango monkey *Cercopithecus mitis*

The samango monkey, known in East Africa as the blue monkey, is the region's only other monkey species. It is restricted to scattered pockets of indigenous forest in northern and eastern South Africa, as well as eastern Zimbabwe, eastern Swaziland and adjacent Mozambique, where habitat usually precludes confusion with the vervet. The samango monkey is in any case larger (a male weighs up to 9kg), darker and furrier, with thick cheek ruffs and a long black tail, black limbs and a white throat that contrast with the otherwise greyish brown body. Samango monkeys are more arboreal than vervets, and spend much of their time in the canopy, where they feed on fruit, flowers, leaves and gum. Troops of up to 35 animals can be located by the crashing of foliage as they leap from one tree to the next, or by their explosive 'Jack!' alarm bark. They are quite easy to find in a few favourite haunts: KwaZulu-

Samango monkey (PRG/FLPA)

Natal's coastal dune forest, particularly around Cape Vidal, harbours numerous troops, which raid cabins and campsites with all the confidence of their vervet cousins; Vumba Botanical Gardens in Zimbabwe is also a good spot. This species is threatened by the continuing loss of the forest on which it depends.

BUSHBABIES

Bushbabies, or galagos, are small primitive primates, sometimes referred to as prosimians ('early monkeys') that are closely allied to Madagascar's lemurs. They are arboreal and nocturnal and move with great agility through trees at night to feed on fruit, insects and gum – which they scrape off using angled incisors. You are unlikely to find a roosting bushbaby by day, but in the right habitat – particularly during a full moon – the beam of a torch or spotlight often reveals their bright, inquisitive eyes.

Of the two common bushbaby species in southern Africa, the thick-tailed or greater bushbaby (*Otolemur crassicaudatus*) is much the larger, weighing about 1.5kg. With its thick grey-brown fur and large eyes and ears it looks superficially like a small, long-tailed cat, especially when walking across open ground holding its tail erect. Thick-tailed bushbabies inhabit indigenous forest and riverine woodland. Small family parties of females and young roost together by day and forage alone by night, urinating on their hands to spread their scent around their territory. Itinerant males visit them, and sometimes small groups gather at a rich food source, such as a gum lick or fruiting fig tree. A litter of one to three young is born in summer and the babies cling to the mother wherever she clambers.

This species occurs to the north and east of the region as far south as Durban, and is absent from Namibia and Botswana. Its eyes shine red in torchlight – often high in the canopy – and in some some camps tame individuals pay nightly visits. However, this animal is more often heard than seen, its repeated eerie wailing call sounding uncannily like the distressed infant from which the whole family gets its name.

The squirrel-sized lesser bushbaby (*Galago moholi*) weighs only 150g and is more agile than its larger relative, with proportionally bigger eyes and ears. Powerful hindlegs enable it to spring between thorn trees with astonishing five-metre leaps,

The lesser bushbaby (*left*, PPK), like all its kind, urinates on its hands before leaping in order to smear its scent wherever it lands. The much larger thick-tailed bushbaby (*inset*, CTS/FLPA) is less of a leaper, and sometimes comes down from the trees to forage on the ground.

landing hind-feet first. On the ground it travels upright in bounding hops, like some lemurs. Like the thick-tailed, the lesser bushbaby roosts communally by day in a nest or tree fork and emerges by night to feed singly in the branches. It has a wide repertoire of calls, including chirps, whistles and barks, but does not wail. Its diet depends less on fruit and more on acacia gum – particularly during winter – so it is not tied to watercourses and is more at home in dry thornveld. A female gives birth to two young, and at about 15 months young males disperse to establish new territories up to 2km from their birth place.

This species occurs in the northern half of the region, not south of the Kruger Park, and westwards across Zimbabwe, northern Botswana and northern Namibia. In torchlight, its seemingly disembodied red eyes dart around like deranged fireflies as the curious animal leaps from branch to branch.

ANT-EATING ODDITIES

The southern African night tempts out some bizarre-looking creatures; none more so than the aardvark and pangolin. These two extraordinary mammals are not related to each other, each being classified in a separate order of its own, and neither are they related to the South American anteaters, with which they are often compared. However, they do share certain characteristics: both eat nothing but ants and both are extremely hard to see.

PANGOLIN *Manis temminckii*

The pangolin looks more reptile than mammal, and, when curled up in a ball, more artichoke than either. Its upperparts are completely encased in sharp, overlapping scales – made of keratin, just like our fingernails – which provide a highly effective defence. This elusive creature reaches a metre in length and weighs 5–18kg. Although it superficially resembles the South American armadillo, it is actually the sole southern African representative of the old-world order Pholidota. Pangolins are nocturnal, solitary creatures that use their long tongue to feed entirely on ants and termites – lacking the teeth to deal with anything larger. They forage by moving slowly on their hindlegs, with their forelegs drawn up and their long tail extended as a counterbalance. When threatened, they curl instantly into a tight ball, wrapping the tail around the head and underparts to present an impenetrable armour of scales. Any predator that attempts to break in may get a nasty shock, as the scything tail can cut deeply into inquisitive muzzles or paws.

Female pangolins carry their young on their backs and males contest fierce territorial wrestling bouts. Otherwise little is known about the private life of pangolins. They inhabit grassland, rocky and wooded habitats, and their range extends from northern South Africa northwards across the region. To find one you will need luck more than advice – as any experienced ranger will testify. And don't be fooled by old car tyres.

Pangolins have long been prized in traditional medicine for the reputed healing and spiritual properties of their scales, though it is hard to ascertain what impact this may have had upon their population. (PPK)

An aardvark at work is a rare and fascinating sight. (ND/FLPA)

AARDVARK *Orycteropus afer*

Aardvark means 'earth pig' in Afrikaans and, with its long snout and almost naked skin, the aardvark – or antbear – does have a certain porcine quality, though this unusual animal is neither pig nor bear and actually belongs in its own unique order, Tubulidentata. Measuring about 1.5m in length and weighing 40–70kg, the aardvark has a solid, hump-backed body, short sturdy legs and a thick muscular tail. The fawn-coloured skin has a sparse covering of hair, longer and darker on the legs, while the long, tubular ears could have been stolen from a rabbit.

The aardvark is found in open habitats almost anywhere except forest or true desert. It is among the few mammals to have benefited from farming, since overgrazing clears the way for termites – its subsistence diet. This champion excavator is hated by farmers for digging holes in roads and dams. Its uses spade-like nails on its front feet to hack into termitaria, and extracts its quarry with a long sticky tongue. Feeding starts some hours after darkness and a solitary aardvark may wander several kilometres in a night, apparently aimlessly, but with nose to the ground and big ears trained for the rustle of termites. By day it holes up in a burrow which, when vacant, often houses other animals – from wildcats to warthogs. Flies around a burrow entrance indicate when an aardvark is in residence, as do its distinctive three-toed tracks nearby. However the animal itself is hard to find. A quiet night drive in an area of fresh diggings may reveal the hump-backed shuffle of the shy excavator, but it quickly retreats from light. Game farms and smaller reserves with fewer predators often produce the best sightings.

SMALL MAMMALS

Although southern Africa's big beasts may catch the eye and imagination, they are heavily outnumbered in every habitat by the small fry. Small mammals comprise several different orders. Some, notably the rodents and bats, are the most diverse and successful of any mammals on Earth. Others, such as the hyraxes and elephant shrews, are unique to Africa.

HYRAXES (Hyracoidea)

Hyraxes, or dassies, are ancient mammals that have changed little in the last 40 million years. Despite looking like big, fat guinea pigs, they actually share their ancestry with the elephant and the dugong – clues to this unlikely lineage being found in the structure of their feet and teeth. There are four species of hyrax in

Rock hyrax or African elephant? Another tricky ID problem for the field naturalist. (MU)

southern Africa, all but one of which live in small colonies in rocky terrain. The rock hyrax (*Procavia capensis*) is the largest and best known. It weighs 2.5–4.5kg, and has brownish upperparts with a dark 'dorsal crest' of hair around a hidden scent gland on the back. Like all hyraxes, it has no tail and its toes are tipped with flat, hoof-like nails. Long, tactile guard hairs help it to feel the way among boulders and crevices, while interdigital glands moisten the feet to provide vital traction on precipitous rocky surfaces.

A rock hyrax colony has a strict pecking order, with a dominant male and female ruling the roost. Each morning, the hyraxes emerge to bask in the sun, before moving off to feed on nearby vegetation – sometimes clambering into low trees to browse (though this does not make them tree hyraxes – see below). By nightfall the colony is usually back in its rocky retreat, except for occasional moonlight forays. Hyraxes never venture far from base, and a sentry is always posted to sound the alarm. The black eagle (see page 148) is their most significant predator and in some areas this raptor feeds on nothing else. Female hyraxes give birth to two to four young after a long gestation period of seven to eight months. The babies emerge fully formed, like miniature adults, and can feed independently within days. Rock hyraxes are common in rocky terrain across the region and in some protected areas, such as Table Mountain, they have become very tame. Colonies can be detected by the long, yellowish urine stains on the rocks and the high-pitched alarm barks of sentries. The similar yellow-spotted hyrax (*Heterohyrax brucei*), found in Zimbabwe and northern South Africa, sometimes shares colonies with the rock hyrax. It is slightly smaller and greyer, with paler face markings and a white or yellowish dorsal crest.

The tree hyrax (*Dendrohyrax arboreus*) is uncommon in southern Africa, occurring only in a small belt of forest along the Eastern Cape coast and another in central

Mozambique. It is solitary, nocturnal and arboreal, browsing among the branches of large forest trees such as white milkwood and depositing its droppings in tree forks. Though seldom seen, the tree hyrax is well known from its blood-curdling call – a repeated descending scream that outdoes even the bushbaby's – and has inspired much local superstition.

HARES AND RABBITS (Lagomorpha)

Though often thought of as rodents, hares and rabbits belong to the separate order Lagomorpha. Hares are longer-eared than rabbits, with more powerful hind legs. They do not use burrows, but lie up in shallow scrapes – or forms – by day, and graze by night. In arid conditions, hares maximise sustenance from their food by re-ingesting their own faeces. They can also use their huge ears as temperature regulators to either gain or lose heat as conditions require. Hares produce up to four litters of furred young per year (unlike the naked young of rabbits), born in a shallow nest lined with fur. Of two very similar species, the scrub hare (*Lepus saxatilis*) is the more widespread, found virtually everywhere except the Namib Desert, but preferring savannah habitats. The slightly smaller Cape hare (*Lepis capensis*) is found in the southwest and prefers drier, more open country. Though the scrub hare has a whiter underside, both species are variable and hard to distinguish in the field. They are commonly seen on night drives, and when confused by headlights will lollop along the road, frustrating a driver who wants to pass. If

By day, scrub hares trust to their camouflage to avoid predators. (PP)

flushed by day, they zig-zag away at great speed, fast enough to elude even a cheetah.

Three very similar species of red rock rabbit (*Pronolagus* spp) occur in rocky habitats in different parts of the region. These stocky animals can be distinguished from hares by their reddish fur and shorter ears. Red rock rabbits are generally solitary, emerging by night from their rocky hiding places to graze. Although they are sometimes flushed from along a trail, you are more likely to spot their latrines of lozenge-shaped pellets among the rocks. The rare riverine rabbit (*Bunolagus monticularis*) has a similar build, but longer hare-shaped ears. It is endemic to South Africa, frequenting dense riverine bush in a restricted area of the Karoo.

RODENTS (Rodentia)

Rodents are herbivorous mammals with chisel-like incisor teeth evolved for gnawing. Eight families, comprising 78 different species, occur in the region. Most are very small and (except for squirrels) nocturnal, so they pass unseen by the average visitor. However, be assured that there are rodents everywhere – and watch where you leave your biscuits.

Porcupine *Hystrix africaeaustralis*

The porcupine is big enough to resent the label 'small mammal'. Up to a metre long and 20kg in weight, it is by far the largest rodent in Africa, although these dimensions are not as impressive as the sight of the animal itself, trundling along beneath a quivering battery of spines like a bush on legs (and a bush to avoid).

Few predators dare tackle a porcupine. (CM/FLPA)

The banded quills are actually modified hairs. Contrary to popular myth, they are not poisonous and cannot be fired at enemies, but are loosely embedded in the skin and easily shed on contact. Those on the back may be 40cm long, while the shorter open-ended tail quills can be rattled as a warning. When threatened, a porcupine erects its quills and turns its back on an enemy. Careless predators who try their luck will retire punctured, at best, and at worst with quills embedded so deeply that crippling, even fatal injuries can develop. Nonetheless, porcupine flesh is prized by many animals, and in some areas lions have perfected the risky technique of flipping a porcupine over to expose its vulnerable underside.

Porcupines occur right across the region, except for the Namib Desert, and can be seen by night almost anywhere – though you are more likely to spot the evidence than the animal. After dark, they emerge from multi-chambered burrows to forage along regular trails, leaving tell-tale diggings, scattered quills and clusters of fibrous droppings. Food includes roots, bulbs and bark, and the porcupine's habit of fatally ring-barking trees has a serious impact on woodland. They will also gnaw bones, both for their minerals and to sharpen their powerful incisors. Porcupines form monogamous pairs which mate throughout the year (carefully, one presumes). The male plays an unusually active role in raising the litter of two to four young.

Springhare *Pedetes capensis*

The springhare is actually a true rodent and not a hare at all. Weighing about 3kg, this bizarre animal looks like a cross between a rabbit and a kangaroo, with its long ears and thick black-tipped tail, and progresses in ambling hops on long hind legs, with forelegs clasped in front and tail balanced behind. Springhares sleep upright in burrows by day, having plugged the hole with dirt. By night they graze on grass and crops and dig for roots, corms and tubers. This animal is prized by many predators, including eagle owls, honey badgers, caracals and – in Botswana – people. It occurs across the region in areas with sandy soil and low vegetation, and can often be found by casting a torch beam around to reveal its bright eyeshine.

The springhare looks like no other rodent. (AZ)

Squirrels (Sciuridae)

Squirrels are among the easiest rodents to get to know, being large, diurnal and often conspicuous creatures. There are seven species in southern Africa, each with a long bushy tail. Most live in trees. However, the ground squirrel (*Xerus inauris*) is entirely terrestrial and inhabits open arid country in the west. Weighing up to 1kg, it has grizzled greyish brown fur and a white stripe along each flank. Males also have conspicuously large testes.

Ground squirrels are highly gregarious, constantly chattering and grooming one another. Colonies of up to 30, led by a dominant female, inhabit a complex burrow system which they often share with suricates or yellow mongooses (see page 56). The young are born underground, and emerge after six weeks. Ground squirrels dig for seeds, roots and bulbs. Like suricates, they stand upright to spot danger, before dashing for cover. When foraging, they also hold their tails up like parasols to deflect the burning sun and cast protective shade. In the Kgalagadi Transfrontier Park (see page 268), colonies of ground squirrels make their home in every camp, foraging between tents and deckchairs.

Ground squirrels share territory and tricks with meerkats. (AZ)

The smaller tree squirrel (*Paraxerus cepapi*) is a woodland species, absent from the arid west. It is brownish in colour and only weighs about 200g. Tree squirrels forage by day in small parties, searching in the branches and on the ground for plants and invertebrates. At night they roost together in tree holes. They are very excitable animals, constantly chasing one another up and down tree trunks. When alarmed they flick their tails furiously over their backs, and their chucking alarm calls often betray the presence of a snake. Tree squirrels can be very common in suitable habitat, particularly mopane woodland. By contrast, the red squirrel (*Paraxerus palliatus*) is restricted to a few pockets of indigenous forest in central Mozambique, the Eastern Highlands of Zimbabwe and northern KwaZulu-Natal, where its scolding trill is often heard from the mid-canopy along forest trails. It is a solitary animal, slightly larger than a tree squirrel, with a reddish face and underparts.

Rats and mice (Muridae)

There are 57 species of rat and mouse in southern Africa. Although the alien house mouse (*Mus musculus*) and house rat (*Rattus rattus*) are notorious pests, no indigenous species does any real damage to people. Most are seldom seen, let alone identified, though many are extremely common. Fat mice (*Steatomys* spp) are docile little rodents that lay down thick fat deposits to sustain them during leaner times, making them a traditional delicacy for people throughout Africa. The pouched mouse (*Saccostomus campestris*) is another dumpy, slow-moving species, and resembles a hamster, with its short tail and capacious cheek pouches for storing food. Climbing mice (*Dendromus* spp) use dextrous toes and a long semi-prehensile tail to

clamber among rank vegetation, often nesting inside old weaver nests (see page 180). Gerbils (subfamily Gerbillinae) are burrowers in sandy soils, and several species have distinct hairy feet and tasselled tail tips. The diurnal striped mouse (*Rhabdomys pumilio*) is a grassland species, identified by the four dark stripes along its back. It is replaced in low-lying eastern areas by the single-striped mouse (*Lemniscomys rosalia*). The tree mouse (*Thallomys paedulcus*) is a larger, long-tailed species that makes conspicuous nests in arid woodland trees such as camelthorns and is often seen scurrying along branches by day. The prolifically fecund multimammate mice (*Mastomys* spp) have up to 12 pairs of teats and produce litters of more than 12 young after a gestation period of only 23 days, making them a vital prey species for many. Vlei rats (*Otomys* spp) resemble miniature cane rats (see below), and build similar (though much smaller) runways to their burrows. The stocky, short-tailed Brandt's whistling rat (*Parotomys brantsii*) is well-known in the Kalahari, where it draws attention to itself by standing on its hindlegs to whistle before diving into its burrow.

Three of many small rodents that nibble their way through southern Africa: the striped mouse (*above top*, ND) is often seen by day; the vlei rat (*above centre*, PPk) clears runways to its burrows; the cape molerat (*above bottom*, PPk) digs kilometres of tunnels.

Don't trust the name

Some rodents are misleadingly named. Dormice (Gliridae) are not mice, but, with their grey fur and bushy tail, they look just like small nocturnal squirrels. The spectacled dormouse (*Graphiurus ocularis*) is the largest and most distinctive of four species and inhabits rocky country in the Cape. Molerats (Bathyergidae) are not moles, but burrowing rodents. They have tiny eyes and ears, short tails, pig-like snouts and formidable incisors which they use to dig extensive tunnel systems for their underground colonies – infuriating gardeners by heaving up mounds of earth. The greater cane-rat (*Thryonomys swinderianus*) is not a true rat but is closely related to porcupines. This big, stocky rodent, weighing up to 5kg, has a short tail and grizzled fur. It feeds on the roots and stems of reeds and grasses, leaving characteristic runways through ground vegetation, and can seriously damage cane plantations if unchecked by natural predators. The dassie rat (*Petromus typicus*) is neither rat nor dassie, but resembles a cross between the two, complete with a long, hairy tail. Like dassies (see page 106), it inhabits rocky terrain (in Namibia and the northern Cape) and basks in the early morning or late afternoon sun.

INSECT EATERS

Unlike the plant-nibbling rodents and rabbits, some small mammals are hunters that prey on insects and other invertebrates. These insect eaters are unrelated to rodents, despite their similar appearance, and have a far more ancient ancestry. Until recently they were all grouped into the single order Insectivora, but ongoing genetic research has revealed the existence of several distinct orders.

Insectivores (Insectivora)

Shrews are true insectivores, and the region is home to 16 species, ranging in size from the 20cm giant musk shrew (*Crocidura occidentalis*) to the tiny 3.5g least dwarf shrew (*Suncus inifinitesimus*). All are superficially mouse-like, but with longer snouts, shorter tails and tiny eyes. Shrews live fast and die young. They feed voraciously to fuel their high metabolism and often tackle prey as big as themselves. The uncommon southern African hedgehog (*Atelerix frontalis*) is another true insectivore and looks much like its European relative. It forages busily after dark for invertebrates and fruits, and trusts its battery of spines to thwart predators – though this defence doesn't always deter the giant eagle owl (see page 157).

Golden moles (Chrysochloridea)

Golden moles are unrelated to true moles, despite being very similar in appearance, with silky fur and no visible ears, eyes or tail. Like moles, they spend life largely underground, feeding on insect larvae and earthworms and using strong front claws to dig long, winding tunnels just below the surface. Unlike molerats (see page 110), golden moles do not create molehills.

Elephant shrews (Macroscelididea)

Elephant shrews, sometimes known by their African name *sengi* to avoid confusion, are slightly larger (about 25cm long) than real shrews and can be distinguished by their big, mouse-like eyes and ears and their eponymous elongated little snouts. They use their long legs to propel them in bursts of high-speed hopping along regular trails, which they keep fastidiously free of obstructions. The rock elephant shrew (*Elephantulus myurus*), one of eight species in the region, is commonly seen by day on granite kopjes, where it shelters from the sun under boulders and dashes out periodically after ants and termites.

Below left African hedgehog (PPK) *Below right* Rock elephant shrew (AZ)

BATS

After snakes, bats (Chiroptera) must surely be the most maligned and misunderstood of all animals; perhaps because their habit of flying by night and hiding by day makes them hard to observe and therefore easy to make things up about. For the record, bats don't become entangled in hair, nor do they transmit disease or suck blood (at least not in Africa). In fact bats are remarkable creatures, whose range of talents – including the power of flight and hunting by echolocation – lies behind their proliferation into the largest single order of mammals in the world. At least 76 of the world's 900-plus species of bat occur in southern Africa.

Fruit bats (Megachiroptera)

An epauletted fruit bat – but is it Peter's or Wahlberg's? To find out, you'd have to check its teeth. (MU)

Bats can be divided into two suborders. Fruit bats are larger, with long, dog-like faces (hence the common name, flying fox) and two claws on each wing for hanging from trees. They feed on fruit, buds and flowers, and occur mostly in moister regions, where they can be spotted by day roosting in fruiting trees. Unlike their insectivorous relatives, fruit bats have no need for echolocation, since they do not eat insects, but rather use their large eyes to navigate by sight. Though they are blamed for damaging orchards, they play a crucial role in pollinating trees (when moving between flowers in search of nectar) and dispersing their seeds (by excreting droppings in flight). Wahlberg's epauletted fruit bat (*Epomorphus wahlbergi*) is typical of this family. The monotonous pinging of territorial males, given as they roost after feeding, is a characteristic night-time sound of riverine forests, orchards and coastal towns in the east. Further west, for example in the Okavango/Chobe region, it is largely replaced by Peters's epauletted fruit bat (*Epomorphorus crypturus*), and mixed colonies form where their ranges overlap.

Insectivorous bats (Microchiroptera)

As their scientific name suggests, insectivorous bats are smaller than fruit bats. Some species live in huge cave colonies, while others frequent human habitation.

In colder regions many hibernate over winter. Insectivorous bats navigate by echolocation: ultrasonic sounds produced in the throat (largely inaudible to the human ear) are bounced off objects and interpreted by the brain to map the immediate environment, enabling them to catch tiny, fast-moving prey on the wing. This technique is so efficient that one bat has been recorded catching over 600 mosquitoes in an hour, and it has been calculated that, in one year, a single colony of 300,000 bats consumes 100 tonnes of insects. Who needs pesticides?

There are six families and at least 69 species of insectivorous bat in southern Africa, classified by the shape of their tail, ears and facial skin adornments. Tomb bats (Emballonuridae) are pale-looking, with pointed faces and larger eyes than other families, and often roost under thatched eaves. Free-tailed bats (Molossidae) show the tail tip projecting 'free' from the interfemoral membrane between the two back legs. They roost in large colonies, often in the roofs of houses, where they start chattering for an hour or two before sunset and can create quite a stink. Vesper bats (Vespertilioninae) are the largest group, each with a simple mouse-like face, and tail fully enclosed by the interfemoral membrane. They include Schreiber's long-fingered bat (*Miniopterus schreibersii*), which roosts in caves in colonies of thousands, the tiny banana bat (*Pipistrellus nanus*), which roosts in the rolled ends of banana leaves, and the widespread Cape serotine bat (*Eptesicus capensis*), which emerges shortly after sunset to fly low and erratically over water. Horseshoe bats (Rhinolophidae) are also mass communal roosters and can be seen in their thousands in the Sudwala Caves in South Africa. Slit-faced bats (Nycteridae) have long ears, silky fur and a split down the length of the face to protect the nose leaves (which are uncovered during flight). The Egyptian slit-faced bat (*Nycteris thebaica*) is widespread in all habitats, often roosting in road culverts, and supplements its aerial forays by capturing small invertebrates on the ground. Leaf-nosed bats (Hipposideridae) have complex facial adornments, which – like satellite dishes – help in echolocation. With its 60cm wingspan, Commerson's leaf-nosed bat (*Hipposideros commersoni*) is one of the largest bats in the region.

The Cape horseshoe bat traps a moth in flight by bouncing ultrasonic 'echolocation' calls off its body.

SEA MAMMALS

The rich oceans of southern Africa harbour a wealth of sea mammals. Many are long-distance wanderers that pass through the region's offshore waters but seldom come within sight of land. Others, such as the southern right whales of the Cape or the Cape fur seals of the Skeleton Coast, provide more dependable and often spectacular viewing.

WHALES AND DOLPHINS

Whales and dolphins, or cetaceans, evolved from land ungulates over 55 million years ago. They are entirely marine (never coming on to land except by accidental stranding) and use forelimbs modified into flippers and a flattened paddle of a tail to power them through the water. Instead of nostrils, a blowhole on top of the head allows them to breathe when they surface – they need to breathe regularly – sending up spouts of spray by which different species may be identified.

Cetaceans fall into two sub-orders: baleen whales and toothed whales. Baleen whales (Mysticeti) comprise the giant filter-feeding 'great whales', among which – at over 30m and 100 tonnes – is the mighty blue whale (*Balaenoptera musculus*), the largest animal ever known. Baleen whales have no teeth, but feed on small marine creatures such as plankton, which they sieve in huge quantities from surface waters through 'baleen' (fronds of keratin) hanging from the upper jaw. Eight species have been recorded off the southern African coast. Toothed whales (Odontoceti) are more numerous and diverse, ranging in size from the little Heaviside's dolphin to the 40-tonne sperm whale. They feed by echolocation, using high-frequency sounds to locate their prey – mostly squid or fish – underwater. Although 30 species have been recorded in southern African waters, many feed far out at sea and only a handful are seen regularly.

Southern right whale *Eubalaena australis*

The southern right whale is the region's best known whale. Every spring, from July, these gentle giants arrive from the sub-Antarctic to breed in the calm inshore waters of the Cape, some remaining until December before migrating southwards with their new calves. They can easily be observed from land at a few prime sites, including False Bay, Plettenburg Bay and Hermanus. Here, whales cavort close inshore, sometimes 'breaching' clear of the water or beating the surface with their tails. The name was coined by whalers, who judged this slow, approachable species to be the easiest and thus the 'right' whale to hunt. Thousands were slaughtered during the 19th century, until formal protection was agreed in 1935, since when numbers have recovered well.

This is the most likely baleen whale to be seen in the region and can be distinguished from others by its V-shaped blow and lack of a dorsal fin. Seen clear of the water, it has no pleats on the throat and its arched upper jaw is covered with whitish growths, or callosities, unique to each individual. After an 11–12-month gestation period, females give birth to a single, 5m-long calf, which suckles for its first six months and may grow up to reach 17m long and weigh over 50 tonnes.

Other baleen whales

Worldwide, the humpback whale (*Megaptera novaeangliae*) is probably the best known, and certainly the most filmed, of all the great whales. It has become famous for its spectacular displays and the complex, haunting songs by which it communicates underwater. A humpback can be identified by its long, largely white pectoral fins, which wave clear of the water as the animal rolls on its side. The short dorsal fin is set far back and the large head is deeply grooved beneath the lower jaw and clustered with knobby tubercles on top. Humpback whales reach 15 metres in length and weigh about 40 tonnes. Small groups migrate up the coasts of southern Africa each autumn from their Antarctic feeding grounds towards their equatorial breeding grounds, returning again in spring. They are often seen passing through the Mozambique Channel, sometimes coming within sight of land at such points as Cape Vidal (see page 246). A small population of Bryde's whale (*Balaenoptera edeni*) is also resident off the southern African coast, often feeding close inshore on shoaling fish such as pilchards, lunging up through the surface among crowds of gannets. This slender species reaches 14m in length and has a mottled appearance.

Whales seldom show much of themselves, so look for obvious identification features when they surface. The humpback whale (*right*, MU) has enormously long pectoral fins which it often waves clear of the water; the southern right whale (*below*, JCS/FLPA) has prominent white growths (callosities) on its head and lacks a dorsal fin.

Dolphins

Dolphins are small to medium-sized toothed cetaceans, many with a distinctive beak. The popular bottle-nosed dolphin (*Tursiop aduncas/truncatus*) is the familiar, acrobatic star of dolphinariums the world over. It occurs in two races off the southern African coast, one in the Indian Ocean (*T. aduncas*) and a larger one in the Atlantic (*T. truncatus*), both usually found in maternity groups of 30 or so. A permanent population along the KwaZulu-Natal coast can often be seen riding the breakers close inshore. In winter, bottlenosed dolphins congregate for the annual 'sardine run' (see page 32), joining other species such as the smaller, more colourful common dolphin (*Delphinus delphis*) which often occurs in schools of hundreds. Risso's dolphin (*Grampus griseus*) is a larger species – up to 3.5m – that occurs in small groups along the coastal shelf. It can be identified by its blunt face, tall dorsal fin, and conspicuously scarred, pale grey body. Heaviside's dolphin (*Cephalorhynchus heavisidii*) is southern Africa's only endemic cetacean, and frequents the west coast in small family groups, often escorting boats around harbours such as Walvis Bay. It is no more than 1.5m long, with a blunt nose, triangular dorsal fin, and complex pattern of black, white and grey. The rare humpback dolphin (*Sousa plumbea*) inhabits shallow, sub-tropical coastal waters and estuaries along the northeast coast. This slow-moving species has a diagnostic thick ridge along its spine, topped with a pointed dorsal fin. Like other dolphins, it faces a barrage of threats to its environment, including pollution, overfishing, the silting up of inshore waters and the deadly tangle of shark nets and fishing trawlers.

Heaviside's dolphin is the only cetacean endemic to southern Africa.

A school of common dolphins race across False Bay, off the Cape, in pursuit of shoaling fish. (MS/FLPA)

CAPE FUR SEAL *Arctocephalus pusillus*

Seals (Pinnipedia) can be divided into two principal families: true, 'earless' seals (Phocidae) can only drag themselves on their belly over land; 'eared' seals (Otariidae), or sealions, have visible ears and move much better on land by raising their bodies on their front flippers. This latter group includes the Cape fur seal, the only species indigenous to southern Africa, which breeds in about 25 colonies on rocky islands and remote shores between Cape Cross in Namibia and Algoa Bay, near Port Elizabeth. Some 90% of the population is on the west coast, where the cold Benguela Current teems with fish, and some colonies here are enormous.

From the 16th to the 19th centuries, Cape fur seals were heavily exploited for their skin and meat, but their subsequent recovery is a rare conservation success story. Today, there are over two million, and the fishing industry is complaining of unfair competition.

Male Cape fur seals weigh 200–350kg, three to four times the weight of females, and measure up to 2.3m long. Their massive neck and forequarters are encased in a thick layer of blubber, covered in coarse fur, which serves as both intimidation and protection during violent territorial skirmishes. Females are slimmer and paler in colour. Breeding starts in November, when bulls come ashore to establish their territories, closely followed by pregnant cows who each give birth to a single pup within two or three days of their arrival. Nursing females leave their young and feed at sea, returning every few days to suckle their pups, which are weaned at about nine months. Under the desert sun and the crush of the colony, the mortality rate is very high. But then so is the birth rate.

Life in a Cape fur seal colony is crowded and smelly, and pups are at great risk from dehydration and the sheer crush of bodies. (AZ)

Wandering fur seals can turn up anywhere along the coast, but only at large colonies, such as Cape Cross in Namibia, can the raw nature of their society truly be appreciated. Here, the rocks and sand are piled high with sprawled and heaving bodies, while the surf churns with thousands more coming and going from their fishing grounds or simply lounging to escape the heat. The pitiful bleating of youngsters and hoarse honking of males fill the air, and the stench of fish and death is overpowering. Massive bulls break into lumbering battles, scattering females and leaving a wake of dead or abandoned pups that draws black-backed jackals out of the desert to pick through the colony, occasionally triggering panic stampedes into the water.

DUGONG *Dugong dugon*

The endangered dugong is the only southern African sea cow. This ancient order (Sirenia) is distantly related to elephants and also includes the West African and tropical American manatees. Dugongs are slow-moving, entirely aquatic creatures of sheltered tropical waters, where they graze seagrass beds with the rising tide. An adult measures up to three metres long and weighs up to 400kg. Its grey, torpedo-shaped body is distinguished from a seal's by the hairless skin and crescent-shaped, whale-like tail. The female's habit of lifting her head from the water while cradling a baby is thought to have given rise to the mermaid myth (showing the effect of a long spell at sea on a frustrated sailor's imagination). Dugongs were once common, but relentless hunting has reduced their population to a few pockets along the Mozambique coast.

Dugongs feed in shallow water, grazing deep furrows through the intertidal seagrass beds. (MP/FLPA)

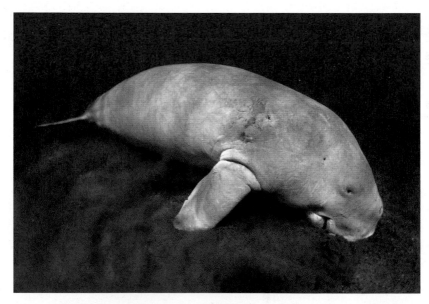

BIRDS

Bateleur eagle (FLPA)

Southern Africa is home to over 900 species of bird. While this is fewer than some parts of central and East Africa, it nonetheless represents an impressive 9% of the world total and includes at least 134 endemic or near-endemic species, most of which occur in habitats – such as the Namib Desert, highveld grassland and Cape fynbos – that are unique to the region. If it's size you're after, then southern Africa has the world's largest bird (ostrich), its largest flying bird (kori bustard), its biggest communal nest (sociable weaver) and its largest flocks (red-billed quelea); if it's looks that count, try the dazzling colours of carmine bee-eater, lilac-breasted roller, Knysna turaco or violet-eared waxbill; for the sheer bizarre, you'd do well to beat the breeding plumage of the pennant-winged nightjar or the display flight of the red-crested korhaan. Other marvels of evolution include an owl that catches fish, a mountain vulture that smashes bones on rocks, sandgrouse that transport water in their belly feathers and a honeyguide that leads people to bees' nests. The following account describes most of the 92 families represented in the region. It does not follow a strict taxonomic order, but is organised according to natural affinities of appearance, behaviour and habitat.

SEABIRDS AND WATERBIRDS

Aquatic habitats, both fresh- and saltwater ones, support a rich variety of birds and offer some of the region's best birding. Abundant food – from fish and frogs to molluscs and mosquito larvae – is the lure; webbed feet, long legs, stabbing bills and waterproof feathers are the tools of the trade. Each species is adapted to its own niche: at sea, gannets plunge-dive for fish, penguins slip beneath the breakers and shearwaters trawl the open ocean; on inland waters, herons spear frogs in the shallows, ducks dabble in the water-weed and sandpipers scuttle along the shoreline.

OCEAN WANDERERS

Beyond the breakers, currents laden with marine life draw pelagic wanderers from across the southern hemisphere. Many of these birds stay well out of sight of land: they breed on remote Southern Ocean islands and arrive in winter to ply the region's offshore waters.

Black-browed
albatross

Nine species of albatross (Diomedeidae) occur in southern African waters. These huge birds spend most of their life at sea, feeding largely on squid and gliding vast distances low over the water on stiff, narrow wings. Most numerous is the relatively small black-browed albatross (*Thalassarche melanophrys*), and in the right weather conditions a steady passage of this species can be seen from headlands such as Cape Point. Shearwaters and petrels (Procellariidae), like albatrosses, have raised tubular nostrils on their bill through which they excrete excess salt. This family includes the albatross-sized southern giant petrel (*Macronectes giganteus*) which sometimes scavenges at seal colonies; the much smaller, all-dark sooty shearwater (*Puffinus griseus*), which gathers in rafts to dive from the surface after small fish; and the pigeon-sized pintado, or Cape, petrel (*Daption capense*), with its distinctive pied plumage. Storm-petrels (Oceanitidae), such as Wilson's storm-petrel (*Oceanites oceanicus*), are small dark birds with a white rump that flutter, bat-like, over the surface, pattering with their feet to stir up tiny organisms.

Cape petrel. (JH/FLPA)

'Wrecks' of petrels sometimes occur around the Cape, when thousands are blown ashore by bad weather. To find pelagic birds, you can take a boat trip from Cape Town, Durban or Walvis Bay to the offshore trawling grounds, where they congregate to scavenge in the wake of the trawlers. The birding can be spectacular, though these trips are not for the queasy.

Cape gannet *Morus capensis*

The Cape gannet is a large, snow-white bird, with bold black wing tips and fine black facial markings. The entire world population breeds in six huge island colonies along the western Cape coast, where thousands of densely packed birds jostle aggressively on the ground while the air above is thronged with hundreds more. Each pair guards its own tiny territory, beak by jowl with its neighbours, and pecks savagely at intruders. Birds trying to negotiate a route through the colony must run the gauntlet of a thousand upturned dagger bills until they find their own nest and partner, whereupon the pair bond is confirmed with a ritual fencing of bills. Gannets catch fish by plunge-diving from high above the surface, folding back their wings to enter the water like a missile. Hundreds may gather for a large shoal, peppering the water in a spectacular aerial bombardment. Outside the breeding season, gannets disperse around the coast.

A cape gannet has no difficulty in identifying its mate among thousands of other birds in the colony; the real problem lies in a negotiating a route back to the nest. (KG)

To Africa's only penguin,
Antarctica is but a chilly rumour. (AZ)

African or jackass penguin
Spheniscus demersus
Africa's one endemic penguin breeds in 27 scattered colonies along the coast of the Western Cape and Namibia, 24 on islands and three on the mainland. Like all penguins, its wings are modified into flippers, which allow great speed and agility in the water but are no use for flight. Each pair occupies a burrow amongst rocks or dug into guano. A male courts his mate with an elaborate 'ecstatic display' in which he slowly raises his head, beats his wings and throbs his breast, while letting out a raucous braying. The whole ritual gets other nearby penguins going, until the air is ringing with their donkey-like crescendo. Penguins fish by diving from the surface. A wonderful spot to watch them is at Boulders, on the Cape Peninsula, where a small colony has taken up residence on the doorstep of the local community.

GULLS AND TERNS (Laridae)
Gulls and terns are primarily coastal birds, with a few species also found inland. Most gulls are larger, and their more powerful bill enables them to exploit a broader diet than the largely fish-eating terns. At 60cm, the kelp gull (*Larus dominicanus*) is the largest, with a distinctive black back and bright yellow bill. This bold opportunist is a familiar scavenger in Cape coastal towns. The smaller Hartlaub's gull (*Larus hartlaubii*) also commonly associates with people and is very common in the Western Cape. The similar grey-headed gull (*Larus cirrocephalus*) is slightly larger than the Hartlaub's, with a grey head and red bill, and is the only species commonly seen inland, where it nests in small island colonies on lakes and dams across the region.

Terns are more lightly built than gulls, with a more graceful and buoyant flight.

The kelp gull nests on cliffs and islands. (MS)

Most species have a forked tail and, in breeding plumage, a jet black cap. Terns fly back and forth over the shallows in search of fish, often dipping swallow-like to the surface or plunging in completely. On the coast, the most common breeding species is the swift tern (*Sterna bergii*), which nests in noisy island colonies, while the common tern (*Sterna hirundo*) arrives in great numbers from the north as a non-breeding summer visitor. At 50cm, the Caspian tern (*Sterna caspia*) is the largest. It is often seen loafing on a sandbank, and is easily identified by its heavy, bright orange-red

Whiskered tern

bill. Inland, two smaller, shorter-tailed terns occur on fresh water: the white-winged tern (*Chlidonias leucopterus*) arrives as a common non-breeding summer visitor right across the region, preferring large bodies of water; the whiskered tern (*Chlidonias hybrida*) breeds on smaller dams and marshes and differs only in its breeding plumage, which shows white cheek patches between the grey underparts and black cap. Both species are constantly on the wing, dipping and darting over the water in search of aquatic invertebrates.

African skimmer
Rhynchops flavirostris

The skimmer is a tern-like bird found along broad rivers in the north, such as the Zambezi, Chobe and Okavango. It has the easy, buoyant flight of a tern, but what most catches the eye is the extraordinary shape of its bright red bill, which has a lower mandible markedly longer than the upper. A skimmer feeds by flying low over the water with this

The African skimmer deploys its elongated lower mandible in a unique fishing technique. (CH/FLPA)

lower mandible dipped beneath the surface, snapping its bill shut on any morsel in its path. Small groups sit quietly on sandbanks, periodically taking off to 'skim' the water and scoring V-shaped wakes in the surface with their bills. Unfortunately skimmers' low-lying nests are often destroyed by the wash of power boats.

PELICANS (Pelecanidae)

Measuring 180cm in length and weighing up to 15kg, the white pelican (*Pelecanus onocrotalus*) vies with the kori bustard and marabou stork for the title of world's largest flying bird. It is quite unmistakable, with its snow-white plumage set off by black flight feathers and a bright yellow fleshy pouch hanging from the enormous bill. White pelicans are usually seen either in a flotilla on the water, or flying in formation high overhead, gliding like great aircraft between ponderous wingbeats. They breed during winter on the Namibian coast and St Lucia, and sometimes at Makgadikgadi Pans.

White pelicans: some authorities claim that their beak can hold more than their belly can. (AZ/FLPA)

At other times they may wander almost anywhere in the region. Pelicans feed cooperatively, corralling fish into the shallows to scoop them up with their capacious bills. The smaller and greyer pink-backed pelican (*Pelecanus rufescens*) is more of a solitary fisherman. It breeds regularly in the Okavango Delta and on Mkuzi's Nsumo Pan (see page 271), though the region's total population numbers no more than 250 breeding pairs.

CORMORANTS (Phalacrocoracidae)

Cormorants are dark, long-necked birds that are often seen swimming low in the water, constantly diving for fish. They have a distinctive habit of perching with their wings spread wide. Opinion differs as to whether this helps the feathers to dry, or whether it serves to warm the bird, or even aid its digestion. Whatever the explanation, cormorants are master fishermen, often surfacing with a hefty, writhing catch, which is then juggled into position for swallowing. Of five species in the region, the white-breasted cormorant (*Phalacrocorax lucidus*) is the largest, and readily identified by its white underparts. It lives in small colonies, inland and along the coast, and often perches in dead trees. The all-dark reed cormorant (*Phalacrocorax africanus*) is the smallest and most solitary species, and is common on inland freshwaters. The Cape cormorant (*Phalacrocorax capensis*) nests in huge west coast colonies, some on artificial platforms built for the collection of guano. Long skeins of these birds snake in formation low over the cold, misty Atlantic waters.

African darter *Anhinga rufa*

The darter, or snakebird, looks like a cormorant taken to extremes, but belongs to a separate family, Anhingidae. It swims so low in the water that only its serpentine neck – held with a distinct kink like a heron's – protrudes above the surface, and perched on a bare tree, wings spread wide, it strikes a gaunt silhouette. The darter also has a dagger-like bill to impale fish, a striped neck and – in breeding plumage – a shawl of long white scapulars. It is common on freshwater bodies and coastal lagoons across the region.

Above Inland, white-breasted cormorants nest in dead trees above water; by the coast they often use manmade structures. (ND) *Below* The African darter can be distinguished from cormorants by its unhooked bill and serpentine neck. (BZ/FLPA)

HERONS AND EGRETS (Ardeidae)

Herons and egrets are long-legged and long-necked wading birds that grab or spear their prey with a sharp, elongated bill. They fly steadily on broad, rounded wings, with legs trailing and neck folded back. There are 20 species in the region. Most hunt alone, but breed and roost in colonies, generally near water. Standing 140cm high, the goliath heron (*Ardea goliath*) is the largest heron in the world. It is a shy bird, found alone or in pairs towards the north and east of the region, and strikes a stately pose as it hunts patiently in the shallows. The goliath heron's stature makes it a conspicuous target for the piratical fish eagle (see page 149), which often steals its catch. The grey heron (*Ardea cinerea*) is very familiar to European birders, and is the region's most common large heron. It frequents lakes and pans, whereas the similar black-headed heron (*Ardea melanocephala*) prefers moist grasslands, where it feeds on rats and small birds. The purple heron (*Ardea purpurea*) skulks in reedbeds, where its thin striped neck is perfectly camouflaged among the reeds.

Egrets are white herons, whose plumes were once coveted fashion accessories. The ubiquitous cattle egret (*Bubulcus ibis*), unlike other species, is gregarious and largely terrestrial, and habitually follows large grazing animals, from cattle to elephants, to feed on insects flushed from their feet. Small flocks of cattle egrets are often seen in fields and parks, rushing around and stabbing at the grass. During the breeding season their white plumage is tinged with saffron. Other egrets are more aquatic. The great white egret (*Egretta*

Rewards will come to those who wait: the purple heron (*above left*, PP) spears fish through a blanket of water plants; the great white egret (*above right*, AZ) has a taste for frogs; the goliath heron (*top right*, MU) is the largest and most patient of anglers; the black-headed heron (*bottom right*, AZ) snaps up its prey on dry land.

The green-backed heron is a solitary species, and does not nest colonially. (AZ)

alba) is the tallest (95cm) and most elegant. It stands motionless in the water for long periods, poised to strike. The smaller little egret (*Egretta garzetta*) is another solitary hunter, identified by its black legs and yellow feet, which sometimes abandons its poise to splash through the shallows after prey. The black heron (*Egretta ardesiaca*) is the size and shape of a little egret, but has slate-grey plumage. It hunts with a unique technique, known as 'canopying', whereby it folds its wings forward like an umbrella to cast a shadow over the water in which its prey becomes visible.

There are several other smaller heron species. Black-crowned night herons (*Nycticorax nycticorax*) roost by day in tree canopies overhanging water, each bird hidden and hunched. At dusk they disperse over their wetland feeding grounds, owl-like in their soft, round-winged flight. The squacco heron (*Ardeola ralloides*) inhabits marshy wetlands, where its subtle, straw-coloured camouflage is undone by pure white wings when it takes off. The green-backed heron (*Butorides striata*) is another camouflaged stalker, but prefers quiet, shady backwaters. The little bittern (*Ixobrychus minutus*) is a diminutive species (only 36cm) that clambers around inside reedbeds and is seldom seen unless flushed, when the male reveals striking black-and-cream plumage.

STORKS (Ciconiidae)

Storks are large, long-legged and long-billed birds. They are sometimes mistaken for herons, though, with the exception of the marabou, all storks fly with their neck extended. Some species are migratory, and often gather on thermals in huge wheeling flocks. Many congregate at grassfires to pick off small animals that are flushed or toasted by the flames. Storks do not call, but communicate with loud bill-clapping at their breeding grounds. Best known of the migrants is the white stork (*Ciconia ciconia*) – baby-carrier of legend, and known in Europe for its huge, untidy nests on ancient buildings. It arrives in Africa each October to disperse across the region's grasslands (although a small population also breeds in the Western Cape). This big bird, 102cm long, is identified by its bold black-and-white plumage and red bill. The smaller Abdim's stork (*Ciconia abdimii*) is an inter-African migrant, breeding in central Africa and arriving in September in great numbers. It is largely black, with a white belly and white rump, and is common in suburban areas, often visiting playing fields and golf courses.

Not all storks are migrants; some stick around all year. The woolly-necked stork (*Ciconia episcopus*) feeds on open ground near fresh water in the north and east of the region. It can be identified by its white, 'woolly' neck of fluffed feathers, which contrast with its otherwise mostly dark plumage. The yellow-billed stork (*Mycteria ibis*) occurs

on large rivers and lakes in the north, often alongside other water birds such as egrets. It wades with its bill held open below the surface, pausing regularly to stir up the mud with its feet, and using the flexible, sensitive tips of the mandibles to seize small aquatic prey. The African open-billed stork (*Anastomus lamelligerus*) nests in large colonies along the Zambezi and other major northern rivers. It has glossy dark brown plumage, and, when closed, the large pale bill shows a clear gap between the two mandibles. This stork is a specialist feeder on freshwater mussels and snails, and is able to winkle them out by using the tips of its mandibles like a pair of tweezers.

Marabou stork *Leptoptilos crumeniferus* and saddle-billed Stork *Ephippiorhynchus senegalensis*

Two storks tower above the others. The marabou stands 150cm high, and is one of the world's largest flying birds. It has a massive bill and a naked head and neck, from which a pendulous inflatable air sac hangs like a great sausage. The marabou's grotesque appearance and its scavenging habits are not everybody's cup of tea. Nonetheless, it cuts a magnificent profile in flight, with its head retracted beneath a three-metre wingspan. Marabous are largely confined to game reserves in the north and east, where they often join vultures at kills, or pick over the local rubbish tips. At breeding colonies the birds communicate with noisy croaking and bill-clapping. One such colony at Gcodikwe Lagoon in Moremi (see page 246) allows an intimate view of marabou society by guided boat trip.

The saddle-billed stork is as tall as a marabou, but more lightly built, with a bright yellow 'saddle' across its black-and-red bill. This uncommon but conspicuous resident occurs on freshwater pans and floodplains to the north and east, where it stalks the shallows, stooping to snap up catfish, frogs and other delicacies. Prey is first washed before being tossed up and gulped down headfirst. Monogamous pairs reinforce their strong bonds with a ritual display in which the male strides deliberately away from his partner, before dashing back with flapping wings.

Different storks with different diets: the African open-billed stork (*above*, PP) specialises in freshwater molluscs; the yellow-billed stork (*centre*, AZ) prefers crustaceans and aquatic larvae; for the marabou stork (*below*, AZ) virtually anything goes, including carrion; while the saddle-billed stork (*overleaf*, RT) is an expert snapper-up of fish, frogs and reptiles.

IBISES (Threskiornithidae) AND SPOONBILLS (Plataleidae)

Ibises are slightly smaller than storks, and use their long curved bill to probe the ground for invertebrates. The sacred ibis (*Threskiornis aethiopicus*), once revered but now extinct in Egypt, is mostly white, with a naked black head and neck. It is a common freshwater bird, and flocks can often be seen over cities returning in formation to their evening roosts. Another familiar town bird is the hadeda ibis (*Bostrychia hagedash*), whose early morning clamour is a wake-up call to suburbanites across the region. It is confident and tame, often feeding on playing fields and lawns, and derives its name from the braying 'ha-ha-ha', or 'waaaaa' call, by which members of the flock keep in contact with one another. The smaller and slimmer glossy ibis (*Plegadis falcinellus*) appears stick-thin in flight, with its long dark legs, neck and bill projecting at either end. It feeds quietly at the edge of dams, lakes and other freshwater bodies, often alone. The rare and endemic southern bald ibis (*Geronticus calvus*) is a high grassland species of eastern South Africa, where a few colonies nest in rocky gorges. It can be seen in reserves such as Hluhluwe (see page 271) and Swaziland's Malolotja (see page 272), where it feeds on burnt areas during winter.

Above African spoonbill (MU)
Centre Hadeda ibis (JCS/FLPA)
Below Hamerkop (GL/FLPA)

Closely related to ibises, the all-white African spoonbill (*Platalea alba*) has an extraordinary spoon-shaped bill which it sweeps from side to side to sift small aquatic organisms from the shallows. It occurs in small parties in freshwater habitats across the region.

HAMERKOP *Scopus umbretta*

The hamerkop is classified somewhere between storks and herons. This unusual, crow-sized bird has a broad flattened bill, rich brown plumage and a shaggy brown crest, from which it gets its name. It is found near fresh water almost anywhere, and after rain often alights on tar roads in search of frogs. In African folklore the hamerkop is feared as a harbinger of doom, and at dusk, when it is particularly active, its strange high-pitched call and silent, floating flight do have a certain eeriness. Stranger still is the enormous domed nest that hamerkops build in the fork of a tree, up to a metre across and two metres high. This nest is constructed of grass and the entrance lined with mud, but cardboard, plastic – almost anything – can be incorporated into its building. Many other species take over hamerkop nests, and eagle owls or Egyptian geese often build their own nests on top.

Greater flamingos (pictured here) are taller than lesser flamingos, with proportionally longer necks. Both species filter-feed by sweeping their inverted bills through shallow water. (MU)

FLAMINGOS (Phoenicopteridae)

Two species of flamingo occur in southern Africa. The greater flamingo (*Phoenicopterus ruber*) is up to 140cm in length, and is pale pink with a black tip to its pale bill. The smaller lesser flamingo (*Phoenicopterus minor*) is a deeper pink with a dark red bill. Both species seem ludicrously proportioned, particularly as they fly overhead in formation, dangling their impossibly long legs and neck. Flamingos feed in shallow water, their heads scything back and forth to filter minute organisms through sieve-like lamellae inside the inverted bill. Though the two species often occur together, greater flamingos feed on larger organisms, whereas lesser flamingos live almost entirely on blue-green algae, so competition is avoided. Both breed in colonies on shallow saline pans, with Etosha and Makgadikgadi being the only regular locations. Here, thousands of birds can be seen displaying in tightly synchronised formation, switching their heads from side to side in a 'flag dance' and 'saluting' with bright scarlet wings. At other times flamingos wander widely, and can turn up on shallow freshwater bodies almost anywhere.

DUCKS AND GEESE (Anatidae)

The freshwater lakes and wetlands of southern Africa are home to twenty species of duck, which, like ducks everywhere, spend most of their time swimming on open water and use their webbed feet to dabble or dive for their food – mostly aquatic plants and invertebrates. Many species of duck are gregarious, and outside the breeding season mixed flocks build up on wetlands across the region.

The comb, or knob-billed duck (*Sarkidiornis melanotos*) congregates on marshes in the north. This big (70cm) duck often perches conspicuously in dead trees, and derives its popular name from the fleshy 'knob' at the base of the male's bill. The white-faced duck (*Dendrocygna viduata*) is a common resident of lakes and dams in the northeast, where flocks dabble for food in the shallows and line up to rest along the water's edge – taking flight with a chorus of whistles when disturbed. The inconspicuous but widespread red-billed teal (*Anas erythrorhyncha*), easily identified by its bright red bill and pale cheeks, is often the first species to move on to newly flooded grasslands. Winter flocks may swell to thousands, but these disperse with the rains to breed. The yellow-billed duck (*Anas undulata*) has a diagnostic bright yellow bill. It is found in pairs or small groups, often on small farm dams, but will also flock with other species to winter flood waters. The handsome South African shelduck (*Tadorna cana*) exploits the labours of aardvarks by nesting in their old burrows.

Strictly speaking, no true geese occur in southern Africa, although several species bear the name. The spur-winged goose (*Plectropterus gambensis*), weighing up to 9kg, is by far the largest. By day, these big, black birds loaf around the water's edge, with territorial males often perched conspicuously on termite mounds. At dusk, large flocks set out in formation for their flooded feeding grounds, passing overhead with an audible whooshing of wings. The Egyptian goose (*Alopochen aegyptiaca*) is a noisy and conspicuous resident of virtually any freshwater body in the region, its rich brown plumage contrasting with striking black-and-white wing markings. Pairs mate for life and defend their territory aggressively, rounding on any intruder – even elephants – with outstretched neck and a hoarse, threatening hiss. Egyptian geese often use the old nests of other birds, especially hamerkops.

Below left Egyptian goose (AZ) *Below right* White-faced duck (AZ)

Above left African finfoot (WD/FLPA) *Above right* Little grebe (AZ)

The African pygmy goose (*Nettapus auritus*) prefers a tree hole, from which the ducklings have a dizzy drop into the world. This shy, uncommon species is best seen from a mokoro in the Okavango Delta, though the male's exquisite markings are hard to appreciate as he crouches among the water lilies or takes flight around the next bend.

GREBES (Podicipedidae) AND FINFOOT
Seen far out on the water, grebes are often mistaken for ducks, but in fact they comprise a separate and more ancient family. These specialist divers have lobed feet, legs set far back on their body and no tail to speak of, and spend most of their time in the water, where they catch fish below the surface and construct large floating nests of vegetation on top of it. The little grebe or dabchick (*Tachybaptus ruficollis*) is well known to visitors from Europe. This dumpy bird is the smallest (only 20cm long) and probably the most widespread waterfowl of the region, popping up on almost any body of water. Also known from Europe is the black-necked grebe (*Podiceps nigricollis*), which gathers in huge rafts off the Namibian coast in winter.

The African finfoot (*Podiceps senegalensis*), unrelated to grebes, is an uncommon bird of quiet, wooded backwaters in the north and east, easily overlooked because of its skulking habits. Male and female differ in plumage, but both have a striped and barred pattern and a stout red bill. A finfoot swims low in the water, suggesting something between a duck and a darter, but in fact it is the only African representative of a completely separate family (Heliornithidae). The Zambezi River upstream of Victoria Falls is a particularly good spot to search for this unobtrusive bird.

COOT, CRAKES AND THEIR ALLIES (Rallidae)
This family comprises a variety of birds that make an amphibious living in the rank scrub and aquatic vegetation of wetland margins. All have long legs and toes, and share the distinctive habit of constantly flicking their short, cocked tail up and down. Many are extremely secretive and skulking. The red-knobbed coot (*Fulica*

cristata) is the most gregarious member of the family, and the only one at home on the open water, where its coal-black plumage and white face topped by two fleshy red knobs makes it unmistakable. Large, loose colonies gather on pans across the South African highveld, where they construct untidy floating nests and pursue each other in continual running fights. The common moorhen (*Gallinula chloropus*) is a familiar sight the world over as it chugs along the water's edge with nodding head and flicking tail, and is quickly identified by the tail's white underside. The chicken-sized purple swamphen (*Porphyrio madagascariensis*) has striking purple plumage and a bright red bill and feet. It clambers clumsily around reedbeds, sometimes

sunbathing on top of the reeds, and uses its long toes as hands to feed on aquatic plants and occasional birds' eggs. The black crake (*Amaurornis flavirostris*) is the only crake species likely to be seen by the average visitor. This small black bird has a yellow bill and forages in family groups, often emerging into the open and duetting with a curious combination of growling and trilling calls. Finding the diminutive and largely nocturnal flufftails presents a real challenge to the most serious birder. However, each species can be located and identified by call, and the buff-spotted flufftail (*Sarothrura elegans*) is well known from eastern regions for its haunting and resonant 'woooo', repeated every three seconds at night for hours on end.

JACANAS (Jacanidae)

Jacanas share the wetland habitats of crakes and rails, but belong to a separate family. The well-known African Jacana (*Actophilornis africanus*) is also known as 'lilytrotter' from its habit of walking over waterlilies and floating vegetation on its extraordinarily long toes. It is a colourful, obvious bird, very common in the northern half of the region, and constantly engaged in energetic territorial disputes, with rivals chasing each other in short flights across the water, feet dangling. Jacana have a polyandrous social system: the female mates with up to four different males and produces several clutches; the males incubate the eggs and perform most

The black crake (*above*, ND) and African jacana (*below*, CH/FLPA) both glean aquatic invertebrates among the floating vegetation of wetland margins

of the parental duties. The much smaller and easily overlooked lesser jacana (*Microparra capensis*) is found only in a few scattered localities in the north and east, of which the Okavango is undoubtedly the easiest place to see it.

WADERS

The term wader loosely describes several families of bird that nest on the ground and feed in or near water by wading on long legs and foraging for small invertebrates. Most have penetrating whistled calls. Some waders prefer fresh water, others are predominantly coastal. To confuse matters, certain African species – including coursers and several plovers – never actually wade, but snap up their insect prey on dry land. Many waders are great wanderers: over half the species recorded in the region are non-breeding summer visitors from the north.

Sandpipers and snipe

Inland freshwater habitats draw many wader species, both resident and visiting. Sandpipers are non-breeding visitors from the north, that tend to feed singly; they

have a distinctive bobbing head and tail. The smallest is the common sandpiper (*Actitis hypoleucos*), which is olive brown above and white below. It gives itself away with a penetrating 'tsee see see' call, and flies low over the water on bowed, flicking wings. The slightly larger wood sandpiper (*Tringa glareola*) has more speckled plumage and shows a white rump in flight. Wood sandpipers feed in the open and wade more readily than common sandpipers – often in the smallest roadside puddle. The marsh sandpiper (*Tringa stagnatilis*) is taller and paler, with long legs and a needle-fine bill, and prefers saline waters. The similar, but larger greenshank (*Tringa nebularia*) has green legs, and feeds by sweeping its long, slightly upturned bill back and forth over the water like an avocet (see page 135).

In the south of the region, sharp eyes may spot an African snipe (*Gallinago nigripennis*) lurking along a marshy shoreline. This wonderfully camouflaged bird uses its exceptionally long bill to probe for worms, and performs a

The common sandpiper (*above*, PP) and wood sandpiper (*centre*, ND) are both non-breeding summer visitors from the northern hemisphere; the painted snipe (*below*, AZ) is a resident which breeds in grasses or sedges set back from the water's edge.

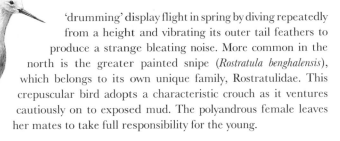

'drumming' display flight in spring by diving repeatedly from a height and vibrating its outer tail feathers to produce a strange bleating noise. More common in the north is the greater painted snipe (*Rostratula benghalensis*), which belongs to its own unique family, Rostratulidae. This crepuscular bird adopts a characteristic crouch as it ventures cautiously on to exposed mud. The polyandrous female leaves her mates to take full responsibility for the young.

Avocet and stilt

The elegant and obvious avocet (*Recurvirostra avosetta*) has striking black-and-white plumage and a long, unusually upturned bill. This bird, familiar to British birders as the logo of the RSPB, occurs sparsely across southern Africa, breeding on shallow, saline pans such as Etosha and Mgkadikgadi. It wades deeply on long legs, sweeping its bill back and forth across the surface to snap up aquatic invertebrates. The more common black-winged stilt (*Himantopus himantopus*) is a similar size, but much skinnier, with extraordinarily long legs that project far beyond the tail in flight. It occurs in small numbers on shallow lakes and pans, and is active and noisy, often taking flight to pursue rivals or dive-bomb intruders.

Black-winged silt

Plovers and lapwings (Charadriidae)

The plover family includes some of the noisiest and most conspicuous birds of the region. All have shorter bills than other waders, and many lead a largely terrestrial lifestyle. The alert, upright crowned lapwing (*Vanellus coronatus*) has been described as 'the sentinel of the veld', being quick to sound the alarm when danger approaches. It is common in open grassland, where it nests and feeds on the ground, and is easily identified by the white 'halo' around its black cap. Crowned lapwings fly with flicking beats of broad wings, boldly marked in black and white. Their shrill 'kiwick' call is a feature of residential parks and playing fields, and is often heard overhead during a full moon. Equally common and similar in general character is the blacksmith lapwing (*Vanellus armatus*). This bird is a beautiful patchwork of black, white and grey, and usually occurs near water in small flocks. Its well-known alarm call is a metallic 'tink tink tink', as of a blacksmith's hammer, and a spirited pair of blacksmith lapwings can divert even an elephant from their nest with a concerted aerial bombardment. Other similar and striking species include the white-crowned lapwing

Crowned lapwing:
'sentinel of the veld' (ND)

The blacksmith plover is a bold and conspicuous resident of any freshwater body in the region. (PP)

(*Vanellus albiceps*), of broad rivers to the north and east, and the wattled lapwing (*Vanellus senegallus*), of moist grassland habitats. Both these species sport colourful fleshy facial wattles. The less common long-toed plover (*Vanellus crassirostris*) breeds on floating vegetation in the Zambezi, Chobe and Okavango regions, often in association with the African jacana (see page 133).

A separate genus (*Charadrius*) of smaller and generally more aquatic plovers includes the three-banded plover (*Charadrius tricollaris*), which breeds across the region and is identified by black bands around its breast, throat and crown. Pairs busy themselves about muddy shorelines, constantly flitting back and forth across the water.

Chasing the tide: coastal waders

From August to April, thousands of coastal waders gather in the region's estuaries and tidal mudflats, with huge concentrations in sites such as Sandwich Bay (see page 263) and West Coast National Park (see page 269). Many also turn up inland, and seek out the invertebrate bonanza offered by sewage works. Most of these species breed in northern Europe, so have moulted their breeding plumage by the time they reach southern Africa. The curlew sandpiper (*Calidris ferruginea*) is the most numerous, and wheels over its feeding grounds in dense, smoke-like flocks, dark backs and white undersides flashing alternately like a shoal of fish. The much larger whimbrel (*Numenius phaeopus*) is more solitary, and uses its long decurved bill to probe deeply into the

mud in search of worms. The coast also supports a few breeding waders: the endemic African black oystercatcher (*Haematopus moquini*) is a conspicuous all-black bird of rocky southwestern shorelines that flies about in noisy piping pairs and uses its long red bill to prise open the shells of molluscs; the diminutive white-fronted plover (*Charadrius marginatus*) scuttles like a clockwork toy along sandy shorelines, almost invisible against the sand and seaweed when it freezes.

African black oystercatchers are endemic to the southwest of the region. (BG/FLPA)

The spotted thick-knee (*above left*, PP) and bronze-winged courser (*above right*, AZ) are waders that have adapted to a terrestrial lifestyle. Both have the large eyes typical of nocturnal birds.

Thick-knees (or dikkops), coursers and pratincoles

Thick-knees (Burhinidae) are skulking, largely nocturnal waders, with a big head, short bill, and large yellow eyes. The spotted thick-knee (*Burhinus capensis*) is found across the region in dry, open country. It roosts by day beneath bushes, heavily camouflaged by its spotted plumage, but at night often forages along roads for insects and small reptiles – always running a few steps before taking off. The smaller water thick-knee (*Burhinus vermiculatus*) can be spotted by day roosting unobtrusively in pairs or small groups along the shoreline; by night its mournful piping call joins the nocturnal chorus along large rivers to the north and east of the region. It can be distinguished from the spotted thick-knee by its unspotted upperparts and bold wing bars visible when at rest.

Coursers (Glareolidae) are plover-like, ground-dwelling birds that stand characteristically erect, and can run fast – only taking flight reluctantly. They inhabit largely open areas, and lay their highly camouflaged eggs in a shallow scrape on the ground. Temminck's courser (*Cursorius temminckii*) is a widespread species of dry grassland, often in small parties on burnt ground. The bronze-winged courser (*Rhinoptilus chalcopterus*) prefers wooded savannah. Its large eyes make it well adapted for nocturnal life, and it is often seen on night drives in the north of the region. The double-banded courser (*Rhinoptilus africanus*) is superbly adapted to withstand the harsh conditions of the arid west (see picture page 256). It does not need any drinking water, and can survive extreme overheating while protecting its single egg from the fierce Kalahari sun.

Pratincoles belong in the same family as coursers, but more closely resemble swallows or terns, with their short bill, long forked tail and graceful, swooping flight. All species are associated with water. The collared pratincole (*Glareola pratincola*) reveals a white rump and rufous underwings in flight. This species gathers on floodplains along the Mozambique coast, and in the Chobe area large flocks can be seen hawking the clouds of insects that follow game herds. The smaller rock pratincole (*Glareola nuchalis*) is restricted to fast-flowing stretches along a few northern rivers, and can often be spotted perched discreetly on rocks upstream of Victoria Falls. It has greyer plumage and a shorter tail than other pratincoles.

GROUND BIRDS

Ground bird is a convenient term used loosely here to describe those families of bird that feed, breed and spend most of their life on *terra firma*. As well as the flightless ostrich, which has no choice, it embraces the bustards and korhaans, the cranes and buttonquails, gamebirds such as guineafowl, francolins and quails, and the pigeon-like sandgrouse (though it does not include some other birds that live in this way, such as the coursers and some plovers, which are officially waders). Most ground birds have long, sturdy legs for walking or running and short, sharp bills for gleaning seeds or invertebrates from beneath their feet. Females generally rely on their cryptic camouflage to escape detection at the nest, while males of some families – especially korhaans – flaunt bold markings in flamboyant courtship displays.

A pair of ostriches in the Kalahari. (CH/FLPA)

OSTRICH *Struthio camelus*

The flightless ostrich is the largest feathered creature on the planet, and could hardly be mistaken for anything else. An adult male stands over two metres tall, weighs more than 80kg and can run at up to 60km/h. His grey neck and black-and-white plumage distinguish him from the smaller, browner female.

Ostriches occur right across the region, except in well-watered and montane areas, though today most are either farmed or descended from domestic stock and the only truly wild populations are in the Kalahari and northern Namibia. They eat a broad variety of plants and insects. Their preferred habitat is semi-desert and short-grass plains, especially burnt areas and the insect-infested patches left by grazing game herds. Contrary to the head-in-the-sand myth, ostriches are extremely vigilant, and their early reaction to danger often rings alarm bells for other nearby grazers. They forage in small groups, but separate into pairs to breed. The nest is a shallow scrape in the ground in which up 30 eggs are laid, often by several females. Each egg weighs more than one kilogram, with the capacity of at least 25 hen's eggs. Incubation rotates between the male at night and the less obvious female by day. The chicks, which are striped for camouflage, congregate in large creches, presided over by one or two adult birds.

The soft plumes of an ostrich do not have stiffened quills or barbed filaments; this, along with the lack of a preen gland, is evidence of a bird that no longer needs its feathers for flight. Instead an ostrich has enormously powerful legs, each of which is balanced on two toes. These power the bird in immense strides, and can also deal devastating kicks to an enemy – including a human one. Both cheetahs and leopards occasionally prey on adult ostriches, but for most predators the eggs are more tempting. The lucrative ostrich-farming industry, once dependent on the feather duster trade, now also supplies meat and leather and has spread as far as Russia and Scandinavia.

BUSTARDS AND KORHAANS (Otididae)

Bustards range from medium-sized to very large birds. They have a short bill, long legs and a long neck that swings from side to side as they stalk slowly after insects. Their habitat is open country. Bustards rely on camouflage to escape detection, and usually crouch or walk away when alarmed rather than take flight. Males are more boldly marked than females, and many have elaborate courtship displays in which they puff out their feathers theatrically and perform aerial stunts. 'Korhaan' is the Afrikaans name, derived from the birds' harsh, grating call; it is used for smaller members of the family.

The kori bustard (*Ardeotis kori*) stands 120cm tall and, weighing up to 17kg, lays a claim to the title of world's heaviest flying bird. It is most easily seen in larger reserves, often feeding on disturbed ground near herds of game or resting during the hottest hours in the shade of a thorn tree. A displaying male inflates his neck and puffs out a white blossom of undertail coverts while uttering a deep booming 'oom oom oom'. Such is the kori bustard's size, that the carmine bee-eater (see page 161) has learnt to use it as a moving perch from which to hunt insects. Denham's bustard (*Neotis denhami*) is a little smaller than the Kori, and prefers moister habitat,

The kori bustard is often seen near herds of grazers, snapping up the insects they disturb. (MU)

Korhaans, like this red-crested korhaan (*above*, MU), generally rely on their camouflage to avoid danger. But breeding males, like this northern black korhaan (*right*, PP) give themselves away with raucous and conspicuous displays.

such as fynbos and high grassland. The male also has a spectacular display, in which he inflates his throat into a balloon of white feathers that is visible for miles. At other times Denham's bustard is a shy bird, and generally takes flight more easily than the Kori.

The red-crested korhaan (*Lophotis ruficrista*) is much smaller. It is a common savannah resident, often seen picking its way slowly across a road. Though generally quiet and inconspicuous, in the breeding season the male performs an extraordinary display: starting with a methodical bill clicking, followed by a slow crescendo of whistles, he suddenly flaps vertically upwards out of the grass for 20 metres or so, before tumbling abruptly to the ground as though shot. The black-bellied korhaan (*Lissotis melanogaster*) is larger and longer necked, and prefers moist woodland and grassland in the north and east. The male displays by flying slowly over his territory with measured wingbeats, before parachuting to the ground. His call, uttered from an anthill for hours on end, is an odd combination of two apparently unrelated sounds: a croaking 'waak', followed three seconds later by a champagne cork 'pop'. The northern black korhaan (*Afrotis afraoides*) is a bird of the arid west, common in the Kalahari. The conspicuous male has black underparts offset by bold white markings. His territorial call is a noisy 'karak karak karak', increasing in urgency as he takes off and circles slowly, before fluttering to the ground with yellow legs dangling. As with all korhaans, the brooding female relies on cryptic camouflage to remain hidden. Ruppell's korhaan (*Eupodotis rueppellii*) is restricted to the stony plains of northwest Namibia. Like many of its family, this species is a favourite prey of eagles, and has developed a twisting, rolling flight that helps it to elude its pursuer.

CRANES (Gruidae)

Cranes are tall, elegant birds that forage on long legs for seeds and invertebrates. Like storks (see page 126), with which they are sometimes confused, they fly slowly on broad wings with neck outstretched, though they have a shorter bill than storks and are more noisy and demonstrative, using bugling calls and flamboyant displays to reinforce their lifelong pair bonds.

Three species occur in southern Africa. Like cranes everywhere, all are highly vulnerable to disturbance and are considered threatened. At 120cm, the wattled crane (*Grus carunculatus*) is the largest, identified by its white neck, long grey plumes and dangling facial wattles. It breeds on scattered wetlands in eastern South Africa and northern Botswana (notably the Okavango region) and builds a nest of flattened vegetation surrounded by water. Wattled cranes are quieter than other species, only uttering subdued honks in flight, but pairs perform energetic leaping courtship dances. The slightly smaller blue crane (*Anthropoides paradiseus*) is South Africa's national bird, but today it is more often seen on stamps than in the wild. This blue-grey bird has dark, trailing tertial feathers and a distinctly bulbous head. The same nest site, on bare ground, may be used for years, and breeding pairs perform extravagant leaping dances, bugling and tossing grass in the air. During winter, blue cranes disperse across central South Africa, and in the Overberg region of the Cape flocks forage on farmland for spilt grain. A separate population breeds in Etosha. The grey crowned crane (*Balearica regulorum*) is the most boldly marked species, with a black-and-white face topped by a spray of golden feathers. It roosts in trees and forages by day in fields and sedge swamps. Pairs build their nest in tall grass on swampy ground, ringed to a 5m radius with flattened vegetation. Crowned cranes have a fragmented distribution across the region, and are most common in Zimbabwe.

Cranes, such as the grey crowned crane (*above*, JC/FLPA) and blue crane (*left*, MS/FLPA), form lifelong pair bonds.

GAMEBIRDS

'Gamebird' is an unfortunate term, suggesting as it does the blast of the twelve-bore and simmering of the pot. It loosely embraces several related families, including, in Africa, the francolins, quails and guineafowls. All are plump, terrestrial birds, generally found in small flocks, or coveys. They forage on the ground for plant and insect food, and, when pressed, fly directly with a rapid whirring of their short, broad wings. Some species have wicked spurs on their legs with which the males do territorial battle, and most have far-carrying, raucous calls.

Guineafowl

Guineafowl (Numididae) are chicken-sized, highly gregarious birds, whose fine polka-dotted plumage appears grey from a distance. Of the two species in southern Africa, the ubiquitous helmeted guineafowl (*Numida meleagris*), with its naked blue face and fleshy red casque, is much the more common, and a great delicacy for human and hawk eagle alike. Quarrelsome flocks occur in all habitats, foraging in open areas and gathering in large numbers at waterholes At night, guineafowls roost in trees, and early morning brings a chorus of clucking and churring as the birds set out for the day, flying down from their perches on whirring wings. Otherwise, guineafowl are reluctant to fly and will bound along in frantic strides for frustratingly long distances in front of a vehicle. The uncommon crested guineafowl (*Guttera edouardi*) inhabits indigenous forest in the far north and east. It is slightly smaller, with a black neck and an absurd black topknot of feathers. Troops move quietly along forest paths, scratching for food in the leaf litter.

Francolins, spurfowl and quails

Francolins and spurfowl (Phasianidae) are smaller and browner than guineafowl, with subtle markings that differ from one species to the next and raucous calls that provide a dawn awakening as rude as any rooster's. There are 12 species in the region, several of which often forage tamely around gardens and campsites. Leg and bill colour are often helpful identification pointers. At 42cm, the Cape spurfowl (*Pternistis capensis*) is the largest, and frequents fynbos and thick scrub along the Cape coast. Its screeching cackle at dawn and dusk is familiar to residents of Cape Town, where coveys feed in local parks. Swainson's spurfowl (*Pternistis swainsonii*) is a common bushveld species, whose rich brown plumage is offset by a bare red face. Like many francolins, it can often be seen picking through dung for titbits. The Natal spurfowl (*Pternistis natalensis*), identified by its orange bill and legs, overlaps with Swainson's in the northeast, where it frequents riverine thickets and rocky outcrops. The red-billed spurfowl (*Pternistis adspersus*) is the dominant species in the arid woodland of Botswana and Namibia, easily identified by its red bill and legs and yellow eye-ring. The crested francolin (*Francolinus sephaena*) prefers well-watered acacia woodland. It has streaked plumage, with a white eyebrow stripe, and cocks its tail like a bantam. Pairs call in a rattling duet. The little coqui francolin (*Francolinus coqui*) is one of the smallest, and behaves more discreetly than others, creeping quietly over the ground in pairs. The male is attractively marked with a cinnamon head and barred underparts.

Above Swainson's spurfowl (AZ)
Above right Helmeted guineafowl (PP)
Right Namaqua sandgrouse (PP)

Quails are summer visitors, travelling by night to arrive across the region's grasslands during September. The persistent liquid 'wet my lips' call of the tiny common quail (*Coturnix coturnix*) can be heard by day and night, though the bird itself stays hidden in the long grass. Likewise, the harlequin quail (*Coturnix delegorguei*) is common in the north of the region, but seldom reveals its rich rufous-and-black plumage unless flushed. The kurrichane button-quail (*Turnix sylvatica*) actually belongs to a separate family, Turnicidae. This widespread resident may be spotted creeping chameleon-like across a track. Button-quail females are polyandrous: each mates with several males, who are responsible for all parental duties.

Sandgrouse

In the arid west, dusk and dawn at the waterhole are heralded by a soft ripple of whistled calls, as sandgrouse wheel swiftly in. The noise swells as more birds arrive in the half-light, each landing a few metres back from the waterhole, before shuffling forward to the water's edge. Thirst quenched, the first birds take to the air with a clatter of wings and disappear towards the dark horizon, while the next rank presses forward to take their place.

Sandgrouse (Pteroclidae) are pigeon-sized birds, perfectly adapted to the arid conditions of the Kalahari and Namibia. Males are ornately patterned, while females have the cryptic camouflage of a ground nester. Their daily visits to water are not only to slake their own thirst. During the breeding season, males will wade in belly-deep to soak up water with their specially-adapted breast feathers, before returning with their precious cargo to the young on the nest, sometimes over 50km away. There are four species of sandgrouse in southern Africa. Most common in the west is the Namaqua sandgrouse (*Pterocles namaqua*), easily identified by the male's long, pointed tail. This species is joined at waterholes by Burchell's sandgrouse (*Pterocles burchelli*), whose ochre plumage is sprinkled with fine white spots. Double-banded sandgrouse (*Pterocles bicintus*) also occur in dry woodland further east. The male is identified by black-and-white bars on his breast and forehead.

RAPTORS

The predatory prowess and dashing demeanour of raptors have fired our imagination since the earliest days of falconry, and southern Africa can boast over 70 species, ranging from the tiny pygmy falcon that snatches birds on the wing, to the immense lappet-faced vulture that can rip open the hide of a zebra carcass. They are divided into three families: the secretary bird (Sagittariidae); vultures, eagles, hawks and harriers (Accipitridae); and falcons (Falconidae). All have the same basic tools for the job: killing talons, a hooked beak for tearing flesh and acute eyesight for pinpointing prey. Since most raptors are usually seen in flight, sometimes at a great height, identification often depends upon flight silhouette and wing markings. By contrast with most birds, female raptors are markedly larger than males.

SECRETARY BIRD *Sagittarius serpentarius*

The secretary bird is out on a long limb; neither quite an eagle nor a vulture. Though its hooked bill is unmistakably a raptor's, its lanky stature (up to 120cm tall), smoky grey plumage and terrestrial habits recall those of a crane (see page 141). Other unusual features are black 'stockings', elongated central tail feathers and a drooping black crest, which, suggesting the quills tucked behind the ear of a Victorian clerk, may explain the 'secretary'. In flight, the broad wings are held in a shallow 'V', and the projecting legs and tail create an unmistakable silhouette.

The secretary bird is widespread but uncommon. It inhabits open country, from montane grassland to semi desert, where it stalks the veld deliberately, cocking its head to detect movement in the grass, and leaping about, wings spread, to batter its prey with fierce blows of its toughened feet. Though famed as a snake killer, its victims also include rodents, reptiles and birds. One pair will occupy a territory of up to 50km, returning at dusk each day to the same roost or nest, prominently sited on top of a thorn tree.

The secretary bird is unrelated to other raptors, and feeds entirely on the ground.(MU)

VULTURES

Vultures, like hyenas, suffer from an image problem, but play a vital ecological role in cleaning up after predators. These big birds are magnificent flyers, riding thermals great distances in search of food and using their prodigious eyesight to spot prey from an extraordinary height. Each is very alert to the activities of others: vultures dropping to the ground in one spot will suck many more out of the sky from miles around. Different species mingle at carcasses, where a strict pecking order is observed. Vultures' naked heads allow them to poke around in the gore without fouling their feathers. They are fastidiously clean birds and visit water daily to drink and wash. The range of many species has shrunk with the decline of game populations, and vultures have now been lost to most farming regions, where dozens can be killed by a single poisoned carcass put out for jackals. Unfortunately, vulture parts are also highly valued in the market for traditional medicines.

At up to 105cm, the huge lappet-faced vulture (*Aegypius trachielotus*) is the largest, and lords it over other species at carcasses. Dark brown, with a red face and massive yellow bill, it is usually seen in pairs, and occurs across the northern half of the region, including deep into the Kalahari and Namib. The smaller white-backed vulture (*Gyps africanus*) is the most common, found from Zululand northwards; adults are identified by a striking white lower back. Hundreds may gather at a large carcass, jostling and hissing as they compete for the spoils. The similar but larger Cape vulture (*Gyps coprotheres*) is endemic, but declining. It nests in cliff-face

Lappet-faced vultures are the largest and most formidable-looking of the vulture family. Their powerful bill enables them to tear into carcasses too tough for other species. (AZ)

The white-backed vulture (*above left*, MU) is the most common vulture of the region; the lammergeier – or bearded vulture – (*above right*, ND) is the rarest, and most unusual.

colonies, with the largest and best-known being in the mountain ranges of northern South Africa's Limpopo Province. Unfortunately, its propensity for perching on power lines often proves fatal. The smaller white-headed vulture (*Trigonoceps occipitalis*), with its distinctive skull-like head, is a shy species, often feeding alone on smaller carcasses, or arriving early at a larger carcass to carry off its share before things get too rough. At 70cm, the hooded vulture (*Necrosyrtes monachus*) is the smallest species, and uses its thin, pointed bill to steal scraps overlooked by its larger cousins. It is very alert to the activities of predators, and will follow the calls of hyenas in hope of a kill.

Bone-breaker

The bearded vulture, or lammergeier (*Gypaetus barbatus*), is quite different from other vultures, and is found only in the high mountains of the Drakensberg, where it builds huge nests on remote crags. Despite a massive three-metre wingspan, it has a slender flight profile, with the long wings and tail suggestive of a smaller raptor, such as a kite. Its underparts are a rich rusty orange, and the feathered head sports a dark 'beard' below the eyes and bill. Lammergeiers are rare and timid visitors to carcasses. They feed on fragments of bone, which they smash open by dropping them from a great height on to rocks below. Legend has it that the Greek playwright Aeschylus met his maker when an 'eagle' dropped a tortoise on to his bald pate. A lammergeier perhaps? Bad luck, certainly.

EAGLES

Eagles enjoy a better press than vultures, being emblematic of power and nobility the world over. Southern Africa has 17 species, grouped into several different genera. Most are hunters, but some also scavenge. Eagles are long-lived birds, and they take several years and a number of plumage changes to reach maturity. Some species lay a single egg; others lay two. Where two chicks hatch, the larger one grows stronger at the expense of the smaller, who seldom survives the vicious bullying of its sibling. This brutal practice increases the chances of at least one healthy chick making it to adulthood.

Large eagles: Verreaux's, martial and crowned

The three largest species of eagle all reach 80–90cm in length. The Verreaux's, or black eagle (*Aquila verreauxii*) is found in rocky terrain across the region. Adults are jet black with bold white markings, while immatures are golden brown. Pairs mate for life and stick close together. They perch conspicuously for long hours near their nest, and glide low over the slopes in search of dassies – their staple diet. This species has been studied intensively in the Matobo Hills of Zimbabwe, where there is an unusually high density. Otherwise, most mountain ranges support a few pairs, and one has nested for years in Johannesburg Botanical Gardens.

The martial eagle (*Polemaetus bellicosus*) has the largest wingspan (2.6m) of any African eagle. This once widespread species has been much persecuted by farmers and is now common only in protected areas. The adult has a dark breast and upperparts and spotted white underparts, and its powerful bill, short crest and penetrating yellow eyes give it an imperious expression. A pair of adults occupies a range of up to 150km. They soar to often invisible heights, and use their superb eyesight to locate large prey such as guineafowl and monitor lizards.

A martial eagle (*main picture*, PD/FLPA) feeds on a young impala. This species and the crowned eagle (*inset*, LLR/FLPA) both regularly capture prey of this size.

The African crowned eagle (*Stephanoaetus coronatus*) has a shorter wingspan than the martial, but is the most powerful eagle of all (see picture, page 119). This species inhabits indigenous forest in the east, where its relatively short, broad wings allow great manoeuvrability among the trees. It hunts monkeys and small antelope, crushing their skulls with formidable talons, and may sit quietly in the canopy for hours waiting for prey to pass underneath. The male soars and swoops in conspicuous spring display flights, calling shrilly and revealing heavily barred, rufous underparts. In some areas crowned eagles have survived the advance of suburbia, and take a heavy toll of the neighbourhood cats.

The broad wings of a Verreaux's eagle are conspicuously narrow at the base. (VG/FLPA)

Bateleur
Terathopius ecaudatus

Bateleur is French for 'tightrope walker', and with its tilting flight on long outstretched wings, the bateleur eagle cuts an unmistakable dash in the air. The combination of its short, almost invisible tail, big owl-like head and the adult's colourful patchwork plumage further prevents confusion with any other species. Bateleurs are widespread in woodland to the north, but are common only in protected areas, particularly big game parks. They frequently take carrion, and their low-level flight often makes them first scavenger at a carcass (and sometimes a useful clue to the location of a treed leopard kill).

African fish eagle *Haliaeetus vocifer*

The ringing cry of the fish eagle has so often been described as the 'sound of Africa' that it's probably time a new contender took the baton. Noisy and conspicuous, with its broad wings, snow-white head and tail and spectacular dives for fish, this is the most obvious of all raptors. Its famous call, a gull-like 'kyow yow-yow', is uttered with the head thrown right back, either in flight or from a waterside perch. Fish weighing up to 3.5kg are plucked from the surface with outstretched talons following a long slanting dive. Fish eagles will also rob ospreys and goliath herons of their catch, and sometimes hunt waterfowl such as coots. They breed on permanent water across the region, being absent only from the arid west, and are common on large rivers and wetlands such as St Lucia, the Okavango and Zambezi.

Other eagles

One step down from the largest eagles, the widespread tawny eagle (*Aquila rapax*) is a common, medium-sized species, whose shaggy plumage comes in various shades of brown. This versatile predator will scavenge alongside vultures, rob other raptors of their kills or snatch live prey, such as doves, from the ground. In summer it often flocks with migrant eagles, such as the very similar steppe eagle (*Aquila nipalensis*), to feed on termite swarms.

The African hawk eagle (*Aquila spilogaster*) is largely dark above and white below, and is found in woodland across the north of the region. This rapacious bird shows a power that belies its modest size, often taking hares or guineafowl as large as itself. Pairs hunt cooperatively. Wahlberg's eagle (*Aquila wahlbergi*) is a common summer visitor to woodland in the north and east. This smaller, uniform brown eagle has a distinctive narrow-tailed flight silhouette and soars high up, drawing attention with its high-pitched whistle.

Snake-eagles are medium-sized, with unfeathered legs, a large, owl-like head and big yellow eyes. They hunt reptiles – especially snakes, which may be seen dangling from their beak in flight and are swallowed headfirst before being regurgitated to youngsters at the nest. The brown snake-eagle (*Circaetus cinereus*) is locally common in dry woodland, where it often perches upright in a bare tree, scanning the ground below for anything slithery. Its warm brown plumage shows paler

Views to a kill: an African fish eagle (*top*, MW/FLPA) plunges feet-first into water to capture fish; a tawny eagle (*centre*, MI/FLPA), muscles in on vultures at a carcass; a long-crested eagle (*bottom*, NB/FLPA) scans the ground for rodents.

flight feathers on the wing. The black-chested snake eagle (*Circaetus gallicus*) could be mistaken for the much larger martial eagle, but has a pure white belly and underwings. This species is more common than the brown in arid western districts, and is the only eagle that hunts by hovering, swooping on its prey in a long slanting dive. Similar in build and behaviour to snake eagles, the smaller, dark-plumaged long-crested eagle (*Lophaetus occipitalis*) inhabits moist woodland and forest edges to the north and east. It is often seen perched on a roadside telegraph pole looking for vlei rats in the rank grass below, its long crest flopping about in the breeze.

BUZZARDS, KITES, HAWKS AND HARRIERS

Down the scale from eagles and vultures is an assortment of other birds of prey. Buzzards are medium-sized raptors that hunt rodents on the ground and often perch conspicuously on telegraph poles. The jackal buzzard (*Buteo rufofuscus*) has broad wings and a chestnut breast and tail. It inhabits hilly country in the south, where it is often seen suspended immobile on an updraught. Further north, this species is replaced by the augur buzzard (*Buteo augur*), which is very similar in shape and behaviour, but is black above and white below. The augur buzzard is common in hill country in Zimbabwe. The slightly smaller steppe buzzard (*Buteo vulpinus*) is a variable brown bird, very similar to the common buzzard familiar to European visitors. Every summer large numbers arrive in southern Africa from central Asia.

Harriers are slimmer and longer-legged than buzzards, and quarter the ground in open country with their wings held in a shallow 'V', often dropping into the grass after prey. They are ground nesters, and perform acrobatic displays in which prey is passed between a pair in mid-air. The dark brown and widespread African marsh harrier (*Circus ranivorus*) hunts over wetlands, while the endemic black harrier (*Circus maurus*), with its striking pied plumage, prefers the dry country and fynbos of the southwest. Some summers see an influx of the elegant Montagu's harrier (*Circus pygargus*) to savannah in the north.

A yellow-billed kite prepares to plunder a picnic. (DD/FLPA)

The black-shouldered kite hovers almost motionless to pinpoint prey on the ground below. (PP)

The black-shouldered kite (*Elanus caeruleus*) is the region's most widespread and distinctive small raptor, with attractive black, white and grey plumage and a graceful tern-like flight. It is usually seen on a prominent perch, its short tail wagging slowly up and down, or hovering above the ground in search of prey. The yellow-billed, or black kite (*Milvus migrans*) is much larger, and dark brown. This intra-African migrant arrives in large numbers across the region from August, drifting buoyantly on angled wings, and constantly twisting its forked tail as a rudder. Yellow-billed kites have learnt to exploit people by gathering around villages and rubbish dumps, and even stealing food from the plates of startled guests at game lodges.

Most hawks are aerial hunters of small birds. Their short, broad wings and relatively long tail allow them to pursue their quarry with great agility through dense cover. In the open, they fly with a characteristic flap-flap glide pattern. The African goshawk (*Accipiter tachiro*) is the largest of several similar species in which the male is grey and larger female brown. It spends long periods sitting quietly on a concealed branch, but the male calls repeatedly in his soaring display flight above the trees. The smaller gabar goshawk (*Micronisus gabar*) has a prominent white rump, and prefers more arid thornveld, where it uses spider webs to help construct its nest. By contrast with the forest hawks, the much larger pale chanting goshawk (*Melierax canorus*) hunts ground prey in arid, open country from a low perch. This conspicuous silver-grey raptor is common in the Cape and Kalahari, and sometimes tags along with foraging honey badgers (see page 52) for leftovers.

The pale chanting goshawk scans for prey from a conspicuous position on top of a thorn bush or telegraph pole. (MS/FLPA)

Some odd ones out

Certain raptors have evolved unique adaptations to exploit an unusual food source. The osprey (*Pandion haliaetus*) is an uncommon summer visitor to southern Africa that feeds entirely on fish. This long-winged, black-and-white

Gymnogene hunting for nestlings

raptor hunts by hovering above the water and, unlike fish eagles, often plunges right in. Long talons and spiny toes help it to grasp its slippery prey. A large flapping bundle of grey feathers spotted dangling awkwardly from a tree trunk or clambering upside-down around a weaver colony is probably an African harrier-hawk, or gymnogene (*Polyboroides typus*). This strange raptor has long, double-jointed legs, which allow it to winkle out nestlings from their holes. The rare bat hawk (*Macheiramphus alcinus*) hunts bats over water or along the forest edge at dusk. Fast, agile flight and sharp eyesight enable it to snatch its evasive prey on the wing.

FALCONS (Falconidae)

Falcons are small to medium-sized raptors with a buoyant, dynamic flight on narrow pointed wings. Most species hunt birds in the air, while kestrels drop on to small mammals or insects from above. The lanner falcon (*Falco biarmicus*) is the largest, and is found across the whole region, even breeding on tower blocks in city centres. It can be distinguished from the similar but much rarer peregrine (*Falco peregrinus*) by the adult's rufous crown. The much smaller Amur falcon (*Falco amurensis*) is a summer migrant to the east of the region, reaching peak numbers in January, when huge flocks gather along roadside wires or at their roosts in eucalyptus stands.

The similar-sized lesser kestrel (*Falco naumanni*) is another gregarious summer visitor, most common in central South Africa, where flocks hawk and hover over fields. Both these species gather with other migrant raptors to feed at seasonal termite emergences. The dashing red-necked falcon (*Falco chicquera*) is an uncommon resident of arid savannah, where it nests in stands of fan palms and hunts birds by ambushing them from cover. Also found in the arid west is the pocket-sized (20cm) pygmy falcon (*Polihierax semitorquatus*) which sits like a shrike on the end of a branch, wagging its tail slowly up and down. It nests in sociable weaver colonies (see page 181), where its own nest can be identified by the whitewash of droppings around the entrance.

The red-necked falcon is an agile aerial predator on other birds. (PP)

NEAR-PASSERINES: LOURIES TO HONEYGUIDES

Falling somewhere between sandgrouse (see page 143) and passerines (see page 167) in the filing cabinet of avian taxonomy is a loose collection of birds known, unhelpfully, as 'near-passerines'. Among the families that make up this disparate group are the fruit-eating parrots and turacos; the night-hunting owls and nightjars; the hole-nesting woodpeckers, barbets and hornbills; the brilliant bee-eaters, rollers and kingfishers; the familiar pigeons, the devious cuckoos and the aerial swifts.

TURACOS (Musophagidae)

Turacos (or louries) are crow-sized, long-tailed birds with prominent crests, raucous voices and, except for one species, colourful plumage. They fly awkwardly, lurching across clearings, but bound rapidly though the tree canopy in a manner thought to be similar to early prehistoric birds. Like other frugivores, louries use their short stout bill for plucking fruit and breaking into kernels. The Knysna turaco (*Tauraco corythaix*) is a species of the indigenous Cape coastal forest, with rich green and blue plumage, delicate facial markings and scarlet wings that flash vividly in flight

(see picture, page 20). It is replaced in Maputaland and eastern Zimbabwe by the very similar but longer crested Livingstone's turaco (*Tauraco livingstonii*) and at Victoria Falls by the even longer crested Schalow's turaco (*Tauraco schalowi*). The purple-crested turaco (*Tauraco porphyreolophus*) has a rounded, purple crest, no face markings, and its loud 'kok kok kok' call is higher pitched than the Knysna lourie's. It is a common riverine woodland species in the east, fond of fruiting fig trees, and its scarlet primaries are used as head adornments by Swaziland's royalty. The grey go-away bird (*Corythaixoides concolor*) differs from the others in its uniform dove-grey plumage and a preference for more open woodland habitats. It inhabits the northern half of the region, as far south as Johannesburg, and small parties perched obviously in tree tops are a common sight in many reserves. It derives its name from its far-carrying, nasal 'kwaaaay' call.

The elusive purple-crested turaco (*above*, PP) seldom emerges from the tree canopy, except to drink; the grey go-away bird (*below*, ND) is much more conspicuous, and sometimes visits flowering aloes.

PARROTS (Psittacidae)

Parrots are highly adapted for a fruit-eating life in the trees, and use strong, dextrous feet to clamber gymnastically among the branches and grasp their food.

The powerful hooked bill is a precision tool for peeling a husk or cracking a nut, but can also double up as a third hand for trickier treetop manoeuvres. Parrots breed in tree holes, and their colourful greens and yellows serve as disruptive camouflage against dappled foliage. They are hard to spot when feeding high up in the canopy, and are more often glimpsed overhead in fast, direct flight on bowed wings, shrieking as they go. Southern Africa has eight species. The brown-headed parrot (*Poicephalus cryptoxanthus*) is a largely green bird, found only in the far northeast; it is common in the Kruger Park, often seen bursting out of a riverine thicket in pairs. It is replaced across Zimbabwe and northern Botswana by the more colourful Meyer's parrot (*Poicephalus meyeri*). The rosy-faced lovebird (*Agapornis roseicollis*) is a much smaller parrot, whose gaudy plumage has made it a popular cage-bird. It frequents arid country across Namibia, where it dashes about in small screeching flocks, sometimes alighting to drink.

The brown-headed parrot (*above*, ND) and speckled mousebird (*below*, PP) both have the short, stout bills of fruit-eaters.

MOUSEBIRDS (Coliidae)

Mousebirds are small, unobtrusive grey-brown birds with soft plumage, a short crest and long thin tail, that clamber nimbly around thickets like small rodents. They feed in small flocks on berries and buds, and are reviled by farmers for the damage they do to fruit plantations. When disturbed, mousebirds fly out on whirring wings, seldom going far before plunging into another thicket. Flocks sleep huddled together and sit on top of bushes to warm up in the early morning. The speckled mousebird (*Colius striatus*) is a common garden bird in the east and south, and has a distinct pale lower mandible to the bill. The red-faced mousebird (*Urocolius indicus*) is found right across the region, generally preferring drier habitats; it has a distinctive trisyllabic whistled call.

PIGEONS AND DOVES (Columbidae)

Southern Africa's 14 species of pigeon and dove include some of the region's most common birds. Most are ground-feeding seed-eaters, often flushed with a clatter of wings from just in front of your wheels. Pigeons breed prolifically, and courtship takes place throughout the year, with much strutting and cooing on the ground, and flap-up, spiral-down aerial displays. Young are raised on a solution of digested seed from the mother's crop, known as 'pigeon's milk'.

The ubiquitous Cape turtle dove (*Streptopelia capicola*) is the most common of several predominantly grey species. It has a thin black half-collar, and a well-known trisyllabic call, 'Ask father' (or 'Cape turrr-tle', according to taste), which continues all day. Non-breeding flocks gather to roost and are numerous at waterholes in drier regions. The red-eyed dove (*Streptopelia semitorquata*) has a similar collar, but is larger and darker, and absent from arid areas. The African laughing dove (*Streptopelia senegalensis*) is a neat little species that frequents towns and woodland. It calls with a quiet, bubbling cooing, and instead of a collar has a fine speckled necklace across the breast. The tiny Namaqua dove (*Oena capensis*) differs from all others by its long, pointed tail, and prefers open country, particularly in the arid west, where pairs are often seen in dashing, agile flight. The equally tiny emerald spotted wood-dove (*Turtur chalcospilos*) is known for its melancholy call: a soft, descending 'du du – du-du-du' that starts aimlessly but gradually gains speed, and is reputed to intone 'My mother is dead, my father is dead, oh woe is me, oh woe, woe, woe...'. It is common in dry woodland to the north, usually in pairs that flash their rufous wings when flushed from the ground. The African green-pigeon (*Treron calvus*) would apparently prefer to be a parrot, with its bright green and yellow plumage, acrobatic antics and taste for fruit. This species occurs in the north and east, often flocking to fruiting riverine trees – especially sycamore figs.

The common and widespread Cape turtle dove gathers in large flocks at waterholes. (PP)

CUCKOOS (Cuculidae) AND COUCALS (Centropodidae)

Cuckoos are brood parasites: they lay their eggs in the nests of other 'host' birds, who stoically raise the interloping cuckoo chick after it has evicted their

own eggs or nestlings. Some species even dupe a host by matching the colour of its eggs with their own. Insects, especially hairy caterpillars, are their preferred food. There are 14 species in the region, all of which are summer visitors. They are generally secretive birds, most often glimpsed in a dashing hawk-like flight. Each has a strident call, evocative of the start of the rains, by which it is easily identified, if not so easily located. The red-chested cuckoo (*Cuculus solitarius*) is known in Afrikaans as 'Piet-my-frou', (meaning, for reasons I've never grasped, 'Pete, my wife'). In early summer, these three descending notes chime incessantly from dawn to dusk and drive grown men to despair. The black-and-white jacobin cuckoo (*Clamator jacobinus*) is found in woodland to the north, and around the east coast. The male uses a conspicuous display to lure the hosts (bulbuls) from their nest, whereupon the female sneaks in unseen to lay her eggs. The smaller diderick cuckoo (*Chrysococcyx caprius*) has metallic emerald upperparts and is less secretive than other species. It calls with a weak but insistent 'dee-dee-deederik', often close to a weaver colony, whose nests it parasitises.

Coucals are medium to large birds with a long tail, powerful bill, and weird bubbling call, often given before rain, that descends and rises like liquid poured from a bottle – hence the popular names 'rain bird' or 'waterbottle bird'. They feed in low, rank vegetation, usually near water, clambering through the tangle in search of insects and nestlings, and flying clumsily for short distances before crashing into the next thicket. Though related to cuckoos, coucals make their own nests. There are six species in the region, all of which inhabit moist habitats to the east and far north. The common Burchell's coucal (*Centropus burchellii*) has a dark head and tail, with a rich rufous back and creamy underparts. The smaller black coucal (*Centropus grilli*) has all-black underparts, and is best seen in the Okavango, where females perch conspicuously on top of reeds and long grass to call.

Above Diderick cuckoo (ND)
Below Burchell's coucal (ND)

OWLS (Tytonidae and Strigidae)

Owls are nocturnal hunters, with the lethal talons and hooked bill of birds of prey, large eyes for night vision and soft plumage to conceal their approach. Most species hunt by swooping from perches on to rodents and other small ground-dwelling prey. Owls are best located at night by their hooting or screeching calls. By day they roost in trees or crevices, hidden by camouflage plumage; the distinctive 'ears' of certain species are actually tufts of feathers to enhance the disguise. There are 12 species in the region.

The barn owl (*Tyto alba*) appears ghostly white in flight, and has a variety of bloodcurdling shrieking and hissing calls. This bird occurs worldwide, and in southern Africa it is common in most habitats, including towns. The little African scops-owl (*Otus senegalensis*) is a master of camouflage, and can flatten its body into virtual invisibility against a tree trunk. In dry woodland regions, its brief, frog-like 'prrrp' call is a classic accompaniment to the crackle of the campfire. Even smaller (only 18cm), the pearl-spotted owlet (*Glaucidium perlatum*) is a rapacious predator of small woodland birds, and is often seen by day, drawing attention with a far-carrying series of whistles that rise in a crescendo before falling gradually away. A good mimic can lure this owl into the open, often attracting other birds, which congregate to mob the offender.

The spotted eagle-owl (*Bubo africanus*) is the most widespread larger owl, and is often glimpsed by car headlights in suburbia. It has long ear tufts and penetrating yellow eyes, and nests in hollow trees or among rocks. This species sometimes falls victim to the formidable Verreaux's eagle-owl (*Bubo lacteus*), which, at 65cm, can take prey up to the size of a hare. Verreaux's eagle-owls frequent woodland habitats, particularly along watercourses, where they use the nests of other birds such as hammerkops. They call at night with a deep grunting 'hu hu hu', and often perch silhouetted on a tree top at dusk before setting out to hunt. Pel's fishing-owl (*Scotopelia peli*) is another giant, found only in riverine woodland beside large rivers or swamps in the far north and east. It hunts fish from a hidden perch, plucking them from the surface with wicked talons.

Owls take different prey according to their size:
the Verreaux's eagle-owl (*above*, MU) can capture hares and guinea fowl;
the spotted eagle-owl (*centre*, MU) feeds on smaller mammals and birds;
the African scops-owl (*below*, MU) is almost entirely an insect eater.

157

NIGHTJARS (Caprimulgidae)

Nightjars are dove-sized, nocturnal birds that hawk insects in flight, using rictal bristles around the bill to help locate their prey and a cavernous gape to engulf it. By day, they roost on rocks or leaf litter, concealed by extraordinary cryptic

camouflage. Seven species occur in the region. Most are very hard to identify by sight, but each prefers a specific habitat and has its own unique call. Many are fond of lying on roads – a habit that often has dire consequences. Here, their large eyes shine red in headlights, and a cautious approach may get you close enough to distinguish diagnostic tail and wing markings.

The fiery-necked nightjar (*Caprimulgus pectoralis*) is found across the region in all but the most arid and hilly regions. By day it lies invisible on the woodland floor. By night, its

The fiery-necked nightjar roosts by day on the ground, where it is almost perfectly concealed among the dead leaves. (MU)

quavering whistle – traditionally interpreted as 'good Lord deliver us' – is one of the most evocative sounds of the African night. The similar square-tailed nightjar (*Caprimulgus fossii*), common in the east, has a very different call; a continuous churring that seems to change gear at regular intervals (see picture, page 239). The one species easily identifiable by sight is the pennant-winged nightjar (*Macrodipteryx vexillarius*), a summer visitor to the north. The male has breeding plumage quite unlike any other winged creature: each wing trails a long white streamer, which twists and loops as the bird drifts over the trees in a bizarre dusk display flight.

Pennant-winged nightjar

158

SWIFTS (Apodidae)

Swifts are the most supremely aerial of all birds, having taken their mastery of flight to such extremes that they not only feed, but also mate and even roost on the wing. They have a characteristic crescent flight silhouette, and tear through the air at breakneck speed, beating their long sickle-shaped wings in short, stiff bursts to maintain momentum. Large mixed flocks often gather high above towns, and surf the air currents of advancing storm fronts. Swifts cannot perch upright, but cling with their toes to the vertical surfaces, such as cliffs and buildings, where they breed. They feed entirely on flying insects and, like nightjars, their large gape is designed for grabbing a bite on the wing. There are 13 species in the region, all mostly dark in colour and distinguished by size, tail shape and rump pattern. Be warned: it is a heinous birding crime to confuse swifts with swallows. Though they might look superficially similar, swifts are most closely related to nightjars, while swallows are actually passerines (see page 168).

Swifts in flight can be identified by a combination of their flight silhouette and any white markings. *From top to bottom*: alpine swift; white-rumped swift; little swift.

The alpine swift (*Tachymarptis melba*) is the largest species (22cm), and identified by its white underside and dark breastband. It often sweeps low over the ground, and is fond of pursuing grassfires. The little swift (*Apus affinis*) is a common urban species, with a square tail and broad white rump, that circles high up in large flocks, pursuing each other with shrill trilling screams and gliding with wings tilted upwards at 45°.

The African palm-swift (*Cypsiurus parvus*) uses saliva to glue its tiny feather nest and eggs to the underside of a palm frond. This bird has expanded its range southwards by using cultivated palms in towns and gardens. It is the most streamlined swift, with a bow-and-arrow silhouette of long, thin wings and tail.

ROLLERS (Coraciidae)

Rollers are colourful, dove-sized birds with a robust bill. They nest in holes, and hunt insects and other small ground prey from prominent perches. The name is derived from their acrobatic display flights, in which they swoop and tumble to flaunt their dazzling plumage, cackling loudly all the while. Five species occur in the region, of which the most common is the lilac-breasted roller (*Coracius cordatus*). This gorgeous and conspicuous bird probably draws more gasps of admiration than any other on safari, and can be distinguished from other rollers by its combination of long outer tail streamers, white forehead and lilac breast. It inhabits savannah woodland in the northern half of the region, where it is often seen perched on a roadside bush or power line, gliding down periodically in a flash of azure wings to snap up a hapless grasshopper. The European roller (*Coracius garrulus*) is a summer visitor to woodland areas. New arrivals disperse widely, in some areas outnumbering the local lilac-breasted rollers. This stocky bird has a square tail and a turquoise head and underparts (see picture, page 6). Being a non-breeding visitor, it does not indulge in the noisy displays of other species. The broad-billed roller (*Eurystomus glaucurus*) is the smallest. It has deep purple underparts, and its short, bright yellow bill gives it a parrot-like appearance. This roller breeds in riverine habitats in the north and northeast and is often seen perched high in a dead tree. It is noisy and acrobatic, and dashes after insects at dusk in a falcon-like flight.

The lilac-breasted roller is known in Zimbabwe as Mzilikazi's roller; its dazzling plumage was once used as decoration by warriors of the ancient chief. (AZ)

Above Southern carmine bee-eater (RT)
Right White-fronted bee-eater (MU) *Below* Little bee-eater (AZ)

BEE-EATERS (Meropidae)

Bee-eaters are agile, colourful birds with long, curved bills that hawk after insects in buoyant, drifting sallies and alight with their prey on low perches – disarming bees by beating them against a branch. They are often seen swooping low over water, sometimes dipping in to bathe, or sunning themselves on top of bushes with their mantle feathers fluffed out. All bee-eaters are hole nesters, and some species form large colonies in riverbanks. The eggs are laid in a small chamber at the end of a tunnel, and a small mound at the chamber entrance prevents them from rolling out. Nine species occur in southern Africa, of which five are summer visitors.

The southern carmine bee-eater (*Merops nubicoides*) is the largest (35cm) and most striking species, with its long tail and rich red and pink plumage. This inter-African migrant breeds in large riverbank colonies to the north and east. Flocks disperse to feed over grassland, often around game herds, where rich insect pickings can be had, and will even hitch a ride on a kori bustard (see page 139) to snatch prey disturbed around its feet. The smaller white-fronted bee-eater (*Merops bullockoides*) is a common resident, with largely green plumage set off by bold red, white and blue markings. Riverbank colonies have a complex social system in which lifelong pairs are assisted in raising their young by family clans of 'helpers'. The European bee-eater (*Merops apiaster*) is a common summer migrant, but also breeds in small numbers in the Cape. This multicoloured bird is identified by its golden mantle and the soft frog-like flight calls uttered by overhead flocks. The little bee-eater (*Merops pusillus*) is the smallest species, and largely green and yellow in colour. It is often seen in pairs, darting out after insects from low vegetation. Like all bee-eaters, the fledged young learn this skill from their parents.

KINGFISHERS
(Alcedinidae and Cerylidae)

Kingfishers, like rollers and bee-eaters, are hole nesters, and also catch the eye with their dazzling plumage and bold behaviour. Ten species occur in southern Africa. Some are plunge-diving fishermen; others seize their prey from the woodland floor. Most are generally seen alone or in pairs, often drawing attention to themselves with strident calls and bobbing their head up and down when alarmed. All have a long powerful bill.

The crow-sized (46cm) giant kingfisher (*Megaceryle maximus*) is much bigger than any other species, and uses its massive bill on crabs and frogs as well as fish. It perches quietly in overhanging vegetation, often along wooded streams, and when disturbed drops out with a harsh 'kak-kak' to disappear around the next bend. At the other end of the scale, the tiny (14cm) malachite kingfisher (*Alcedo cristata*) is usually seen perched like a blue and orange jewel on a reed, or darting across the water on whirring wings. The pied kingfisher (*Ceryle rudis*) can be found beside any permanent water. It is entirely black and white, and often hovers above the water, kestrel-like, before swooping down on fish. Away from the water's edge, the woodland kingfisher (*Halcyon senegalensis*) hunts insects on dry land. This brilliant blue bird is an inter-African migrant, arriving each October in the north of the region. Males set up their territory with a shrill, far-carrying two-part call, 'trip-trrrrrrrr', and pairs display on a bare branch with semaphore-like wing flashing. The brown-hooded kingfisher (*Halcyon albiventris*) is a common resident of parks and gardens, where it spices up its insect diet with the odd lizard. It is a drab, unobtrusive bird when perched, but reveals its bright blue wings and tail in flight.

The pied kingfisher (*above*, PP) and malachite kingfisher (*centre*, MU) are both tied to aquatic habitats; the brown-hooded kingfisher (*below*, AZ) catches its food on the woodland floor.

162

HOOPOES, WOOD-HOOPOES AND SCIMITARBILLS

Three distinct families of bird, all hole-nesters with a long, curved bill, are commonly grouped together. The hoopoe (*Upupa epops*) is a largely terrestrial bird, whose soft, insistent 'poop poop poop' call can be heard in woodland, parks and gardens across the region. It covers the ground on short legs in a methodical, nodding walk, probing deeply for insect larvae. Though inconspicuous when feeding, the hoopoe explodes into colour like a giant butterfly when disturbed, displaying bold black-and-white wing markings in a floppy, undulating flight. Its long crest, when folded, gives the head a pick-axe profile, but can be fanned forward when the bird is alarmed.

Hoopoe (MU)

The green wood-hoopoe (*Phoeniculus purpureus*) is an arboreal species. Long-tailed, with glossy green-black plumage, it moves from tree to tree in small flocks, clambering acrobatically among the branches and cackling madly – hence its Zulu name, *Inhleka bafazi*, which means 'laughing women'. As with hornbills (see below), the male seals the female into her tree-hole nest during incubation. The similar common scimitarbill (*Rhinopomastus cyanomelas*) is a smaller, quieter bird, with a more deeply curved, black bill, that works its way through woodland in pairs, keeping in contact with a high-pitched whistling call.

Green wood-hoopoe

HORNBILLS (Bucerotidae and Bucorvidae)

Hornbills are medium-sized to very large birds, with a heavy, decurved bill. They nest in tree holes, and – with the exception of the southern ground-hornbill – the female seals herself inside for the entire incubation period by plastering up the entrance with mud and droppings, leaving only a narrow slit through which her mate feeds her. The female undergoes a full moult inside the hole, and only breaks out once the eggs have hatched. Some hornbills are forest birds, feeding on fruit and berries in the canopy. Others inhabit woodland, and glean most of their food from the ground, including insects and small reptiles. There are nine species in southern Africa.

The trumpeter hornbill (*Bycanistes bucinator*) inhabits riverine forest to the east and far north of the region, and is very partial to fruiting fig trees. This big black-and-white bird (60cm) carries a heavy casque on its bill, and announces its presence with a raucous braying, not unlike a bawling baby. At Victoria Falls, noisy parties can

Above Southern yellow-billed hornbill (AZ)
Below Southern ground-hornbill (MU)

be seen lurching across the Zambezi towards their evening roosts, their wings whooshing as they flap heavily overhead. The southern yellow-billed hornbill (*Tockus leucomelas*) and red-billed hornbill (*Tockus erythrorhynchus*) are common woodland residents in the northern half of the region, the red-billed being dominant in mopane lowveld, while the yellow-billed prefers acacia savannah. Both species are bold camp visitors. Where they occur together, they avoid competition by using their different-sized beaks for different foods (the smaller red-billed is more adept at winkling insects out of holes). Both species call during the heat of the day, and their monotonous, rising clucking often provokes a chorus of rivals. The African grey hornbill (*Tockus nasutus*), another widespread woodland species, has a more plaintive, whistling call. Unlike its yellow-billed and red-billed cousins it seldom feeds on the ground and is less bold around camp.

The southern ground-hornbill (*Bucorvus leadbeateri*) only resembles other hornbills by the shape of its great hatchet-like bill. Otherwise this masssive bird (over 90cm) looks more like a turkey, with its black plumage, bare red face and flabby throat pouch. Ground-hornbills are found in open woodland, where they feed entirely on the ground, stalking the veld in loose gangs of four or more for prey such as insects and lizards. They will gather around a snake to peck it to death, and fling a baby tortoise into the air to swallow it whole. If pressed, ground-hornbills lumber reluctantly into low heavy flight, revealing startling white primaries. They roost in dead trees, from where they greet the dawn with a far-carrying booming phrase, mistakable only for a distant lion. The female is not sealed into the nest hole, and – unlike other hornbills – incubation rotates among adults. Fledged young, identified by their yellow facial skin, tag along ineptly with feeding parties. Common only in game parks, this charismatic bird is increasingly threatened elsewhere, and reintroduction efforts are now underway in some former haunts.

BARBETS (Capitonidae)

Barbets are dumpy, bull-headed birds with a stout bill that they use to excavate their own nesting holes in trees. Like woodpeckers (see page 166), they have zygodactyl feet, with two toes facing forward and two backward. Most species feed in the canopy on fruit and insects. Some are brightly coloured, and all can be identified by their distinctive repetitive calls. The crested barbet (*Trachyphonus vaillantii*) is the largest, and shows a shaggy crest and distinctly angry expression as it hops around boldly on the ground and investigates holes for grubs and larvae.

Above left Crested barbet (DD/FLPA) *Above right* Black-collared barbet (AZ)

This common woodland and garden bird calls throughout the day with an incessant reeling trill, like a muted alarm clock. The slightly smaller black-collared barbet (*Lybius torquatus*) has a scarlet face and throat framed in black. It frequents fruiting riverine forest and woodland, where pairs duet high in dead trees, warming up with a low growling before bursting into a frantic 'one puddly-two puddly, one puddly-two puddly' (or words to that effect). The acacia pied barbet (*Tricholaema leucomelas*) is the only species found in much of the arid west. It feeds mostly on fruit and berries, and helps to spread mistletoe by wiping the sticky seeds off its beak on to branches. The tiny yellow-fronted tinkerbird (*Pogoniulus chrysoconus*) feeds high in the forest canopy, and often joins mixed bird feeding parties. It is hard to spot, but easily detected by its monotonous 'dink dink dink' call that chimes from the tree-tops during the hottest hours of the day.

WOODPECKERS (Picidae)

Woodpeckers are small to medium-sized birds that move vertically around trees, clinging to the bark with zygodactyl feet (see barbets, page 165) and bracing their stiffened tail against the trunk. The stout bill is used to chisel for grubs (extracted with a long sticky tongue), excavate nest holes and, in some species, drum a loud territorial tattoo on a dead branch. All woodpeckers have a loud call and an undulating flight.

Ten species occur in the region, several of which share very similar plumage of barred upperparts, golden-shafted tail and scarlet crown. The cardinal woodpecker (*Dendropicos fuscescens*) is the smallest and most widespread, and often feeds in pairs, continually tapping branches to test for cavities. The larger golden-tailed woodpecker (*Campethera abingoni*) frequents open woodland and is usually first detected by its piercing nasal shriek. The bearded

Bennett's woodpecker
(*Campethera bennettii*) (MU)

woodpecker (*Dendropicos namaquus*) is the largest arboreal species, and its powerful drumming on a resonant branch can be heard from a kilometre away. The pinkish-hued ground woodpecker (*Geocolaptes olivaceus*) breaks all the rules by feeding entirely on the ground. This shy bird lives in small family parties around rocky outcrops on the high grasslands of South Africa, Swaziland and Lesotho, where it laps up termites and excavates nesting tunnels in earth banks.

HONEYGUIDES (Indicatoridae)

Honeyguides may look unremarkable, but their drab appearance belies a crafty nature. Like cuckoos (see page 156), they are brood parasites, choosing hole-nesting birds such as barbets and woodpeckers as their hosts. However, of six species in the region, only the greater honeyguide (*Indicator indicator*) performs the eponymous trick of deliberately leading people – and possibly honey badgers – to bees' nests. It does this by flitting on from tree to tree whilst keeping up a constant chatter, then falling silent when it reaches the nest. Once the nest has been ransacked, the bird takes its own share of the spoils – grubs and bee's wax. One warning though: local folklore warns that anybody led to honey in this way should always leave some behind for the bird, or next time it will lead them to a black mamba. Don't doubt it.

Success for a greater honeyguide (ND)

PERCHING BIRDS

The term perching bird – or, more correctly, passerine – is used to describe a mixed bag of over 400 species (nearly half the birds of the region), ranging from the hefty raven to the minuscule penduline tit and including garden favourites such as sparrows, robins and thrushes. Some, such as whydahs and sunbirds, are flamboyantly colourful. Others, such as larks, pipits and cisticolas, are the 'little brown jobs' that often defy identification. Bill shape helps in sorting different families: flycatchers use a fine bill to catch insects; waxbills use a short, stout bill for splitting seeds; sunbirds probe for nectar with a long, curved bill. First prize for nest-building goes to the weavers, while robins and bulbuls are among the most accomplished songsters. Voice is vital for locating and identifying many species, so keep your ears open.

LARKS AND FINCHLARKS
(Alaudidae)

Larks are drab brown birds of open country that feed and nest on the ground, and 18 of the region's 27 species are endemic. Though many are very similar, most can be identified by their distinctive songs and displays. The rufous-naped lark (*Mirafra africana*) advertises itself by whistling the same short phrase over and over again from the top of an anthill. The Cape clapper lark (*Mirafra apiata*), another grassland species, derives its name from the resounding volleys of wingbeats given in its cruising spring display flights, though the bird itself may be invisible against a bright sky. The sabota lark (*Calendulauda sabota*) is a woodland species, whose long rambling song, uttered from the top of a bush, incorporates mimicked phrases from other

A male rufous-naped lark sings from the top of a termite mound. (DD/FLPA)

birds. The dune lark (*Calendulauda erythrochlamys*) is the only permanently resident bird of the Namib sand dunes, where small parties feed on wind-blown seeds and insects. The chestnut-backed sparrowlark (*Erymopterix leucotis*) has a short finch-like bill, and, like finches, small flocks often visit water to drink.

PIPITS, WAGTAILS AND LONGCLAWS (Motacillidae)

Wagtails are energetic birds that constantly wag their long tail and dash about in an erratic way after insects. All species have a characteristic dipping flight and shrill call. The striking African pied wagtail (*Motacilla aguimp*) forages along shorelines much like a sandpiper (see page 134), while the greyer Cape wagtail (*Motacilla capensis*) is a common garden bird in many regions.

Pipits wag a slightly shorter tail, and with their nondescript brown plumage they look more like slim larks. Several similar species occur in the region, and can be identified (with experience) by call and habitat. Most widespread is the African pipit (*Anthus cinnamomeus*), which is particularly fond of cleared or burnt areas.

African pied wagtail

Longclaws are grassland birds, whose extremely long hindclaws baffle scientists. They are slightly larger and more conspicuous than pipits, and display colourful throat markings while calling from the top of bushes (see picture, page 17). The yellow-throated longclaw (*Macronyx croceus*) inhabits moist low-lying areas, whereas the more common Cape longclaw (*Macronyx capensis*) prefers coastal and upland regions.

SWALLOWS AND MARTINS (Hirundinidae)

Swallows and martins, like swifts (see page 159), are aerial birds that spend much of their time chasing insects, but have a more darting, fluttering flight on shorter, more flexible wings, and – in most species – long outer tail feathers. Unlike swifts, swallows often alight on prominent perches such as power lines. Many species are summer visitors. Some come to breed, arriving just before the rains to build their mud nests beneath eaves or bridges, or in riverbanks and culverts. The European, or Barn Swallow (*Hirundo rustica*) comes to escape the northern winter. Tens of millions arrive every October, and loose flocks flicker over grasslands and along roads in agile pursuit of insects. The smaller, resident wire-tailed swallow (*Hirundo smithii*) has almost imperceptibly fine tail streamers. It frequents rivers in the northeast, dashing over the

Lesser-striped swallow. (AZ/FLPA)

water in fast, erratic flight and often alighting on bridges. The larger red-breasted swallow (*Hirundo semirufa*) occurs in open woodland, where pairs can be seen perching quietly on top of a bush near their nest in a roadside culvert. The common lesser striped swallow (*Hirundo abyssinica*) differs from the similar greater striped swallow (*Hirundo cucullata*) in its smaller size, bolder markings and preference for woodland, rather than grassland, habitats. Where their ranges overlap, these two species often build their mud nests side by side in shared colonies under eaves. The rock martin (*Hirundo fuligula*), like most martins, is shorter-tailed and less colourful than most swallows. It breeds on cliffs and quarries, and is often seen hawking quietly over rock faces in a slow fluttering flight.

DRONGOS (Dicruridae) AND CUCKOOSHRIKES (Campephagidae)

Drongos are all-black, bull-headed birds that use a stout, hooked bill to hawk small prey from an exposed perch. They are noisy, aggressive and resourceful, and will dive-bomb raptors many times their own size and pirate food from other birds – even mimicking the alarm calls of meerkats (see page 55), to dupe the little carnivores into bolting, before snatching their catch. Drongos frequently join mixed feeding parties, and their wide repertoire of harsh, metallic calls includes much mimicry of other birds. The common fork-tailed drongo (*Dicrurus adsimilis*) is found in woodland, parks and gardens, where it is the only all-black perching bird with a strongly forked tail. The smaller and

A fork-tailed drongo is seldom silent. (JCS/FLPA)

much less common square-tailed drongo (*Dicrurus ludwigii*) is confined to eastern forests. The superficially similar male black cuckooshrike (*Campephaga flava*) is neither drongo, cuckoo nor shrike, but belongs to a completely different family. It behaves very differently from a drongo, moving quietly through the canopy in search of insects.

CROWS (Corvidae) AND ORIOLES (Oriolidae)

Crows are much the largest of the passerines. The common pied crow (*Corvus albus*), is a versatile, streetwise omnivore, seldom seen far from towns, where large cawing flocks gather at evening roosts. Pied crows hassle other scavengers at carcasses, and are quick to exploit road kills, caching any food that they cannot bolt on the spot. The larger white-necked raven (*Corvus albicollis*) has a formidable bill and a short tail. It is found in upland areas in the east, often seen in pairs performing noisy aerobatics, and in some hill towns, such as Mbabane, flocks gather at evening roosts like pied crows.

Pied crow

Above left The black-headed oriole gives its diagnostic fluting whistle from high in a tree, where it feeds on fruits, pollen and nectar. (MU)
Above right The arrow-marked babbler is never seen alone. Beyond this picture, the rest of the gang are rummaging noisily through the thicket. (ND)

Orioles are bright yellow, starling-sized birds that feed on fruit and insects in the woodland tree canopy. The most common of four species in the region is the resident black-headed oriole (*Oriolus larvatus*), which joins mixed feeding parties in winter and will probe flowering aloes for nectar. Like all orioles, it has a melodic, liquid call, often given in a bounding overhead flight between trees.

BABBLERS (Timaliidae) AND BULBULS (Pycnonotidae)
Babblers are noisy, sociable, thrush-sized birds that feed on the ground in small groups of a dozen or so, hopping about in search of insects, muttering all the while, and regularly bursting into a crescendo of rattling calls, like a chorus of wind-up toys. They are close, cooperative breeders, with last year's young helping their parents raise this year's chicks, and family parties often huddle together to preen each other. The arrow-marked babbler (*Turdoides jardineii*) is a widespread woodland species, often seen rummaging through the leaf-litter on the edge of a clearing, before flying off low to work the next thicket. The southern pied babbler (*Turdoides bicolor*) is a striking black and white bird of Kalahari thornveld, associated with camelthorns.

Bulbuls are thrush-sized birds that feed on fruit, pollen and insects. Three similar species, each with a yellow vent and black crest, are common birds of garden and thicket, and displace each other across the region: the Cape bulbul (*Pycnonotus capensis*), found only in the Cape, has a white eye-ring; the black-eyed bulbul (*Pycnonotus barbatus*), found in the east, has a black eye-ring; the red-eyed bulbul (*Pycnonotus nigricans*), found in the west, has a red eye-ring. These spirited, restless birds share similar liquid calls, and are often active at dusk. The quite different terrestrial brownbul (*Phyllastrephus terrestris*) is a sociable species of dense woodland and riverine thickets, where small groups scratch about in the leaf litter, chattering quietly. The sombre greenbul (*Andropadus impotunus*) is common in eastern forests and coastal bush – hard to see, but easily detected by its strident 'Willie' call. The yellow-spotted nicator (*Nicator gularis*), closely related to bulbuls, is another supreme skulker. Though its yellow spots usually remain hidden, its loud, jumbled song, bursting from a dense thicket, has the rich timbre of a nightingale's.

The black-eyed bulbul is one of the most common birds in the eastern half of the region. (ND)

THRUSHES, CHATS, ROBINS AND ROCKJUMPERS ✓
(Turdidae)

This large family of small to medium-sized birds comprises 43 species, all of which have the typical slim bill of insect eaters and forage for their food on the ground. Many are celebrated songsters. The unobtrusive kurrichane thrush (*Turdus libonyanus*) is a common garden bird in the east, often seen crossing a lawn in a characteristic stop-start run. Pairs defend their territory vigorously, returning to the same nest site year after year. This species is replaced to the south by the similar but darker olive thrush (*Turdus olivaceus*). The groundscraper thrush (*Psophocichla litsitsirupa*), with its boldly spotted breast and upright stance, is a conspicuous bird of open and newly cleared areas. By contrast, the colourful Cape rock-thrush (*Monticola rupestris*), is a shy bird of rocky habitats. Though it sings energetically from a prominent perch, it takes great care not to reveal the location of its nest, hidden in a crevice.

The trim, alert groundscraper thrush usually feeds on the ground. (AZ)

Chats are smaller than thrushes, and prefer more open habitats where they perch characteristically upright, flicking their wings and calling with various harsh staccato notes. The mountain wheatear (*Oenanthe monticola*) is a black-and-white bird of rocky terrain, and a tame campsite visitor in desolate regions. The capped wheatear (*Oenanthe pileata*) nests in a disused rodent burrow; it thrives on burnt grassland, where small family groups snap up insects. The southern ant-eating chat (*Myrmecocichla formicivora*) also nests underground, using the roof of an aardvark burrow; it is a conspicuous bird of termitaria-studded grasslands, where it lives up to its name. The handsome mocking cliff chat (*Thamnolaea cinnamomeiventris*) is found in pairs on

Above left The capped wheatear is found on arid grasslands – especially around burnt areas. (PP)
Above right Like many of its kind, the white-browed robin-chat is usually betrayed by its melodious song. (MU)

rocky kopjes in woodland areas, often alighting on rocks with a burst of song before running a few paces forward, jerking up its tail and singing again. The bull-headed little stonechat (*Saxicola torquata*) is a common grassland bird, most often detected by its 'chack chack' call, like two stones being struck together.

Robin-chats, with their bright colours and memorable songs, are popular garden favourites. The champion songster is the white-browed robin-chat (*Cossypha heuglini*), which selects a repeated phrase, usually a liquid whistle, and, starting quietly, gradually accelerates into a crescendo. Once this subsides, a new phrase is chosen and the pattern repeated. The red-capped robin-chat (*Cossypha natalensis*) has no great song of its own, but is a gifted mimic of other birds, including even the fish eagle. It frequents eastern forests, where it forages on the forest floor and is most active at dusk. The Cape robin-chat (*Cossypha caffra*) is a common garden bird in the south. It is less retiring than other species, singing from an exposed perch and feeding in the open.

Erythropygia Scrub-robins are more soberly marked in brown than robin-chats, and each is tied to a specific habitat: the white-browed scrub-robin (*Cercotrichas leucophrys*) is a widespread bushveld bird that calls at dawn and dusk with a sibilant whistle; the eastern bearded scrub-robin (*Cercotrichas quadrivirgata*) inhabits woodland thickets in the northeast and plunders the songs of many other birds, including pied kingfisher and crowned hornbill, in its rich repertoire of mimicry; the Karoo scrub-robin (*Cercotrichas coryphoeus*) is a western species of arid scrub and fynbos that bands together in noisy family parties to scold predators such as mongooses.

Closely related to robins, the colourful Cape rockjumper (*Chaetops frenatus*) is an endemic bird of fynbos-covered hillsides, where small parties hop about among the boulders. It nests beneath a rock, and sometimes a second male will attend the sitting female.

TITS (Paridae) AND PENDULINE TITS (Remizidae)

Tits are small birds with a big head and a short bill. They feed acrobatically amongst the outer branches, gleaning insects – particularly caterpillars – from leaves and bark, and are the life and soul of mixed feeding parties. The southern black tit (*Parus niger*) is a common woodland bird, and nests in tree holes. In winter it works through the pods of combretum trees, popping out the larvae of parasitic insects with an audible snap. The tiny (9cm) Cape penduline tit (*Anthroscopus minutus*) prefers drier regions, and is common in the Kalahari. Its pendulous nest, woven from plant down and animal hair, is an ingenious structure; the entrance can be 'zipped up' by the adult's bill, while a false tunnel constructed above acts as a decoy to predators.

WARBLERS AND ALLIES (Sylviidae)

Warblers and their allies are quintessential LBJs – the 'little brown jobs' that excite the ardent twitcher and frustrate the less dedicated. There are 72 members of this insect-eating family in southern Africa. With time and patience, each reveals its own unique character, though some species are more common or conspicuous than others. The lesser swamp-warbler (*Acrocephalus gracilirostris*) constructs its nest in reedbeds just above the waterline, and sings from a hidden position in a jumble of improvised phrases. The tit-babbler (*Parisoma subcaeruleum*) is a lively bird of arid thornveld, with a rich chestnut vent and sweet whistling song. The easily-overlooked willow warbler (*Phylloscopus trochilus*) is one of the most common European migrants, with over a billion estimated to winter in sub-Saharan Africa each year. The yellow-breasted apalis (*Apalis flavida*) creeps about woodland thickets; pairs duet with a strange combination of clicking and squawking to produce a rolling trill. This species is often joined in mixed feeding parties by the long-billed crombec (*Sylvietta rufescens*), a restless, almost tailless little bird, that clambers acrobatically around the branches and suspends its tiny purse of a nest from a tree fork. Cameropteras (*Camaroptera* spp)

Zitting cisticola at the nest (KC)

feed low down in thickets, with cocked tail and a rhythmic 'chop chop chop' song. Males display by pinging rapidly up and down from a branch as though on a rubber band.

Cisticolas are small grassland warblers, all with similar streaked brown plumage, and their names – croaking, chirping, tinkling, singing, wailing etc – suggest, correctly, that most species are best identified by voice. The rattling cisticola (*Cisticola chiniana*) is a ubiquitous bushveld species. It calls from the top of a low bush with a harsh 'cher, cher, cher', followed by a short tumbled phrase. The tiny zitting cisticola (*Cisticola juncidis*) is one of several smaller species that display in flight, and its bottle-shaped nest is the source of the name cisticola, which means – in the original Latin – 'inhabitant of a woven basket'. Prinias are closely related birds, usually seen working their way through low vegetation with their tail cocked, calling insistently.

The common tawny-flanked prinia (*Prinia subflava*) is found right across Africa, and ranges as far east as Java.

WHITE-EYES (Zosteropidae)

White-eyes look superficially like small warblers, but can immediately be distinguished by their conspicuous white eye-rings and their habit of creeping about the tree canopy in small flocks, keeping in contact with soft, sibilant calls. They feed primarily on nectar and fruit, and are found in woodland, parks and gardens, often in stands of exotic trees. There are two species in the region: the Cape white-eye (*Zosterops pallidus*) is found in the southern half; the yellow white-eye (*Zosterops senegalensis*) replaces it further north.

FLYCATCHERS AND BATISES (Muscicapidae)

Flycatchers are small passerines of forest and woodland that hawk insects in brief sallies from a fixed perch, sitting quietly for long periods before darting out in an agile flutter of wings to snap up their prey. Most species build camouflaged, cup-shaped nests in tree forks. There are 22 species in the region, including the spotted flycatcher (*Muscicapa striata*), a widespread summer visitor from Europe, and the marico flycatcher (*Bradornis mariquensis*) of arid savannah regions, which supplements its insect diet with small fruits. Many are predominantly brown or grey in colour. However, the all-black plumage of the southern black flycatcher (*Melaenornis pammelaina*) is thought to serve as protective mimicry of the more aggressive fork-tailed drongo (see page 170), with which it is often confused. The African paradise flycatcher (*Terpsiphone viridis*) is an active, noisy bird of gardens, thickets and forest edges. The unmistakable breeding male sports extravagant red tail plumes that twirl 30cm behind him as he dashes

Above African paradise flycatcher (MG)
Below Chinspot batis (MU)

out after insects. Batises are boldly marked little flycatchers that glean their insect prey from the branches. The attractive chinspot batis (*Batis molitor*) is a familiar savannah bird, often in the thick of mixed feeding parties; its descending three-note whistle has been likened to 'three blind mice' in a minor key. The male feeds his mate while she incubates, calling her 20–30 metres from the nest to collect her food.

SHRIKES (Laniidae)

Shrikes are smallish passerines with stout, hooked bills. There are 26 species in the region, falling into several distinct groups. True shrikes (Laniidae) perch conspicuously in open country with a trim upright stance, and are sometimes known as 'butcher birds' from their grisly habit of impaling prey on a thorn or barbed wire 'larder'. The ubiquitous fiscal shrike (*Lanius collaris*) is aggressively territorial, often terrorising the other birdlife of a garden lawn. It preys on insects, reptiles and occasional small birds. The red-backed shrike (*Lanius collurio*) is a non-breeding summer visitor from Europe to acacia savannah regions, where it perches on top of thorn bushes, scrutinising the ground below for insects. The slightly larger lesser grey shrike (*Lanius minor*) arrives at the same time, and is dominant over the red-backed wherever the two species occur together. The resident magpie shrike (*Corvinella melanoleuca*) is very untypical of this family. Small flocks occur in dry savannah, their long tail plumes dangling from thorn bushes or telegraph wires. They feed on insects, keeping in contact with mellow whistled calls and often associating with other birds, such as glossy starlings. The southern white-crowned shrike (*Eurocephalus anguitimens*) is a dumpier bird of open acacia woodland, where it perches obviously on telegraph wires or thorn bushes, often dropping to the ground to feed on insects.

Above Red-backed shrike (PP)
Below Magpie shrike (ND)

Bush-shrikes, boubous and tchagras (Malaconotidae)

This diverse family contains a number of species best known for their call, which is lucky, since they are skulking birds of woodland and riverine thicket that tend to keep their bold markings hidden. The orange-breasted bush-shrike (*Telophorus sulfureopectus*) whistles a short phrase all on the same pitch, as though calling a dog. The similar, but slightly larger, grey-headed bush-shrike (*Malaconotus blanchoti*) has a haunting whistle, hence its colloquial name 'ghost bird', and a bill powerful enough to dispatch mice and small birds. The bokmakierie (*Telophorus zeylonus*) flouts the rules by hopping around in the open, and with its ringing, bell-like call and striking livery of black, yellow and green, is a conspicuous bird of gardens and scrub in the south and west.

The southern boubou (*Laniarius ferrugineus*) is one of three very similar boubou shrikes, all of which are predominantly black and white. Pairs duet with such precise timing – one bird whistling, its mate answering with a growl – that only a single bird appears to be calling. The closely related crimson-breasted shrike (*Laniarius atrococcineus*) has vivid scarlet underparts, and occurs in arid western regions, often seen picking about in the lower strata of a camelthorn. Looking like a small, scruffy boubou, the black-backed puffback (*Dryoscopus cubla*) feeds higher in the tree canopy, often in mixed feeding parties, and derives its name from the male's display, in which he fluffs out his rump into a snowball of white feathers. Tchagras are brownish shrikes of woodland and thicket, with chestnut wings and a boldly marked head, that prefer to scuttle into cover rather than take flight. The three-streaked tchagra (*Tchagra australis*) gives a distinctive rippling call as it spirals downwards from its brief display flight, while the lilting whistle of the black-crowned tchagra (*Tchagra senegalus*) is the essence of a hot summer's day in the bushveld.

HELMET-SHRIKES (Prionopidae)

Helmet-shrikes are gregarious birds, with bright eye-rings and bristled foreheads. They pass through woodland in small flocks, leapfrogging one another as they work their way from tree to tree. These birds are cooperative breeders, each group containing only one breeding pair, with other young birds from previous broods remaining to help raise the young. The white-crested helmet-shrike (*Prionops plumatus*) is a common bushveld species, and a flock on the move resembles a fluttering of large pied butterflies. The less common, all-dark, Retz's helmet-shrike (*Prionops retzii*) prefers woodland with granite outcrops.

Below left Crimson-breasted boubou (PP) *Below right* White helmet-shrike (PP)

STARLINGS (Sturnidae)

Starlings are medium-sized passerines with a strong pointed bill. They feed mainly on the ground, on a variety of plant and insect food, and progress by waddling, rather than hopping like thrushes. Most species are noisy and sociable, some being communal breeders that form large flocks outside the breeding season, and several live commensally with humans.

Identifying the glossy starling species by colour is tricky, since all have iridescent plumage that reflects a constantly changing spectrum of blues, greens and violets. The Cape glossy starling (*Lamprotornis nitens*) is most widespread. However, in woodland to the north, it may be outnumbered by the very similar, greater blue-eared starling (*Lamprotornis chalybaeus*), which flocks to picnic sites with all the discretion of Trafalgar Square pigeons. Burchell's starling (*Lamprotornis australis*), another woodland species, is larger, with

The greater blue-eared starling is a common and tame visitor to lowveld camps and picnic sites during the dry season. (MU)

a heavier flight and longer-legged stride, while southern long-tailed starling (*Lamprotornis mevesii*) has (surprise, surprise!) a long tail, and prefers mopane woodland in low-lying river valleys such as the Zambezi. The red-winged starling (*Onychognathus morio*) inhabits cliffs, gorges and towns, where its pleasant, fluting whistle is often heard overhead. This is one of the few birds that eats millipedes, seemingly undeterred by their noxious secretions.

The pied starling (*Spreo bicolor*) is a common farmland bird in South Africa, where it often feeds around sheep, combing their wool for ticks and other delicacies. These starlings are communal, cooperative breeders, whose fledged young help to feed the next brood in the nest. Wattled starlings (*Creatophora cinerea*) are highly nomadic, and large flocks will colonise an area for a few weeks, timing their breeding to coincide with the hatching of locust larvae – their staple diet – then quickly moving on. The violet-backed starling (*Cinnyricinclus leucogaster*) is an inter-African migrant that arrives in October to nest in woodland tree holes. Pairs are often seen feeding quietly in fruiting trees – the speckled brown female being quite unlike the beautiful violet male. In South Africa, foreigners have muscled in on local starlings: the Indian myna (*Acridotheres tristis*) is a common suburban bird of Durban and Johannesburg, while the European starling (*Sturnus vulgaris*) has invaded the Cape.

Red-billed oxpeckers prefer hairy mammals, such as this impala. (PP)

OXPECKERS (Buphagidae)

Oxpeckers spend much of their life on the back of large animals, where they find food, rest, nest material (hair) and even partners. They feed by clambering around the bodies of their hosts, removing ticks with a neat scissoring action of their bill. Although this sounds like a useful service, their habit of pecking into wounds and sores is less welcome. Of two species in the region, the more common red-billed oxpecker (*Buphagus erythrorhynchus*) likes giraffe, impala and other antelope, whereas the yellow-billed oxpecker (*Buphagus africanus*) prefers less hairy mammals such as rhinos, hippos and buffalo. The rattling, hissing calls of oxpeckers can be a useful indication of a large mammal close by (see page 237).

SUNBIRDS (Promeropidae) AND SUGARBIRDS (Nectariniidae)

Sunbirds are often thought of as Africa's hummingbirds. Although incorrect, this association is understandable, since both families share colourful iridescent plumage and an ability to plunder nectar from flowers with a long decurved bill. Though zippy little movers, sunbirds cannot buzz about or hover with the speed and control of a hummingbird. However, like hummingbirds, they do help pollinate plants by transferring pollen from one flower to another. There are 27 species in the region. Many are best seen in winter, when they gather to feed on flowering aloes. Breeding males are easy to identify, but the drab females are more challenging.

The tinkling song of the white-bellied sunbird (*Cinnyris talatala*) is a characteristic sound of lowland savannah, where this is a common species – though seasonal numbers depend on the flow of nectar. The handsome male scarlet-chested sunbird (*Chalcomitra senegalensis*) is one of the most belligerent of his kind, constantly darting about after rivals and intruders, and is a familiar garden bird in northern regions.

The tiny collared sunbird (*Hedydipna collaris*), with its shorter bill, cannot reach into flowers, so vandalises them by piercing the corolla to extract the nectar. It also feeds on insects, clambering around like a white-eye (see page 174). Its nest is camouflaged with a dangling 'beard' of twigs, leaves and webs.

The floral riches of the Cape create an ideal habitat for a variety of sunbirds. The malachite sunbird (*Nectarinia famosa*) is the largest (25cm); the male of this species is easily identified by his long tail and iridescent emerald plumage that flashes in flight as he bullies rivals off his patch. The smaller orange-breasted sunbird (*Anthobaphes violacea*) is endemic to the coastal fynbos, where it feeds on and pollinates ericas, while the southern double-collared sunbird (*Cinnyris chalebeus*) prefers valley bush and often enters gardens to feed on aloes (see picture, page 34). Closely related to sunbirds, the Cape sugarbird (*Promerops caffer*) is a common bird of mountain and coastal fynbos, where the male flaunts his long tail in an aerial breeding display. Sugarbirds feed largely on proteas (see page 26), and animate winter hillsides in the Cape with their dancing flights and jangling songs.

Left to right White-bellied sunbird (ND); orange-breasted sunbird (MW/FLPA); malachite sunbird (MW/FLPA)

SEED-EATERS (Ploceidae)

This large, diverse family comprises 35 species, divided into several distinct groups including sparrows, weavers, bishops, queleas and widows. All are seed-eaters, and use a short stout bill for prising out or splitting open seeds and grain. Many are sociable birds that nest communally and flock outside the breeding season. Some, notably the weavers, construct elaborate nests, and most show marked sexual dimorphism – the drab brown female outshone by her gaudy mate.

Sparrows: faithful and familiar

Sparrows are unusual among this family in being monogamous, and most species thrive around human settlement. The ubiquitous house sparrow (*Passer domesticus*) was imported to southern Africa from India (via KwaZulu-Natal) and from Europe (via the Cape). Today its familiar chirrup can be heard in towns, villages and farms across the region. The indigenous Cape sparrow (*Passer melanurus*) is found in the south, and distinguished by its bold black and white head. It too shows a fondness for human company, and often nests on telegraph poles. The southern grey-headed sparrow (*Passer diffusus*) is a more unobtrusive bird, often seen feeding on the ground in mixed flocks. Around buildings this species is displaced by its urban relatives, but in woodland habitats it holds its own.

Cape sparrow

Weavers: art and craft

Weavers are among nature's great artisans. Males spend much of their short life frantically building one nest after another and attempting, like desperate estate agents, to lure females onto their property with vigorous fluttering displays. A successful male secures several females and, having mated, leaves all parental duties to them. Weaving is an acquired art and each species works to a unique design. Rejected nests are torn down, and novices can be seen toiling away on misshapen practice nests that impress nobody. Most male weavers have bright breeding plumage, but at other times resemble the drab brown females.

The southern masked-weaver (*Ploceus velatus*) is the most widespread of several predominantly yellow species. Large colonies are usually found near water, and the noisy 'twizzling' chorus of displaying males carries for some distance. These colonies often harbour other species, such as the lesser masked-weaver (*Ploceus intermedius*), distinguished by its white eye, or the slightly larger village weaver (*Ploceus cucullatus*), and may attract diderick cuckoos (see page 156), which lay their eggs in weaver nests.

The plump Cape weaver (*Ploceus capensis*) is common on South African farm dams, where noisy colonies nest in overhanging trees, defoliating the branches around their nests to display their work to its best advantage. By contrast, the spectacled weaver (*Ploceus ocularis*) nests in solitary pairs. This species often joins mixed feeding parties, and uses its finer bill to supplement its diet with insects.

Not all weavers are yellow: the thick-billed weaver (*Amblyospiza albifrons*) is largely dark brown, with a powerful nutcracker bill, and weaves

Cape weaver (PP)

Above The massive communal nest of the sociable weaver is among the biggest in the bird world. (PP)

Right The lesser southern masked-weaver constructs a short entrance tunnel to its nest, by which it may be distinguished from that of the similar masked-weaver. (PP)

its beautifully compact nest from shredded leaves across the gap between two reed stems; the white-browed sparrow-weaver (*Plocepasser mahali*) inhabits arid regions, where its untidy nests festoon acacias like windblown bundles of grass; the red-billed buffalo weaver (*Bubalornis niger*) is a mostly black species that often builds its big, communal nests in dead trees over water.

The communal spirit is taken to extremes by the little sociable weaver (*Philetairus socius*), which constructs one of the largest nests of any bird. These huge haystack-like structures are built in camelthorns, or sometimes on top of telegraph poles, and are a distinctive feature of the southern Kalahari and Namibian landscape. With over 50 separate downward-opening entrance tunnels, each nest is an apartment complex that supports up to 300 birds. It is also a miracle of air conditioning, with the temperature inside kept over 10°C cooler than the blistering Kalahari midday sun, or conversely 10°C warmer than the cold winter nights. Birds seldom wander far from the colony, where they spend their entire life. Pygmy falcons (see page 152) sometimes commandeer a chamber for themselves, and live alongside their hosts. Cape cobras (see page 192) are less congenial neighbours, and often plunder a nest for eggs or hatchlings.

THE SWARM

The red-billed quelea (*Quelea quelea*) is a small relative of the weavers that gathers in the largest-known flocks of any bird – sometimes millions strong – to feed on grass seeds in dry savannah. Unreliable rainfall can cause populations to plummet, and in hard times queleas move on to farmland, descending locust-like to strip a winter wheat harvest clean overnight. A single breeding colony may cover 100 hectares, and predators of every description, from mambas to marabous, gather for the bonanza of eggs and nestlings. A quelea flock is often detected by the rush of air as it passes overhead in tight formation. When gathering to drink, smaller flocks combine into a huge swarm that twists and flexes like smoke before settling at the water's edge. On the ground, the flock has a collective forward movement, as individuals who have taken their fill are leap-frogged by the massed ranks behind.

Red-billed quelea drinking. (VG/FLPA)

Bishops and widows: putting on a show

These thick-billed seed-eaters are best known for the breeding colours of the males, who display gaudy costumes in spring, far removed from their dowdy, sparrow-like attire at all other times. The southern red bishop (*Euplectes orix*) breeds in reedbed colonies, where males puff up their fluorescent red plumage and buzz about the marsh to attract females, gyrating around reed stems and 'swizzling' in a continuous stream of song. Widows prefer damp grassland habitats. A breeding male long-tailed widow (*Euplectes progne*) dangles extravagant black tail plumes while cruising back and forth over his territory in a laboured display flight. Reputedly, in wet weather, these birds become so bogged down by their bedraggled plumes that they can be caught by hand. Other male widows, such as the red-shouldered widow (*Euplectes axillaris*) and the yellow-rumped widow (*Euplectes capensis*), also have black breeding plumage offset by bright flags of colour. All species form nomadic flocks in winter, when they become much harder to tell apart.

The extravagant plumes of the male long-tailed widow are a heavy burden in flight, making him very vulnerable to predators during the breeding season. (RD/FLPA)

WHYDAHS AND INDIGOBIRDS (Viduidae)

Like cuckoos (see page 156), whydahs are brood parasites. Each species exploits a particular species of waxbill, though, unlike cuckoos, whydahs do not evict their hosts' eggs or nestlings, so young whydahs grow up alongside their step-siblings, not instead of them. To complete the deception, a whydah's eggs mimic the colour of its host's and whydah nestlings have exactly the same arrangement of gape spots inside their bill as their host's chicks. Breeding male whydahs are lively and conspicuous birds that flaunt fancy tail plumes in dancing, dipping display flights.

The paradise whydah (*Vidua paradisaea*), with broad black plumes, frequents mixed woodland, where it parasitises the green-winged pytilia. The pin-tailed whydah (*Vidua macroura*), with thin splayed plumes, is a common garden bird that harasses other species – especially its host, the common waxbill. The shaft-tailed whydah (*Vidua regia*), with pennant-tipped plumes, is common in the arid west, where its host is the violet-eared waxbill (*Uraeginthus granatina*). Indigobirds are closely related to whydahs, but breeding males are black with no showy plumes. Each of the three different species parasitises a different firefinch. The dusky indigobird (*Vidua funerea*) is identified by its white bill and red legs, and its host is the blue-billed firefinch (*Lagonosticta rubricata*).

The male paradise whydah appears superficially similar to the long-tailed widow, but is found in savannah woodland rather than moist grassland. (NB/FLPA)

WAXBILLS, FIREFINCHES AND MANNIKINS (Estrildidae)

Waxbills are dinky little seed-eaters that feed in small groups on or near the ground, and are regular visitors to bird baths. The widespread common waxbill (*Estrilda astrild*) has the short, conical red bill – like a blob of wax – from which the group derives its name. Small flocks flutter weakly from tangle to tussock in rank waterside vegetation. The blue waxbill (*Uraeginthus angolensis*) is a common woodland bird with powder-blue colouring unlike any other's (see picture, page 184). It is often revealed by its sibilant contact call – 'tsee see see' – as it flits up

into a low thicket. Blue waxbills habitually nest near wasp nests for protection, as does the tiny red-billed firefinch (*Lagonosticta senegala*), which is easily overlooked as it creeps around in pairs, despite its rich red plumage. Firefinches and waxbills often feed in mixed flocks, and are sometimes also joined by the colourful green-winged pytilia (*Pytilia melba*), with its pretty, trilling song. In eastern towns, the tiny (9cm) bronze mannikin (*Spermestes cucullatus*) is often seen in small flocks on overhead wires, or buzzing about lawns and pavements, always returning to the same spot after being disturbed. A breeding male displays to his mate by waving a grass stalk in his bill to advertise his nest-building potential.

CANARIES AND BUNTINGS (Fringillidae)

There are 14 canary species in the region, all of which show some yellow in their plumage. The yellow-fronted canary (*Crithagra mozambicus*) is a gregarious bird of woodland and gardens that often joins mixed seed-eater flocks. The duller black-throated canary (*Crithagra atrogularis*) reveals a bright yellow rump in flight, and is common in more arid regions. The Cape canary (*Serinus canicollis*) has an attractive pastel plumage of green, yellow and blue-grey. It thrives in parks and gardens in southern and upland areas, where it performs its fine, twittering song in a butterfly-like display flight.

The golden-breasted bunting (*Emberiza flaviventris*), usually seen in pairs, is a discreet, ground-feeding bird, common in mixed feeding parties, that progresses with a quiet walk – unlike the jaunty hop of sparrows. In farming areas it often lines its nest with cattle hairs.

Top to bottom
Blue waxbill (MU);
yellow canary (AZ);
red-billed firefinch (MH/FLPA);
golden-breasted bunting (VG/FLPA).

REPTILES AND AMPHIBIANS

Cape cobra in defensive posture
(WD/FLPA)

R eptiles have never been popular. Perhaps it is the myth about their cold, slimy skin, or the fact that some species are venomous, that has inspired the general revulsion. But if these fascinating animals never interested you before, then southern Africa is the place to get started. With more than 480 species recorded – many more than mammals – this is one of the world's reptile hotspots. Highlights include giant sea turtles that haul themselves onto beaches to breed by moonlight, snakes that can swallow an egg larger than their own head, the riotous colour displays of breeding agama lizards, and crocodiles that carry their own hatchlings in jaws strong enough to drown a buffalo. Herpetologists will also find a wealth of endemic lizards and 30% of the world's species of land tortoise. Reptiles are ectothermic, deriving body heat from their surroundings rather than generating it internally as mammals do. This makes them more active in warm weather, so you will see the greatest variety in summer, especially at the start of the rains.

TORTOISES, TURTLES AND TERRAPINS

When your body is encased in a tank-like armoured shell, there's no need to outrun your enemies. Flourishing on this principle, the chelonians, or shield reptiles, are found right across southern Africa. The shell is fused to the skeleton and consists of two parts: the carapace, which is the shield on top, and the plastron, which is the protective plate below. Chelonians also have a horny beak to pluck food, but lack the teeth to grind it. The common terms tortoise, turtle and terrapin have no scientific weight, but refer to those that live on land, in the sea and in freshwater respectively. All chelonians lay eggs, buried by the female in a pit she digs herself. Males can be distinguished from females by a longer, narrower tail – when visible – and, in some species, by a concave depression in the plastron that helps them balance on the female while mating.

LAND TORTOISES (Testudinidae)

Southern Africa has the world's greatest variety of land tortoises, and 12 of the 14 species are endemic to the region – each identified by the shape and pattern of its thick, domed shell. Being too slow to catch anything that moves, land tortoises are vegetarians, though they will gnaw bones – and even hyena droppings – for precious shell-building calcium. Their head can be retracted into the shell for protection, and their powerful forelimbs are tipped with strong claws for digging.

The widespread leopard tortoise (*Geochelone pardalis*) is much the largest and most widespread species. It is named for the spotted pattern on its carapace (rather than any cat-like athleticism), though this fades with age. Adults average 8–12kg in weight, and exceptionally reach an impressive 40kg. Though impregnable to predators, the burnt-out, whitened shells that litter the bush show that fire is a much worse danger to this animal. Males often sustain a cracked carapace during the rough and tumble of their territorial disputes, and mating is also a strenuous affair, with males butting the larger females into submission before levering themselves up to copulate with much wheezing and straining. The 6–15 eggs,

What tortoises lack in speed, they make up for in determination. The broken shell of this male leopard tortoise was probably sustained in a battle for the female.(MU)

buried in a shallow trough, are a great delicacy for enterprising mongooses, and hatchlings are also snapped up by a variety of predators. Survivors, however, may lumber on to reach an age of over 50 years.

The angulate tortoise (*Chersina angulata*) is a common species of sandy coastal regions in the Cape, where it feeds on succulents. It has an elongated carapace with a border of black triangles on the marginal scutes (around the rim). The smaller Kalahari tent tortoise (*Psammobates oculiferus*) has a serrated rim to its intricately patterned carapace. Its shell was traditionally used by the San people of the Kalahari as a pouch, and today this species is often a victim of the curio trade. Speke's hinged tortoise (*Kinixys spekii*) can close the hinged rear part of its carapace to protect its hindquarters. It is found in northeastern savannah, aestivating through the dry winter in a burrow or termite mound, and emerging at the start of the rains.

TERRAPINS (Pelomedusidae)

Terrapins are aquatic chelonians that live in pans, marshes and slow-moving rivers. They are usually seen basking on a protruding log or rock, or floating close to the surface with their snout and eyes protruding. After good rains they disperse overland to new territories – if they can make it across the roads. Terrapins have a flatter shell and longer neck than tortoises, and webbing on the feet. Most species are omnivorous, eating water-weed, freshwater mussels, invertebrates, fish and frogs. The marsh terrapin (*Pelomedusa subrufa*) is the most widespread, and pops up at small pans in surprisingly arid places, such as Etosha. When threatened, it withdraws its head and neck sideways into the shell, leaving only one eye showing. This is a voracious little predator, and will even ambush drinking doves. The serrated hinged terrapin (*Pelusios sinuatus*) can close the front of the plastron to protect its head and forelimbs. It is common in freshwater to the northeast, where it often scavenges from crocodile kills (though it may itself fall victim to the larger reptile).

SEA TURTLES (Chelonioidea)

Sea turtles evolved from ancestors that forsook their primeval swamps for a life on the ocean wave. These gentle giants feed on sea-grass, squid and jellyfish, and their adaptations to a marine lifestyle include limbs modified into flippers and tear ducts that can excrete excess salt. Sea turtles travel great distances through the oceans in search of food, but all return to coastal waters to breed. Five species occur in southern Africa, two of which breed in colonies on the warm Indian Ocean coast, gathering each spring to mate in the shallows off the beaches where they were born. On moonless nights, gravid females haul themselves up the beach to lay their soft, round eggs. One female may lay over a thousand in a season, in batches of a hundred or more. She digs a pit in the sand, and when the last egg has been squeezed out, buries them all with laborious strokes of her front flippers before returning to the sea. After an incubation of 50–70 days, the tiny hatchlings emerge *en masse* to run the gauntlet of predators in a frantic scramble for the sea. Today, turtles are endangered the world over – trapped in fishing nets, hunted for turtle-shell knick-knacks and driven from their breeding grounds by development and pollution. Southern Africa's few protected turtle 'rookeries' offer a rare chance to witness this awesome spectacle.

The leatherback turtle (*Dermochelys coriacea*) is one of the world's largest reptiles, measuring up to 1.7m and weighing over 800kg, and is the only member of an ancient family of sea turtles. Unlike other turtles, its shell is not horny, but is composed of a thick, leathery material, and divided by 12 longitudinal ridges. The leatherback is the only living reptile that is regularly endothermic –

able to control its body temperature by metabolising fat – and so can survive in cold waters and at great depths. It feeds mostly on jellyfish, which are prevented from escape by spines in the throat. Small numbers nest each year along the Indian Ocean beaches, as far south as Maputaland. The loggerhead turtle (*Caretta caretta*) is a 'modern' sea turtle, and the best-known species in the region. It has a hard, patterned shell and, though smaller than the leatherback, can still weigh up to 130kg. About 400–500 females breed on the beaches of Maputaland each year in early summer, before moving north to feed in the warm Mozambique Channel.

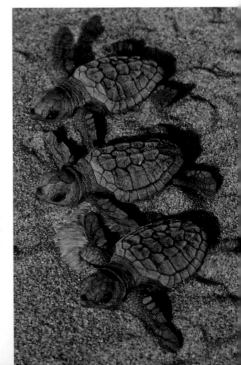

Loggerhead turtle hatchlings usually emerge at night. Exposed by daylight, they must race for their lives to reach the sea. (SA)

Boomslang? Green mamba? Snakes are hard to identify by colour alone. This one is actually a harmless Natal green snake. (GE/FLPA)

SNAKES

Snakes have suffered a bad press since Eden; the mere sight of one generally provokes hysteria, which often culminates in its slaughter. However, of 143 species in southern Africa, about half are non-venomous, only 15 have life-threatening bites, and all of them – venomous or not – do their best to avoid people (see *Snakebite*, page 234). Like lizards, snakes are scaly reptiles (Squamata) that shed their skin regularly as they grow. In fact, snakes evolved from lizards, with their limblessness being an adaptation for moving through habitats such as sand or long grass, where legs just get in the way. Slithering technique depends upon the terrain (see page 225, *Snake tracks*). In place of ears, snakes have evolved some remarkable adaptations for getting around: a retractable tongue flicks in and out to test the air, Jacobson's organ (in the roof of the mouth) interprets what the tongue finds so the snake can 'see' by taste; heat-sensitive pits along the lip scales of pythons and vipers can even detect the infra-red radiation of prey. All snakes are carnivores, and can dislocate their lower jaw in order to swallow live prey whole. Most lay soft-shelled eggs, although a few – including vipers – give birth to live young.

BURROWING SNAKES

Several families of small, primitive snake spend their lives largely underground, but may be seen when they come to the surface on warm, wet nights. Most have a cylindrical, worm-like body, hidden eyes and no neck, so it can be difficult to tell one end from the other. Schlegel's blind snake (*Rhinotyphlops schlegelii*) is the most common and largest of eight blind snake species in the region. It feeds mainly on termites, and is sometimes seen on roa ds during the rains. The Cape centipede eater (*Aparallactus capensis*) is a common species in the east, and is found

Caught above ground, Schlegel's blind snake waves its tail as a mock head to fool predators. (MU)

Young pythons are much more often seen than large adults, which have learnt the value of concealment. (LH)

in loose soil and old termitaria where it feeds almost entirely upon centipedes. By contrast, some thread snakes, such as the widespread, all-dark Peter's thread snake (*Leptotyphlops scurifrons*), are small enough to count big centipedes among their predators. The common burrowing asp (*Atractaspis bibronii*) is a larger, more venomous snake that feeds on other burrowing reptiles. It is aggressive when disturbed, and can deliver a very painful – though not dangerous – bite.

AFRICAN ROCK PYTHON *Python sebae*

The African rock python is by far the largest snake in Africa. Exaggerated claims for its length and appetite abound. In southern Africa it is seldom known to exceed five metres, but this is large enough to capture and swallow a bush pig, and outsized individuals have occasionally claimed human victims. Whatever its size, a python is easily recognised by its muscular body and long triangular head, with a dark spearhead mark on top. Its ornate pattern is such effective camouflage that it is possible to step over a 5m python without seeing it (though unnerving once you realise your mistake). Pythons are constrictors. They lie in wait to ambush their prey, seizing and throwing coils around it before it can escape. The prey dies by asphyxiation and is swallowed immediately, starting with the head. A huge meal may take months to digest. Pythons inhabit savannah and scrub, usually near water, where they take refuge when disturbed. They are fond of caves, kopjes and disused aardvark burrows – where a female will lay up to 50 round eggs. Although not venomous, pythons are aggressive in defence and can inflict nasty wounds with their sharp curved teeth, so are best left alone.

TYPICAL SNAKES (Colubridae)

The large colubrid family comprises 73 species – over half the region's total – and includes many of the most common 'typical' snakes, divided into several subfamilies. The mole snake (*Pseudaspis cana*) is a large, solid constrictor that hunts moles and rodents underground. It varies from pale brown in arid regions to black in the south, and reaches two metres long in parts of the Cape. The brown house snake (*Lamprophis fuliginosus*) is also a constrictor, and has a well-defined, python-like head, though it seldom reaches more than 70cm in length. This attractive, red-brown species makes itself useful around buildings by preying on rats. The common slug eater (*Duberria lutrix*) is a slow-moving, gentle snake often found in gardens.

It feeds entirely on slugs, by following the slime trail and swallowing the slug on the end of it. Sand snakes, such as the Karoo sand snake (*Psammophis notostictus*) are extremely slender, fast-moving and difficult to approach. They hunt lizards and other small ground-dwelling vertebrates in arid regions, and are often seen crossing roads. The larger olive grass snake (*Psammophis mossambicus*) inhabits savannah, where its speed, length (up to 1.5m) and grey-brown colour often cause confusion with the black mamba (see page 193). The spotted bush snake (*Philothamnus semivariegatus*) is more at home in the trees, where it uses camouflage and agility to hunt arboreal prey such as geckos, chameleons and tree frogs and – with its huge eyes – is often mistaken

A juvenile mole snake is more boldly marked than adults. (MB)

for a boomslang (see page 192). The closely-related green water snake (*Philothamnus hoplogaster*) prefers aquatic habitats, where it hunts reedbeds for frogs and birds.

The common or rhombic eggeater (*Dasypeltis scabra*) is remarkable on two counts. Firstly, it can swallow a whole egg several times the size of its own head.

Egg-eating snake in action

To do this, it dislocates its jaws and works its toothless, elasticated mouth slowly over the egg, forcing the shell against the back of the throat, where it is pierced by the 'gular tooth' – a projecting vertebra from the spine. The contents are then swallowed and the collapsed shell is spat out. Secondly, though harmless itself, the eggeater's markings exactly mimic those of the venomous night adder, and it can even produce ·a mock hiss by rubbing its coils together. Though widespread and common, this snake is nocturnal and rarely seen.

Juvenile boomslang. This species can be identified at all ages by its large eyes. (LH)

Back fangs: boomslang and vine snake

Most colubrids are harmless, or only mildly venomous. This is manifestly not true of the boomslang (*Dispholidus typus*), which produces one of the most potent venoms of any snake – though it took until 1957, and the death of a top Chicago herpetologist, to discover exactly how potent. This common, widespread snake grows up to 1.3m in length, varying in colour from olive brown (females) to leaf green (males), and has bulging eyes with round pupils. It is an arboreal hunter, using excellent vision to capture birds and chameleons, and often raiding weaver nests. Boomslang venom is haemotoxic, and may prove fatal to humans. That's the bad news. The good news is that, being back-fanged, the boomslang cannot easily deliver an effective bite to a human and, being fairly mild-mannered, isn't generally inclined to try. So, despite the notoriety, serious bites are rare.

The vine snake, or twig snake, (*Thelotornis capensis*) is also arboreal, back-fanged and equipped with a deadly haemotoxic venom. Its pointed head and thin, twig-coloured body are perfect camouflage among the branches, where it will freeze for concealment or, if rumbled, disappear with fluid ease. Prey is swallowed upwards as the snake hangs upside down. Like a boomslang, a threatened vine snake inflates its throat to display the dark underskin.

COBRAS, MAMBAS AND THEIR ALLIES (Elapidae)

The elapid family contains the most feared snakes of all. Alert and responsive, cobras and mambas have a reputation for belligerence. In reality, none has any interest in pursuing an argument and, given the chance, will flee any human intrusion. Nonetheless, all should be treated with respect.

Cobras (*Naja*) are known for their dramatic habit of rearing up to spread a hood when threatened, though, since this hood is rarely visible (see page 242), they often go unrecognised. They are medium to large snakes, with fixed front fangs, that hunt small vertebrates such as mice, birds and lizards. Most species are ground-dwelling and nocturnal. The snouted cobra (*Naja annulifera*) is a stocky, blunt-headed snake that can reach 2.5m in length and comes in two colour phases: one plain yellow-brown, the other banded. It generally hunts by night and basks by day near its lair in a hollow log or termite mound. A bite from this cobra is very serious, and requires large doses of anti-venom. The Cape cobra (*Naja nivea*) is endemic to the arid southwest. It is slighter than the snouted cobra, and no more than 1.5m in length, but has even more powerful venom. Cape cobras come in various shades of brown, with a golden-yellow race being common in the Kalahari (see page 185). They are active, diurnal hunters that often forage around farms, and will climb trees to raid sociable weaver nests.

A venomous bite is not the only hazard with cobras. When threatened, the Mozambique spitting cobra (*Naja mossambica*) will also spray its venom. The spray is angled at the eyes, and over 2–3 metres it can be very accurate. Although the pain is excruciating, lasting damage can be prevented by bathing the eyes immediately in clean water. This smallish, widespread cobra is readily identified by the banding on its throat, and often forages around buildings at night in eastern districts. The rinkhals (*Hemachatus haemachatus*) can also spread a hood and spit its venom, though it is not a true cobra. This stocky, black and white snake is found in highveld and coastal grassland. If spitting doesn't work, it may sham dead in an attempt to fool its attacker.

No other snake in Africa has inspired such fear and mythology as the black mamba (*Dendroaspis polylepis*) and, perhaps because of this, other snakes are often misidentified as mambas. The genuine article is unmistakable: averaging about 2.5m in length, this elegant reptile can exceptionally reach over 3.5m – the longest venomous snake in Africa – and moves with impressive speed. It is not black, but a uniform grey/brown, with a long, narrow head (ominously described as 'coffin-shaped' in most field guides) and prominent brow-ridges that create a penetrating expression. If a

Only a black mamba rears this high. So keep your distance. (LH)

black mamba is left no room to retreat, it will rear up the front third of its body (sometimes to shoulder height), spread a narrow hood and hiss menacingly, exposing the black lining of its mouth. This is a warning worth heeding, since the copious neurotoxic venom can cause death through paralysis unless treated immediately with anti-venom. However, bites and fatalities are rare. Black mambas inhabit savannah and coastal bush to the north and east, where they make their home in a termite mound or hollow log, and hunt by day for prey such as rats and dassies. The green mamba (*Dendroaspis angusticeps*) is a more arboreal species, and hunts birds and small mammals in the tree canopy. Though also highly venomous, this shy and elusive snake does not deserve its bad reputation. It is smaller (up to 1.5m) and less aggressive than the black mamba, and its emerald coils are hard to spot in the forest tangle. In southern Africa, green mambas are restricted to coastal bush in KwaZulu-Natal and pockets of forest in Zimbabwe's Eastern Highlands.

VIPERS (Viperidae)

Vipers are stocky, venomous snakes with a large head, vertical pupils and long poison fangs that hinge forward when the mouth is opened to strike. They hunt by night for small vertebrates, striking at their prey from a concealed position then tracking it down by scent when it succumbs to the venom. Most vipers hunt on the ground, where they are concealed by excellent camouflage. The puff adder (*Bitis arietans*) is responsible for 60% of serious snakebites in the region. Though it has less powerful venom than a cobra, it is common, sluggish and aggressive – a dangerous combination in a snake. The flat triangular head and chevron pattern are unmistakable, and big specimens can exceed a metre in length, growing very fat in the process. When disturbed, a puff adder coils into a strike posture and hisses threateningly. It hunts at night for rodents, birds and other snakes, and often basks on warm roads – not always a wise habit. Puff adders usually give birth to 30–40 live young, though one litter of 156 in Kenya was the world record for any snake.

The gaboon viper (*Bitis gabonica*) grows even bigger than the puff adder, reaching

The gaboon viper is the most beautifully camouflaged of forest floor predators. (M&PF/FLPA)

a length of up to 1.3m, and has the longest fangs of any snake. It is a protected
species in the region, restricted to pockets of indigenous forest in Maputaland and
eastern Zimbabwe. Here it uses spectacular camouflage to ambush unwary rodents
and birds in the leaf litter. Though its strike is lightning fast and its venom copious
and powerful, this is a mild-mannered snake, and bites to humans are rare.

The horned adder (*Bitis caudalis*) takes its name from a horn of skin projecting
above each eye. This small viper of the arid west lurks beneath rocks and may
conceal itself in the sand to ambush its prey. The little Peringuey's adder (*Bitis
peringueyi*) lives in the dunes of the Namib Desert, where it moves just like the North
American 'sidewinders', using a series of sideways undulations to lift its body off
the hot, unstable sand. It may also bury itself entirely (see picture, page 21), and
wiggle its protruding tail tip as a lure to its lizard prey. The common or rhombic
night adder (*Causus rhombeatus*), with its narrow head, round pupils and large (rather
than fragmented) head scales, belongs to a separate, more ancient group of vipers.
It hunts its prey at night by scent, and can be identified by the distinct 'V' shaped
mark on the back of its head.

LIZARDS

Lizards form the largest group of reptiles, with at least 291 species recognised in southern Africa and more being discovered every year. Like snakes, they belong to the order Squamata (scaly reptiles). Most have four well-developed limbs and a long tail, but some, such as legless skinks, have no legs and are frequently confused with snakes. If in doubt, only snakes have enlarged belly scales, while only lizards have external ear openings and movable eyelids. Many lizards can shed and regenerate their tail as a defensive strategy. Their diet ranges from plants and invertebrates to – in the case of monitors – any animal small enough to kill and swallow. You needn't look far to find one: lizards are common in all habitats, including houses, and the greatest variety occurs in rocky, arid areas. Most species lay eggs, though a few will give birth to live young. No lizard is venomous.

SKINKS (Scincidae)

Typical skinks are small lizards with short legs, a long tail, and dense overlapping scales with a polished, almost iridescent veneer. Most live on the ground, on trees

or on rocks, moving regularly between sunlight and shadow to control their temperature. A few legless species live underground. The striped skink (*Mabuya striata*) is common in towns, except in the Cape, and forages tamely around houses. It is easily recognised by the two pale stripes along its sleek body. The Cape skink (*Mabuya capensis*) is stockier, with short, stubby legs. This gentle creature is found in the south

The striped skink is a familiar reptile about town. (MU)

where it lives in burrows and hunts in gardens and sandy clearings, often among the debris of fallen aloes. The five-lined or rainbow skink (*Mabuya quinquetaeniata*) is a fast-moving species that inhabits rocky outcrops in eastern bushveld. Females and young have a striped body and electric-blue tail, while adult males are olive brown with a golden-yellow tail. These colour differences help to establish hierarchies and so settle territorial disputes.

OLD WORLD LIZARDS (Lacertidae)

This large family comprises 37 species in eight genera, all of which – like their European relatives – are small to medium-sized 'typical' lizards, with a long tail, well-developed legs, large head scales and spotted or striped patterning. They dash around by day among rocks or on the ground, using speed and agility to hunt insects and escape predators. Among various similar sand lizards (*Pedioplanis*), sandveld lizards (*Nucras*) and others, the shovel-snouted lizard (*Meroles anchietae*) of the Namib Desert deserves a special mention. This species races across the sand dunes after

Lizards have adapted to fill every habitat niche: the shovel-snouted lizard (*top*, LH) withstands the burning heat of the desert by raising its feet from the sand in a curious 'thermal dance'; the smooth scales of the giant plated lizard (*above*, LVH) allow it to slip easily into rock crevices; the giant girdled lizard (*below*, LH) jams its spines into the roof of its underground tunnel to thwart the efforts of a predator.

insects and – in the dry season – wind-blown seeds, obtaining all the moisture it needs from its food. To survive the burning surface temperatures, it performs a comical 'thermal dance', in which its feet are lifted clear of the sand in alternating diagonal pairs. If disturbed, it swims deep down into the dune.

PLATED LIZARDS (Gerrhosauridae)
AND GIRDLED LIZARDS (Cordylidae)

Plated lizards are big, diurnal lizards with a long tail, sturdy legs, large head scales and a lateral fold of skin along each flank. Measuring up to 60cm long, the giant plated lizard (*Gerrhosaurus validus*) is the largest lizard in the region after the

monitors (see page 199), from which it can be distinguished by its flatter, shinier body. This shy creature is common on granite kopjes to the northeast and in parts of Namibia, where it supplements an insect diet with figs and other fruit. When pursued, it will slip into a crevice and wedge itself securely by inflating its body.

The common flat lizard is particularly abundant among rocky kopjes in Zimbabwe, where dense colonies may form. (AZ)

Girdled lizards are a southern African speciality, with 26 of the 32 known species being endemic to the region. Most are associated with rocky terrain, where they live in loose colonies presided over by territorial males. They are medium-sized lizards, with a large head, sturdy limbs and rough, crocodile-like skin which comprises overlapping whorls of serrated scales. This armour protects them when wriggling through crevices where, like giant plated lizards, they inflate their bodies so nothing can winkle them out. The armadillo girdled lizard (*Cordylus cataphractus*), which feeds on insects among the flowers of the succulent Karoo, takes self-defence a step further by gripping its tail in its mouth and rolling into a spiky, unswallowable ball (see page 23). The giant girdled lizard (*Cordylus giganteus*) – also known as the 'sungazer' from its habit of basking on termite mounds – is the largest, and inhabits the rocky grasslands of central South Africa, where loose colonies live in individual burrows several metres apart.

Flat lizards (*Platysaurus*) belong to the same family as girdled lizards, and also live in small colonies among rocks. The common flat lizard (*Platysaurus intermedius*) prefers exfoliating granite outcrops, where it can squeeze its flattened body into the narrowest of cracks. Breeding males flaunt a gaudy livery of red, blue, green and orange to intimidate rivals and attract the plainer, striped females. Rhodes' Grave in Zimbabwe's Matobo Hills (see page 276) supports a large colony and offers an intimate close-up of their energetic and colourful life.

Rock monitors often take refuge in trees. Their blunt snout immediately distinguishes them from water monitors. (MU)

MONITORS (Varanidae)

Monitors – popularly known by the Afrikaans *leguaan* – are by far the largest lizards in the region. Two species occur, both of which have strong limbs, a long whip-like tail, a sinuous neck and loose skin composed of tiny beaded scales. The colourful patterns of juveniles fade with age to a dirty grey. Monitors are predators, and prey on anything from insects to small mammals, which they track down by scent – flicking their forked tongue in and out like snakes. They can climb trees, using their long claws for traction, swim well, and run fast – adopting a high-limbed, bounding gait, their heavy body swinging from side to side.

The water or Nile monitor (*Varanus niloticus*) can reach a length of over two metres, over half of which is tail. It occurs in aquatic habitats, where it is usually

Nile monitors will feed on any food they come across, alive or dead. This one is scavenging from a dead catfish. (WD/FLPA)

The colours of the male southern tree agama are most intense during the breeding season. (MVL/FLPA)

seen basking or foraging at the water's edge or using its long oar-like tail to swim powerfully across the surface, head protruding. When disturbed in waterside undergrowth it crashes noisily away, sounding alarmingly like something much bigger. Water monitors feed on crabs, mussels, fish and nestlings, and will ransack an unattended crocodile nest for its eggs. They themselves may fall prey to an adult croc, though their biggest enemy is the martial eagle (see page 147). In spring, a female breaks into a live termite mound to lay up to 60 eggs inside. The termites repair the damage, leaving the eggs to incubate in perfect warm, humid conditions until they hatch with the following spring rains, when the damp soil allows the hatchlings to break out.

The rock monitor (*Varanus albigularis*) is shorter and stockier than the water monitor, seldom exceeding 1.5m, and has a blunter snout, shorter tail and often a dirty and flaking skin. It prefers arid and rocky habitats, where it lives beneath rocks, in old animal burrows or in large tree holes. Rock monitors eat anything they can find or kill, including carrion, and, if under attack themselves, will lash out with their tail and bite fiercely. In winter they become semi-dormant, and may hibernate. Females generally prefer to dig their own nest hole, but will use a termite mound.

AGAMAS (Agamidae)

Agamas are chunky lizards, with long legs, a long thin tail, a spiny crest and a big triangular head. They feed mostly on ants, and breeding males of many species assert their territorial claims with colourful displays. The southern tree agama (*Acanthocerus atricollis*) is always found either on tree trunks or scuttling between them. The male nods his bright blue head vigorously in display, and pursues his rivals in spiralling battles around the trunk – the victor usually chasing the vanquished right out of the tree. The duller female is well camouflaged against rough bark. Despite popular belief, tree agamas are not poisonous, but if captured they gape their bright orange mouth lining and bite fiercely. Kirk's rock agama (*Agama kirkii*) is largely confined to Zimbabwe, where it clambers around granite outcrops flaunting a dazzling purple body and orange head. It often feeds around the roots of rock fig trees, browsing on ants that stream up for the fruit. The ground agama (*Agama aculeata*) is a ground-living species, concealed on rocky and sandy soils by its cryptic patterning. It sometimes climbs into low scrub to bask, and scuttles away from trouble with tail held high.

CHAMELEONS (Chamaeleonidae)

Despite being completely harmless, chameleons play many sinister roles in African folklore. This can perhaps be explained by their bizarre-looking adaptations for a hidden life in the trees: a hunched, flattened body with flaps and crests that mimic a leaf; long legs, opposable toes and a prehensile tail for clambering through flimsy foliage; conical eyes that move independently to focus on prey while the body remains stock still; and a sticky, telescopic tongue that can shoot out twice the body length to capture unsuspecting prey. Last, but not least, the famous colour changing – achieved by the rapid compression of pigment cells – provides a versatile language with which to express everything from distress (a dark colour) to arousal (a more intense flush). By day, chameleons are almost impossible to find in foliage, but are

The flap-neck chameleon green cross code: look left, look right, change colour. (MU)

often seen hesitantly crossing a road, where their trembling leaf act is little use against a truck. By night, they glow strangely white in torchlight.

There are 18 species in the region, including several rare and localised dwarf chameleons. The best-known is the larger and more widespread flap-neck chameleon (*Chamaeleo dilepis*), which is essentially green, with a bright orange throat that it inflates in a defensive bluff. This species feeds primarily on grasshoppers and beetles, but must itself avoid predatory birds and boomslangs. Females take 24 hours to lay up to 50 small eggs in a small pit that they dig themselves. The similar-sized Namaqua chameleon (*Chamaeleo namaquensis*) has a shorter tail and is more terrestrial, inhabiting arid western regions, where it climbs into low scrub during the heat of the day. It eats anything it can swallow, even other small lizards.

Bibron's thick-toed gecko (WC)

GECKOS (Geckonidae)

Geckos are unusual little lizards, notable for their big, jewel-like, lidless eyes which they lick clean with a long windscreen-wiper tongue, and their miraculously adhesive toes, equipped with pads of hair-covered scales called scansors, that allow them to grip surfaces as smooth and vertical as glass. Most species lay just one or two eggs. Many are nocturnal, and live in colonies, using sound to communicate in the dark. Geckos can endure cooler temperatures than the average lizard, and so have evolved to colonise mountains, deserts and cities.

Of at least 89 species in southern Africa, the majority are endemic. Many are highly localised, and only likely to be identified by an expert, but a few are more easily seen. Tropical house geckos (*Hemidactylus* spp) are medium-sized geckos (8–10cm) that have spread all over the tropics by hitching rides on boats. They thrive in houses, and are often seen clustered around porch lights (see page 34) waiting to snap up unwary moths – many showing broken or regenerated tails as evidence of their territorial disputes. The Cape dwarf gecko (*Lygodactylus capensis*) is a smaller house guest in the east of the region, but feeds by day – picking off ants from their trails. Bibron's thick-toed gecko (*Pachydactylus bibronii*) is a larger, more pugnacious-looking gecko with a big head, pimply skin and segmented tail, that inhabits rock outcrops in the Cape and Karoo and takes prey up to the size of large centipedes. The common barking gecko (*Ptenopus garrulus*) is a ground-dwelling species of the arid west, where it emerges onto the surface after dark to forage for insects. Each territorial male calls from his burrow entrance with a short series of clicks, creating a strange echoing chorus that fills summer evenings across the empty expanses of the Kalahari.

NILE CROCODILE

Crocodiles and alligators are descendants of the great archosaurs that dominated the Earth for over 150 million years. Certain anatomical features, such as a four-chambered heart and improved limb articulation, reveal that they are more closely related to birds than today's other reptiles, though you might not guess this at first glance. The Nile crocodile (*Crocodylus niloticus*) – the only species found in southern Africa – is a formidable predator. Large adults may exceed 5m in length, weigh over 1,000kg and live over 100 years, although today such monsters are rare. Whatever its size and age, a crocodile is unmistakable, with its powerful serrated tail, horny plated skin and up to a hundred peg-like teeth crammed into a long, sinister smile. Youngsters are boldly marked in black and green, but these colours fade to a muddy grey-brown with age.

Crocodiles inhabit lakes, rivers and swamps to the north and east of the region. Here they lead an amphibious life: either basking on land, jaws agape to lose heat, or cruising the waters, raised eyes and nostrils allowing them to see and breathe undetected. Youngsters take small prey such as invertebrates, frogs and small fish. Adults take larger fish, such as bream and barbel, and will ambush mammals up to the size of buffalo, grabbing them with an explosive sideways lunge from the water before dragging them under to drown. Large numbers of crocodiles gather to demolish big carcasses, churning up the water as they thrash and spin to dislodge chunks of flesh. They will even leave the water to steal a nearby lion kill.

Crocodiles reach sexual maturity at 12–15 years, and show more complex breeding behaviour and more devoted parental care than any other reptile.

A crocodile can raise itself on sturdy limbs in order to move rapidly over land. When in less of a hurry it slithers on its belly. (MU)

A big crocodile waits in the rapids to snap up unwary fish. Anyone for white-water rafting? (PP)

A male establishes his territory along a defined stretch of water, wooing females with thunderous roars and noisy displays of jaw champing, tail thrashing and bubble blowing. The female digs a pit in a dry, sunny sandbank, and lays about 80 hard-shelled eggs, guarding them aggressively against intruders – including male crocodiles – until, after 85–90 days, a muffled chorus of cheeping reveals that the young are ready to hatch. She then breaks into the nest to release the hatchlings, and carries them delicately in her mouth to a nursery in the shallows, where they remain under her guard for six to eight weeks until ready to strike out alone. Hatchlings are vulnerable to any predator who can sneak past their formidable mum, and monitor lizards, baboons and honey badgers will grab any chance to plunder the buried eggs.

VICTIM OR VILLAIN?

From Kariba to St Lucia, there are enough gruesome stories about crocodiles to scare the nervous from the water for ever. Though crocs generally avoid people (understandably, given the slaughter they have suffered), humans are still potential prey for a big crocodile, and in remote regions tragedies do occasionally occur. Contrary to the more lurid myths, crocodiles will not launch themselves into boats or come galloping after you on land. However, when in crocodile country, it is sensible to keep your distance from the water's edge: a torch beam at night will often reveal tell-tale red eyes where not a ripple had been visible by day. Crocodiles are integral to the ecology of many rivers and wetlands, where they clean up carrion and control numbers of larger, predatory fish, but today they are increasingly threatened by poaching and habitat destruction and are rare outside protected areas. At crocodile farms, such as those of St Lucia and Victoria Falls, captive-bred animals are harvested for their leather and meat, and hatchlings are reintroduced to the wild to boost local populations.

Crocodiles lie with jaws agape in order to lose heat. (MU)

Dollops of candyfloss hanging from a waterside tree (*above*, MU) are actually the nests of the foam-nest frog (*right*, MU), whose tadpoles develop in a ball of frothy mucus before dropping into the water below.

FROGS

Frogs (Anura) are the only order of amphibian found in southern Africa. Like most amphibians, they begin life as tadpoles, before shedding their tail, growing legs and venturing on to land, where they must keep their smooth, permeable skin permanently moist in order to absorb oxygen. Most hide in damp retreats by day and come out after dark to feed on invertebrates, which they capture with a long sticky tongue and gulp down whole. All have big eyes for hunting at night, and large tympana (eardrums) for tuning in to the courtship ritual of the frog chorus. Mating itself often involves a chaotic struggle between rival males to grab a female and deposit their sperm on her eggs. Eggs (frogspawn) are usually laid in water, though some frogs use a moist burrow or nest. Southern Africa boasts over 130 species of frog, but perhaps not loudly enough to attract the attention they deserve. South Africa's recent *Frog Atlas Project* has revealed that many are in serious decline.

The frog chorus

No visitor to southern Africa's wetlands during summer can fail to be impressed by the crescendo of croaks, barks and whistles that gets underway at sunset, especially following rains, as the frog chorus tunes up. Some frogs sing high, some low; some mutter erratically, others chirp relentlessly. Combined, they can swell into a pulsing wall of sound, amplified by their balloon-like inflatable vocal sacs. The purpose of these calls, just like bird song, is for males to claim territory and attract females. The trained ear can identify each member of the chorus by its unique call. The bubbling kassina (*Kassina senegalensis*) has a loud liquid 'quoip', like a heavy drop of rainwater, uttered at irregular intervals, while the brown-backed tree frog (*Leptopelis mossambicus*) barks its spasmodic 'yack-yack' from a woodland tree. The painted reed frog (*Hyperolius marmoratus*) generates a shrill, piping chorus of whistles

Above left African bullfrog in defensive posture (AZ/FLPA)
Above right A bushveld rain frog inflates its body (LH)

from reedbeds (see picture, page 29), while the snoring puddle frog (*Phrynobatrachus natalensis*) gathers to call in temporary pools, with a combined rhythmic bleating not unlike the honking of distant geese. The African bullfrog (*Pyxicephalus edulis*) is the giant of the order, and has a bellow to match. This massively fat frog aestivates for much of the year, but emerges during the rains to breed in temporary pans, which it defends aggressively from intruders – even lunging at lions.

Climbers, leapers and waddlers

A frog's legs reflect its lifestyle. Treefrogs and reedfrogs have adhesive suckers on the tips of their fingers and toes that allow them to clamber up any surface – even glass. The foam-nest frog (*Chiromantis xerampelina*) lays its eggs in a tree, depositing them on a branch in a mucus ball, which it whips into a frothy meringue-like 'nest' with its back legs. Inside, the eggs stay moist and develop into tadpoles, which then plop down into the water below. The common river frog (*Rana angolensis*) is the most widespread of several 'typical' frogs of the genus *Rana*, all of which use their large, muscular legs for leaping, and can spring athletically away from trouble. The common platana (*Xenopus laevis*) is almost totally aquatic, with a slimy skin and feeble forelimbs that are useless on land. Underwater, it propels itself efficiently with powerful kicks of its massive hindlegs and clawed feet. Platanas disperse during the rains, when they often turn up in ditches and drains.

Toads (*Bufonidae*) are simply frogs that tend to walk rather than hop. The common or guttural toad (*Bufo gutturalis*) often waddles around buildings at night, snapping up insects attracted by the light. Being unable to leap to safety, it inflates its body when confronted by a hungry snake. Rainfrogs (*Breviceps* spp) also prefer to walk. These short-limbed little frogs have a rotund, inflatable body and a squashed face like a tiny Pekinese dog. They use toughened pads on their back legs to dig burrows in the soil, where they aestivate in a cocoon of mucus during the dry season, emerging during the rains to feed and breed. The bushveld rainfrog (*Breviceps adspersus*) may be seen on warm summer nights at termite emergences, wings plastered around its mouth as it tucks away a serious helping.

INVERTEBRATES

Citrus swallowtail (LH)

L ions, elephants and other 'charismatic megafauna' may steal the headlines, but southern Africa's wildlife is actually much more prolific lower down the scale. Here, munching through the vegetation, tunnelling into the ground and swarming through the skies, a vast army of creepy-crawlies powers the engine room of the great food pyramid. More properly known as invertebrates (animals without backbones), these comprise a bewildering variety of forms. The more primitive 'lower' invertebrates include soft-bodied annelids, such as burrowing earthworms and blood-sucking leeches, and molluscs – such as the giant African land snail (*Achatina fulica*) – which have eyes on tentacles and use a single muscular foot for locomotion. The more advanced invertebrates, with many limbs and segmented bodies, are known as arthropods. These range from simple crustaceans, such as woodlice (Isopoda) and freshwater crabs (Decapoda), to the more complex insects (see page 213) and arachnids (see page 209). Invertebrates are far too many and varied for anything but the most cursory overview here. To guide the newcomer, I have introduced a few of the better-known and more visible groups.

MILLIPEDES AND CENTIPEDES

Different orders of arthropod can be distinguished by their number of legs, and none has more than the millipedes (Juliformia). Millipedes are among the most familiar of southern African invertebrates, often seen trundling across roads on a twinkling forest of tiny legs and rolling into a tight ball when disturbed. Their local name, *tshongololo* (steam train),

The giant millipede can reach an impressive size. (C&TS/FLPA)

is a perfect description of their motion. Many people regard tshongololos with suspicion. In fact, they are harmless vegetarians, but can secrete a noxious fluid in defence and are considered unpalatable by most – civets and red-winged starlings being notable exceptions. A millipede's body is formed of up to 60 segments, with two pairs of legs on each. Hatchlings start with only three pairs of legs, but acquire more at each moult. Centipedes, by contrast, are carnivores, and have only one pair of legs on each of their 25 body segments. The large centipedes (Scolopendromorpha) are the best known of several different groups. These aggressive, fast-moving predators have a painful (though not dangerous) bite, and big specimens – up to 25cm long – will even prey on frogs and geckos.

They are largely nocturnal, but can be active on overcast days, when their bright orange colouring should be warning enough not to touch. By curling around their young to protect them, female centipedes show more parental care than many vertebrates.

Scolopendra centipede

SPIDERS AND SCORPIONS

Spiders and scorpions are arachnids. This class of arthropods differs from insects by having eight legs, no antennae and a body divided into two, not three, principal sections. Southern Africa's rich complement of arachnids numbers over 3,000 species of spider (Araneae) and 160 species of scorpion (Scorpiones). Most are predators, though some, including ticks and mites, are parasites.

SILK ENGINEERS

Spiders do amazing things with silk. As well as for web design (without the benefit of HTML), this remarkable substance is used for making egg sacs, lining burrows, luring mates and hitching rides on the breeze. Golden orb-web spiders (*Nephila* spp) are the original web masters: the big black-and-yellow females string a concentric cat's cradle of golden rings on a hammock of radiating support wires, then wait at the centre for a catch. Nearby lurks the much smaller male, and often a number of tiny, dew-drop spiders (*Argyrodes* spp) which scavenge any leftovers. These webs

A female banded-legged golden orb-web spider is much larger than her minuscule mate (this picture is roughly life-size). (MU)

are so strong that birds up to the size of swallows are sometimes ensnared, and their tensile properties have reputedly been studied by NASA scientists. Kite spiders (*Gasteracantha* spp), whose spiny, triangular abdomens look like something out of Star Wars, also build an orb web – as do bark spiders (*Caerostris* spp) which dismantle theirs by day and retire to a camouflaged position on a nearby branch. Community nest spiders (*Stegodyphus* spp) nest socially in a large, spherical web, which becomes strewn with debris, while daddy-long-legs spiders (*Smeringopus* spp) hide from predators by hanging upside down beneath their web and shaking it when disturbed. Other web designs include tunnels built into crevices, sheets spread over the ground and the complex 'scaffold' webs of button spiders (*Latrodectus* spp), with thread snares that lead to their refuge. Some spiders dispense with a web and instead wield their silk as a weapon: net-casting spiders (*Deinopis* spp) dangle from low vegetation to fling a silken net over prey passing below; sand divers (Ammoxenidae) pounce on their termite victims, and bind them in silk.

Spiders have perfected many other hunting techniques beside the silken snare. Common baboon spiders (*Harpactira* spp) lurk down neatly drilled, silk-lined tunnels, about 3cm across, from which they ambush prey when alerted by its footfalls. Robust, hairy and the size of a small rodent, these impressive spiders are the stuff of an arachnophobe's nightmare. They can be manoeuvred gently to the surface with a grass stem inserted into the burrow, which they grip. Other ambush hunters include trapdoor spiders (Ctenizidae), which construct a cork-like lid to their tunnel, and white lady spiders (*Carparachne* spp), which dig deep into desert sand to escape burning surface temperatures, and will fold up their legs and cartwheel down a dune to escape predatory wasps. Rain spiders (*Palystes* spp) are not tied to a web or a tunnel, but hunt their prey by speed – often around houses at night. These large spiders are perfectly harmless, despite the alarm they cause. Jumping spiders (Salticidae) leap on to their victims, first securing themselves to the ground with a silken line. Fishing spiders (*Thalassius* spp) pursue insects, tadpoles and small fish across the water's surface, using their legs as a lure.

The white lady spider (*Carparachne aureoflava*) of the Namib Desert escapes predators by folding up its legs to form a wheel shape and rolling away down a sand dune. (M&PF/FLPA)

FANGS

Spiders use fangs to subdue prey with venom. Very few can penetrate human skin, and most of these are not dangerous – although the 'black widow' button spiders (*Latrodectus* spp) are among a handful whose bite demands urgent medical attention. Ironically the 'spider' with the most impressive fangs is neither a spider nor venomous. Sun spiders, better known as solifuges, belong to the separate order Solifugae. These large, voracious hunters (up to 8cm long) are identified by their red or yellowish colouring, soft hairy body, massive fangs and their habit of dashing around after prey with their front legs held off the ground. Victims, including large beetles and even small frogs, are killed without venom and crunched up audibly. Solifuges are common in hot, dry areas and frequently seen scuttling around camp fires.

A sun spider, or solifuge, with its grasshopper prey. (PN/FLPA)

A STING IN THE TAIL

A scorpion's venom is in the sting on the end of its tail, which it arches forward over its head to strike prey and intimidate enemies. The fearsome-looking pincers are used to grip and grab, but are not venomous and hold no threat to people. All scorpions can deliver a painful sting, but only those with thin pincers and a thick tail (*Parabuthus* spp) are dangerous – their potent venom requiring urgent medical attention. Some thick-tailed scorpions will also spray their venom in self-defence, and can even produce a warning sound by scraping their sting across their tail. Scorpions with thick pincers and a narrow tail are less venomous. These include black rock scorpions (*Hadogenes* spp), which inhabit rocky crevices, and smooth-headed digging scorpions (*Opisthophthalmus* spp), which use heavy lobster-like pincers to dig complex spiral burrows.

The greatest variety of scorpions occurs in arid western areas, where they can survive for a long time without food or water (over one year has been recorded in captivity). Being nocturnal, scorpions are seldom seen by day – unless, like a hungry baboon, you are prepared to grub about under rocks for them. At night they venture from their hiding places in search of prey, which they detect on air currents using tiny sensory body hairs. Scorpions are remarkable among invertebrates for their breeding behaviour. Mating partners lock pincers in a grappling courtship pirouette, clearing the ground for the male to deposit his sperm sac, which the female picks up with her abdomen. New born young are carried on their mother's back for protection.

Scorpions with impressive claws but thin tails, such as this smooth-headed digging scorpion, are not dangerous to humans. (FL/FLPA)

BLOODSUCKERS

Ticks (Acari) are the strongest disincentive to wearing shorts in the bush, especially during the rainy season in long grass. These tiny parasitic arachnids wait on grass tips and clamber aboard animals that brush past. Once on, they pierce the skin with their sharp mouthparts, and gorge themselves on the host's blood, swelling up like peas. Different species choose different hosts. Cattle and dog ticks (Ixodidae) infest domestic livestock, and the minuscule, red 'pepper ticks' that plague hikers are actually their larvae. The tampan tick (*Ornithodorus moubata*) is a particularly nasty species of Kalahari regions. Colonies lurk in the sand beneath camelthorns, waiting for an animal to lie down in the inviting shade, whereupon, chemically alerted by its exhalation of carbon dioxide, they swarm over their host. Some species of tick can transmit diseases. The common form of 'tickbite fever' (ricketsia) is not dangerous, but is very unpleasant, causing intense headaches and a malaria-like delirium. Antibiotics will deal with it quickly, but letting the disease run its course – if you can bear it – will produce a resistance that prevents it from ever recurring. Ticks can be discouraged with insecticide spray, and removed by carefully pinching them out – taking care not to leave the mouthparts embedded. Oxpeckers (see page 178)

have honed this skill to a fine art, and with up to 20,000 ticks being recorded on a single giraffe, they're seldom short of a meal.

Mites are parasites on larger invertebrates, including spiders, scorpions and millipedes. Most are microscopic, but the larger red velvet mites (*Dinothrombium* spp) look like minuscule (5mm) scarlet cushions, and can be seen in open, sandy areas in the early morning after rains.

Red velvet mite (MM/FLPA)

INSECTS

Insects are distinguished from other arthropods by having a three-segmented body (consisting of head, thorax and abdomen), three pairs of jointed legs and – in most cases – two pairs of jointed wings. They are the most abundant life form on Earth, with millions of species worldwide, of which at least 80,000 have been identified in southern Africa. To many people insects are simply pests, and certainly cockroaches, house flies, head lice, clothes moths, mosquitoes and timber beetles have not always made themselves welcome. However, insects play an integral role in the natural environment, whether as pollinators (bees, flies, butterflies), waste-disposal machines (dung beetles, termites, blowfly larvae) or providers of such precious natural resources as silk and honey. In southern Africa many also form a valuable food source, with locusts, termites and caterpillars all spicing up the human menu in various parts of the region.

Insects fall into 26 different orders, with a bewildering variety of families and lifestyles. Some, such as dragonflies and damselflies (Odonata), are predators. These dashing hunters patrol their wetland territories and capture other insects in flight, using amazing aerial agility and the keen vision of their large compound eyes. The larvae of antlions (Neuroptera) are ambush specialists: they dig a conical pit in loose sand and wait for their ant prey to stumble in, seizing it in powerful jaws and sucking it dry. Praying mantids (Mantodea) hunt using stealth and disguise: some are leaf green, and hide among foliage; others use elaborate camouflage to resemble bark or petals. All have huge eyes, mounted on a mobile, triangular head, and lethal forelegs, held clasped together as if in prayer, with which they snatch victims. In some species, the female chews off her mate's head during mating – though he usually manages to finish the job, since his copulatory movements are regulated by the last ganglion of the abdomen. Mantid eggs are laid in a foamy nest called an *ootheca*.

Left Huge compound eyes give a dragonfly predatory omniscience. (LH)
Right A praying mantis holds its front legs ready to strike. (MM/FPLA)

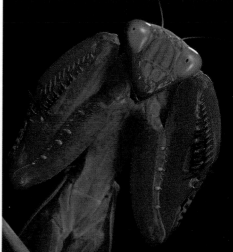

Above Pyrgomorphid grasshoppers flaunt bright warning colours. (LH)
Left Brown locust nymphs – or hoppers – gather in huge, hungry swarms. (PP)

Crickets and grasshoppers (Orthoptera) are vegetarians, not hunters. They have powerful hind legs for leaping, and proclaim their territory with a symphony of bleats and chirrups, produced by rubbing various body parts rhythmically together. Long-horned, nocturnal species are generally known as crickets, and include the armoured ground crickets (Tettigoniidae), the big king crickets (Stenopelmatidae) – known to Johannesburg residents as 'Parktown Prawns' – and the lawn-burrowing mole crickets (Grylloptalpidae). Short-horned, diurnal species are generally known as grasshoppers, and include the superbly camouflaged toad grasshoppers (Pamphagidae), the bright-green bladder grasshoppers (Pneumoridae) that inflate their entire abdomens as resonators, and various locusts (Acrididae), whose nymphs may descend on crops in voracious swarms. Stick insects (Phasmatodea) are also vegetarians, and have a body that exactly mimics a twig or grass stem. Like some mantids and grasshoppers, many flash bold markings on their hindwings to confuse a predator. The largest stick insect species can reach a length of 25cm.

Bugs (Hemiptera) use piercing and sucking mouth parts for extracting juices. There are over 4,000 species, ranging from predatory assassin bugs (Reduviidae), which can deliver a painful bite from their strong, curved proboscis, to herbivorous stink bugs (Pentatomidae) which suck sap from plants, and cicadas (Cicadidae), whose nymphs feed on root sap below ground, taking up to 17 years to develop. Adult cicadas live for only a fortnight or so, during which males attract mates with their ear-splitting zinging call, created by the rapid vibration of a membrane in their hollow resonating abdomen. Cockroaches (Blattodea) look superficially similar to some bugs, but are identified by their flattened shape and long, fine antennae. Some exotic species, such as the American cockroach, are much reviled for infesting homes and spreading disease. However, many harmless indigenous varieties can be found living beneath bark or under stones. All cockroaches are omnivorous, and most can fly.

BEETLES

Beetles (Coleoptera) constitute by far the largest single order in the entire animal kingdom. Over 18,000 species have been identified in southern Africa alone, all of which have biting mouthparts and forewings modified into hardened cases (elytra). The sheer variety among beetles is staggering. Some, such as ground beetles (Carabidae) and tiger beetles (Cicindellidae), are fast-moving, wingless predators that hunt down their prey by sight. Others, such as fruit chafers (Cetoniinae), are day-flying vegetarians that feed on flowers, fruit and fermenting sap. Many, including the ominously named blister beetles (Meloidae), pack a noxious defensive spray and sport bright warning colours to advertise the fact. Among the most extraordinary beetles are those of the cantheroid group, better known as glow-worms and fireflies (Lampyridae), whose adults illuminate their abdomen to attract a mate. Female glow-worms remain immobile and emit a steady glow, while male fireflies emit regular pulses in flight. This is the most efficient form of light known to science, being entirely chemical and generating no heat.

Above Fruit chafer (LH)
Below Dung beetles (AZ)

Dung beetles (Scarabaeinae) are robust black or brown beetles that can be seen piling into fresh animal droppings and rolling away balls of dung backwards, often crashing into obstacles and battling violently with each other in their haste to secure the prize. Inside these balls, called brood balls, a female lays her eggs. One brood ball can be 40 times the weight of its roller, which gives some idea of the beetle's strength. Some species roll their brood balls away, others lay their eggs right underneath the mound. Either way, dung beetles play a vital role in soil fertilisation. Their efficiency at waste disposal has even led to them being exported to Australia, which lacks indigenous invertebrates to clear up the countless tonnes of alien cattle dung smothering the outback.

DESERT SPRINTERS

The Tenebrionidae are a group of mostly flightless, ground-dwelling beetles, many of which are indigenous to southern Africa – including the 'tok-tokkie' beetles, which tap their abdomen audibly against the ground to attract a mate. Most are well adapted to hot, arid habitats. They bury themselves in sand or sprint on long legs between patches of shade, while fused wing cases prevent dehydration through the spiracles (breathing holes). In the rainless Namib, some species obtain water by 'fog basking': they plant themselves head-down on a dune crest and allowing condensing fog droplets to run down into their mouthparts.

Fog-drinking beetles in the Namib Desert. (WD/FLPA)

FLIES

It is hardly surprising that flies (Diptera) are among the most unpopular of insects, given their general association with putrefaction and disease. However, like all other 'pests', each species has evolved to suit its environment, and many perform vital ecological services such as waste disposal and pollination. All flies have mouthparts adapted to feeding on liquid matter, which they digest outside the body. There are 6,260 species in southern Africa, including predators such as robber flies (Asilidae), which snatch other insects in flight, and nectar-eaters such as hoverflies (Syrphidae), which dip into flowers with their long proboscis. Blowflies (Calliphoridae) are carrion-eaters, and lay their eggs in carcasses from which their larvae – or maggots – hatch in huge numbers to feast on the rotting flesh.

BLOOD LUST

While some flies lap up nectar and juices, others have more carnal tastes. One such bloodsucker, the tsetse fly (family Glossinidae), has proved a historical ally to wildlife by spreading the devastating livestock disease *nagana* and thus impeding the advance of cattle farming. Today, however, insecticides have eradicated the tsetse fly from all but the most northern, subtropical areas, and although it can transmit sleeping sickness (Trypanosamiasis) to livestock, this fly is not a serious threat to people.

A female *Anopheles* mosquito quenches its thirst for blood. (NC/FLPA)

Unfortunately, the same cannot be said of mosquitoes. These innocuous-looking little flies are primarily nectar-feeders, but females also suck blood from vertebrate hosts and it is females of the *Anopheles* genus – identified by a body angled downward at rest – that are responsible for transmitting malaria, estimated to kill more than two million people in Africa each year. Malaria is caused by a microscopic parasite carried in the mosquito's saliva, and the anaesthetic properties of this saliva leave the victim unaware of being bitten. Since mosquitoes lay their eggs in water and their larvae are aquatic, they are rare in the arid west. But low-lying, well-watered areas in the north and east are all potentially malarial and that irritating whine in the ear should be taken seriously by any visitor (see page 234).

BUTTERFLIES AND MOTHS

Gaudy, harmless (mostly) and fond of flowers, butterflies (Lepidoptera) are the hippies of the insect world and enjoy a better press than most other insects – including their cousins, moths. Actually there is little distinction between the two. Broadly speaking, butterflies are colourful, day-flying insects with thin, clubbed antennae that hold their wings vertically at rest, whereas moths are drab (with some garish exceptions), night-flying insects with feathery antennae that fold their wings roof-wise. Adults of both uncoil a long proboscis to sup on nectar, sap and fruit juices. Their eggs hatch into voracious caterpillars that develop into pupae from which new adults emerge. Butterfly pupae are naked, whereas moth pupae are often encased in a silk cocoon.

Top left African monarch – or one of its many imitators? (MU) *Top right* The garden acraea has a taste for the flowers of *Passiflora* vines. (WM/FLPA) *Above* Emperor moths flash eye-markings to baffle nervous predators. (MU)

Anyone brought up on a more limited selection of butterflies – in my case, the UK's 55 resident species, each with a handy common name – is easily dazzled by southern Africa's pageant of 800-plus. Rotting fruit, fresh dung and evaporating puddles often draw many different species in search of food and mineral salts, while some, such as the brown-veined white (*Belenois aurota*), migrate in countless millions. Thankfully a number of common species are instantly recognisable by their markings and behaviour: the yellow pansy (*Junonia hierta*) often suns itself to display the diagnostic purple spots on its black and orange wings; by contrast, the gold-banded forester (*Euphaedra neophron*) affords only brief glimpses of its brilliant metallic blue, black and gold wings as it swoops along forest trails. Some species use markings for self-defence: the African monarch (*Danaus chrysippus*) is toxic to predators, and its bold black, white and orange warning pattern (see page 217) is mimicked for protection by several other species. Many butterflies, such as swallowtails (Papilionidae), sport eye markings and tails on their hind wings to distract a predator's attention from their head. Confusingly, the common citrus swallowtail (*Papilio demodocus*) is tail-less (see page 207), though its caterpillar does a great bird-dropping impression. The emperor swallowtail (*Papilio ophidicephalus*), found in forest glades from the Cape to eastern Zimbabwe, is the largest butterfly in the region, with a wingspan of up to 12cm.

Stingers, loopers and munchers

If you find butterflies hard to identify, then moths – of which there are ten times as many species – may drive you to despair. A few larger ones are distinctive, such as the spectacular emperor moths (Saturniidae), with their broad wings (up to 15cm across), bold eye markings and – in some species – long tails, and the dashing hawk moths (Sphingidae) with their thick-set body and delta-shaped wings. However, many moths are better known by their caterpillars. Slug moth caterpillars (Limacodidae) are fat, green and armed with painful, poisonous spines. Tiger moth caterpillars (Arctiidae) are also best left alone, since their coat of woolly hairs contains a nasty toxic irritant. Looper moth caterpillars (Geometridae) take a more discreet approach to self-preservation by disguising themselves as twigs – invisible until they start 'looping' along a branch.

Some caterpillars are serious pests: the notorious crop-devouring army worms and stalk borers are the larvae of owl moth species (Noctuidae). By way of compensation, the caterpillars of one emperor moth species, known as mopane worms, are harvested in large numbers from mopane woodland. Cooked up with a tomato and onion relish, they make a delicious accompaniment to mealie pap.

The 'mopane worm' is the caterpillar of the emperor moth *Gonimbrasia balina*.

TERMITES

Termites (Isoptera) are perhaps the most amazing, though in evolutionary terms the most primitive of the social insects. Popularly known as 'white ants', they are actually unrelated to ants, but have evolved many similarities of lifestyle. So successful are termites, that it has been estimated they constitute the largest biomass (combined weight) of herbivores in African savannahs – in other words, their total weight exceeds that of antelope. The many varieties of termite all share similar social structures. Each colony has soldiers that protect the nest, workers that care for young and forage for food and an egg-laying queen who is fertilised by a resident king. All termites are vegetarian: some carry micro-organisms in their gut that enable them to digest plant cellulose; others cultivate a fungus (*Termitomyces*) to do this job for them. Although termites can cause serious damage to timber and crops, on balance this is outweighed by the essential work they do in draining, enriching and aerating the soil.

Not all termites build mounds – harvester termites (Hodotermitidae) leave little evidence of their underground tunnels above the surface – but those that do, the Macrotermitidae species, are responsible for one of the true wonders of nature. Communicating entirely through pheromones (chemical signals), millions of blind workers can raise several tons of soil, particle by particle, into an enormous structure – over three metres high in some subtropical species – in which separate

A termite mound makes a useful territorial marker for this black-backed jackal. (AZ)

chambers house brood galleries, food stores, fungus combs and the queen's royal cell. The queen produces up to 30,000 eggs a day, which means – since she lives for many years – that the millions of inhabitants of the colony are all brothers and sisters. The whole structure is prevented from overheating by a miraculous air-conditioning system. Warm air rises from the nest chambers, up a central chimney, into thin-walled ventilation flues near the surface (you can feel the warmth by placing your hand inside one of the upper vents). Here it is cooled and replenished with oxygen, before circulating back down through separate passages and cavities into the nest chambers, passing *en route* through specially constructed cooling vanes, kept damp by the termites. In this way, termites maintain the 100% humidity and constant temperature of 29–31°C required for successful production of eggs and young. During the rains, when conditions are right, the queen produces a reproductive caste of winged males and females – known as imagoes – who leave the colonies in huge 'emergences' to mate, disperse and establish new nests, providing a seasonal feast for many other creatures (see page 236).

ANTS, BEES AND WASPS

Like termites, ants, bees and wasps (Hymenoptera) are largely social insects, though they belong to a more advanced order in which all species pass through a larval and pupal stage. Ants (Formicidae) are the most advanced of all. Some species live in underground colonies of millions. Others live in smaller colonies inside hollow acacia thorns or use chewed plant matter to build their nests in trees. All colonies contain one queen and many wingless workers, some of which are soldiers responsible for defence. When conditions are right, the queen produces winged males and females that leave the nest in mass nuptial flights. Males die immediately after mating, but females disperse in search of new nest sites. Different species of ants feed in different ways. Some, such as driver ants (Dorylinae), swarm over large areas in a relentless quest for food, devouring any prey unable to escape (and ruining many a promising picnic). Others, such as Myrmicine ants, 'farm' aphids inside their nests, stimulating them to produce 'honey dew' (excreted plant sap) for their larvae. Communication within the colony involves a combination of scent trails, pheromones and, in some species, chirping calls. Threats are repelled with bites or stings, and formicine ants (Formicinae) can also spray formic acid at an attacker, leaving a distinct vinegary smell.

A female sand wasp drags a paralysed caterpillar to feed her larvae in the burrow. (PN/FLPA)

Parasites and architects

Wasps, closely related to ants, are day-flying insects, with two pairs of wings and usually a thin waist between the thorax and abdomen. The females of many species use their modified ovipositor to inflict a powerful sting in self-defence. This lethal weapon is also used by parasitic species, such as spider-hunting wasps (Pompilidae), to paralyse prey, which they feed to their carnivorous young. Some parasitic wasps cache their victim in a burrow and lay their eggs on it, so that the newly hatched larvae have a ready, live food source. Ichneumon wasps (Ichneumonidae) use their long ovipositors to burrow into plant stems and lay their eggs directly into the larvae of wood-boring moths and beetles. Other wasps construct nests for their young: potter wasps (Eumenidae) create a variety of ingenious chimneys and pots out of mud; paper wasps (Vespidae) work with wood pulp to build delicate multi-celled apartment structures, which they defend against all comers.

Dancing for honey

Bees (Apoidea), unlike most wasps, feed their young on nectar and pollen – helping to pollinate plants in the process. Some varieties are solitary, such as the hole-drilling carpenter bees (Xylocopinae) – which resemble European bumble bees. Others, such as the honey bee (*Apis mellifera*), are highly colonial. A honey-bee colony, often located in a tree hole, can house many thousands of individuals, all graded within a rigid caste system. Female workers collect food and maintain the colony, while males mate with the queen who lays her eggs in the wax cells of the comb. Communication inside the nest includes an extraordinary 'sun dance', in which workers use a strictly choreographed dance routine to indicate the precise direction of food in relation to the sun. Though honey is considered a great delicacy by man and beast alike, honey bees can be extremely dangerous when their nest is threatened.

African honey-bees swarm outside their tree trunk nest hollow in the Kruger Park. (C&TS/FLPA)

TRACKS AND SIGNS

Lion tracks after Kalahari rains (PP)

nimals seldom parade across the bush the way they do across a TV screen. In fact, the untamed wilderness, far from teeming with wall-to-wall wildlife, can sometimes seems a disappointingly empty place. But there is much more to see than simply the animals themselves, and the trained eye will find the land littered with evidence of their presence or passing: tracks and trails, pellets and droppings, diggings and rubbings, torn branches, flattened grass, feathers, nests and bones. These clues, often known by

An elephant's tracks show a criss-cross of cracks on the soles, with the oval hindfoot printed over the larger, rounder forefoot. The indentation and mound of sand at the leading edge shows that this jumbo exited stage left. (HB)

the Afrikaans word *spoor*, tell the story of what happened when nobody was looking. The Khoisan people once depended for their survival on a remarkable ability to find and interpret them. Today, some awareness of tracks and signs will greatly enrich your own understanding of wildlife. Trackers, like forensic detectives, combine acute eyesight and vigilance with great patience, a photographic memory and the imagination to reconstruct a complete picture from a few scattered fragments. It is a humbling experience to watch an expert in action: a mere scratch in the soil can not only identify the animal responsible, but also reveal its age, sex, size, where it was heading, how it was moving, when it passed by and why.

MAKING TRACKS

Every animal that touches the ground leaves tracks. Some are easily recognised; others are more puzzling. Most small creatures, such as lizards, can only be identified to a broad generic level, but many larger mammal species have unique signatures. No two individuals of any species are identical, and the tracks of many show marked differences of size and shape between forefeet and hindfeet or between male and female. Conditions underfoot are critical to tracking. The clearest tracks are laid on surfaces that hold an impression, such as firm mud or damp sand. Hard, baked soil is too resistant, while soft sand allows slippage that distorts the shape. Weather is also important: wind and rain can help to date tracks, but may erode or completely obliterate them. Neither overcast weather nor a midday sun are very helpful to trackers. Early morning is the best time to look – partly because tracks are still fresh, but also because the low light and slanting shadows throw any imprint into sharper relief.

The cloven-hoofed tracks of a gemsbok spread out in the soft sand of the Namib Desert. (MU)

THE HEAVY BRIGADE

The bigger the animal, the harder its footfall. Elephants leave huge, round tracks, up to half a metre across, with the hindfeet smaller and more oval than the forefeet. In soft mud they create knee-deep craters that become sunbaked into a treacherous pitted moonscape. On hard ground, the latticework of cracks on their soles leaves a distinct, mosaic-like impression, even though the circular track outline may be invisible. A small heap of soil in front of each print indicates the elephant's direction (the rear of each track shows a clean edge). Rhino tracks have a clover-leaf shape, with each foot showing three distinct toes. On hard ground only the curved outer rim of each toenail may be visible. White rhinos have larger tracks (up to 30cm long) than black rhinos (about 24cm), with relatively broader toe marks. Hippos leave tracks of a similar size, but spaced more closely together and showing four clear toes on each foot. Their regular trails to and from water leave two, deep, parallel ruts either side of a central ridge.

ON THE HOOF

Most ungulates leave symmetrical cloven-hoofed tracks. Those of antelope differ in little other than size, though some, like an impala's, are pointed, while others, like a kudu's, are more rounded. Identification often depends upon other clues: for example, an impala's tracks are likely to be in a herd and unlikely to be on a hillside. A few antelope show more unusual tracks: a sitatunga's are very long (over 15cm in the male) and widely splayed for bounding over marshy terrain, while klipspringers drill neat round holes with their cylindrical tip-toed hooves. A giraffe's enormous hooves (up to 20cm long) leave imprints like a steam iron, spaced far apart by its great stride. A buffalo has tracks like a cow – larger and rounder than any antelope's except an eland. A warthog's are also quite rounded, with the two halves clearly separated. Zebra, with only a single big hoof on each foot, leave horseshoe tracks, the size of a donkey's.

Above Conditions underfoot determine the form and clarity of tracks. These three prints were each left by a white rhino, in mud (*top*), very soft mud (*centre*) and on harder ground after rain (*below*). Each one shows the tell-tale clover-leaf shape, with the curved edges of the three toenails. (MU)

Below A giraffe's tracks reveal its cloven hooves – just like an antelope's, only much bigger. (MU)

223

PADS, PAWS AND CLAWS

Most predator tracks show the typical pad and toes arrangement of domestic cats and dogs. The crucial things to look for are size, shape, number of toes and whether or not claws are visible. The male lion's are the biggest (up to 15cm long) and, like

The long claws of a white-tailed mongoose are clearly visible in its tracks. (MU)

all cats, each shows four well-spaced, rounded toes and two small indentations in the back of the pad (see page 221). Except for the cheetah, whose claws are permanently extended, cats do not leave claw marks. Conversely, all dog tracks show claws, and most have a longer, narrower shape than a cat's, with all four toes set in front of the pad. A hyena's tracks also show claws, but the curved toes are tucked closer together and the back of the pad slopes at a distinct diagonal. Spotted hyena tracks are about 10cm long, similar in size to a leopard's, and are commonly found around camp sites. Mustelid tracks have five toes: an otter's show the hand-like spread of its dextrous fingers; a honey badger's show the furrows of its long claws, set well ahead of the toes. A genet's neat tracks resemble a tiny cat's – four-toed, clawless and rounded – but spaced close together by its short-legged gait. Most mongooses leave small, clawed tracks, some showing a fifth hind toe set back behind the four in front.

MAMMAL VARIATIONS

An aardvark's tracks show only three toes on each foot, each one capped with a heavy claw mark, and its meandering trail is scattered with freshly excavated soil. Monkeys leave five-toed hand prints, with the opposable thumb or big toe clearly visible on each. The larger baboon's look particularly human, and are often confusingly overlaid where a whole troop has been active. A lesser bushbaby hops upright between trees, so leaves only the prints of its hindfeet. Squirrel tracks show longer hind feet than forefeet, and usually lead to and from a burrow or tree. A hare leaves tracks in sets of four, each of which shows the two front feet placed in line, one ahead of the other, and the overlapping back feet placed side-by-side in front. Rat and mice tracks are tiny and show four front toes, five hind toes and sometimes the drag mark of the tail.

BIRDS

Bird tracks can be roughly classified by the shape and arrangement of the toes. Most have three toes pointing forward and one back. In some, such as starlings or hornbills, the hind toe points straight back, while in others, such as doves, it is set at a slight angle. Korhaans and dikkops show no hind toe at all, while an ostrich shows only two toes in each of its enormous (20cm long) tracks and at least a metre's stride between them. The pattern of a bird's tracks reflects the way in which it moves: robins place both feet together in a series of well-spaced hops; doves follow a winding trail in which the feet move alternately in quick, short steps.

SCALE TRAILS

The undulating motion of a typical snake leaves a series of S-shaped ripples, where each curve has pushed against surface irregularities to propel the body forward. Heavy-bodied snakes, such as pythons and puff adders, can also grip the ground with their belly to push themselves along caterpillar-fashion, leaving a broad, straight furrow, stamped with the impression of belly scales and bisected by the thin drag-line of the tail tip. The sidewinding Peringuey's adder (see page 195) leaves a strange sequence of disconnected bracket marks where each violent undulation has flung its body off the hot sand.

Other distinctive reptile tracks include the metre-wide beach trail churned up by a sea-

Crocs may wander far over dry land during the dry season. Here, the distinct tail mark and – top right – hind foot, reveal where one crossed a patch of mopane woodland on its way to water. (MU)

turtle coming ashore to lay its eggs, the riverbank mud-chute of a crocodile – whose tracks show five splayed toes on the forefeet, four toes on the longer back feet, and a heavy furrow gouged by the tail – and the large, long-clawed prints of a monitor lizard, spaced either side of its wavy tail drag-line. Smaller lizards inscribe neat, winding tramlines of closely spaced prints which, in soft surfaces such as sand, can be hard to distinguish from those of beetles and other larger invertebrates.

DROPPINGS

Unsavoury as they may seem, droppings can speak volumes about the whereabouts and behaviour of animals. Many male mammals delineate their territory using the strategically placed whiff of dung. Some, such as rhino and civet, build up big middens with regular deposits; others, such as hyena and many antelope, roll in theirs to soak up the scent and spread it around. Some droppings are visible from a great distance: a splash of white often reveals the nest or roost of birds such as vultures or cormorants, while dassie colonies stain the rocks yellow and brown with their viscous urine.

A young male impala adds his contribution to a communal dung pile. Scent is a vital tool in the demarcation of territory. (MU)

Fresh elephant dung is quickly worked over by an army of dung beetles. (MU)

DEPOSITING A LOAD

An elephant scatters its fibrous, football-sized droppings anywhere, and elephant country remains littered with dung long after the herds have moved on. When fresh, these droppings are full of goodies, and a host of foragers, from baboons to francolins, pick through the steaming contents in search of seeds, fruits and pods. White rhino dung is fine in texture, consisting entirely of grass, whereas black rhino dung is full of twigs and other woody matter. Over time, a bull rhino builds up a waist-deep midden, spread over several square metres, into which he scrapes deep grooves with his hind feet to pick up the scent. In areas where both rhino species occur, one may deposit its dung on the midden of the other (see page 65). Hippo scatter their dung with their tail, plastering it messily over vegetation beside their trails. Buffalo droppings are black and loose, falling in folded 'pats' like domestic cattle's, and are often left trampled and smeared by the traffic of the herd.

PILES OF PELLETS

Antelope leave neat piles of dark pellets, each pointed at one end and indented at the other. Many, such as impala, use communal dung heaps. Antelope are so efficient at deriving moisture and sustenance from their food that even the largest species have remarkably small, dry droppings – though a wildebeest's may congeal in sticky clumps. A giraffe's droppings, also amazingly small, are widely scattered by their great drop. Zebras deposit their dark, kidney-shaped droppings in neat mounds, which grow paler with age and break down into heaps of fine, dry grass.

Hyena droppings (*below*, MU) are whitened by crunched-up bone. Lion droppings (*bottom*, PP) are full of fur and blood, and seemingly irresistible to butterflies.

SMELLY SCATS

Carnivore droppings – or scats – are cylindrical sausages, often pointed or twisted at one end – as any dog-owner will confirm. Because of their meat content, they tend to be smellier than those of herbivores. Hyena droppings are green when fresh, but turn to a conspicuous chalky white because of their high bone content. A lion's may also whiten with age, but can be black with blood, and are usually full of fur. Civet droppings are surprisingly large, and often contain the hard undigested exoskeletons of millipedes, as well as berries and insect husks. Otter droppings, or spraints, consist mostly of crushed crab shell and are deposited on rocks at the water's edge.

WHO'S AT HOME?

Many animals can be detected by the homes they build. Bird nests are the best known, and some, such as the enormous thatches of sociable weavers (see page 181) or hammerkops (see page 129) often provide shelter for a whole community of other animals. Tree holes offer a desirable residence to anything from hornbills and hoopoes to bushbabies and squirrels, and a promising-looking cavity is always worth watching during the breeding season. Burrows should be checked for signs of life: a complex of small holes may indicate a mongoose or ground squirrel colony, while a big burrow may house either the aardvark that dug it, or more recent tenants such as warthogs, wild cats or porcupines – so look out for signs of occupation, such as a snake skin or porcupine quill.

The state of an area's vegetation can also betray local residents with no permanent home. A flattened depression in long grass might be where a reedbuck bedded down for the night, while tattered bushes could be the work of a territorial bull sable, who thrashes them with his horns. Deep parallel gashes gouged into a tree trunk are the calling card of the local leopard, and a shiny tree stump beside a mud wallow is a 'rubbing post', polished to a smooth finish by generations of itchy rhinos.

FEEDING SIGNS

A good look at the landscape soon reveals who had what for dinner. Elephant are the messiest of eaters: freshly broken branches, peeled strips of bark and tussocks of grass tossed across the track are all sure signs of their presence, as are deep holes dug in sandy riverbeds for fresh water. Big grazers such as hippo or rhino trim clearly defined and well-managed lawns. Giraffe prune thorn trees up to a height of six metres, creating a visible browse line, and leave glistening strings of saliva in overhead branches. Kudu leave bushes frayed and nibbled at head height, while black rhino will even munch thorny, poisonous euphorbias, sometimes demolishing them entirely. Many smaller animals also refashion the landscape in their search for food: bark stripped from the foot of a tree trunk is probably the work of porcupines; excavations at the base of an anthill show where an aardvark dug for termites; shallow grubbings along a forest trail mark a bush pig's search for tasty tubers; a hillside littered with overturned stones shows the methodical foraging of baboons for lizards and scorpions.

Dry season concentrations of elephants can lay waste to large areas of bush, as seen here in Moremi, Botswana (MU)

A vervet monkey makes a decent snack for a leopard. No need to bother with the chewy bits. (MU)

Mortal remains

Predators usually leave evidence of their kills, though even a large carcass quickly disappears beneath an army of scavengers, as hyenas scatter the bones, vultures strip the skin, blowfly maggots consume the final shreds of flesh and ants clean the last drops of blood from the soil. Even the keratin of an antelope horn is food for the larvae of the horn-boring moth, which leave strange tubular casts along its length. Leopards often cheat scavengers, at least for a while, by hoisting their kill into a tree, so look out for hooves overhead. A scattering of feathers may reveal the regular plucking post of a raptor – which tears out tough flight feathers individually, leaving small, V-shaped punctures on the shafts, whereas a mammalian predator rips them out in clumps, shearing right through the quills with its teeth. Owls and other birds of prey regurgitate pellets of undigested bones and fur, often found beneath their roosts, while some shrikes (see page 175) impale prey such as lizards and grasshoppers on acacia thorns and barbed-wire fences.

Left A withered carcass found in one piece – such as this kudu – suggests a victim of drought, not predators. (MU) *Right* Flight feathers plucked out, not bitten through, reveal that this guineafowl fell victim to a raptor; probably a martial eagle. (MU)

MAKING THE MOST OF IT

Exploring the Okavango by mokoro (CM)

PLANNING YOUR TRIP

With such riches on offer, planning a wildlife trip to southern Africa can be bewildering. You can't see everything, so try to strike a balance between quantity (of sightings) and quality (of experience), and beware of over-stretching yourself. Although it is tempting to tick off all the seductive 'must-sees' of a guidebook, a thorough immersion in just one or two places is often more fulfilling, allowing you time to absorb the unique character of each, and also offering a better chance of finding their wildlife.

There is no wrong time to visit southern Africa, nor any wrong place to go, but be selective. Decide what you would most like to see and find out where and when this is to be found. You won't find rhinos in the Kalahari, nor will you spot whales off the Cape in April (they only arrive in June). In most big game parks, the end of the dry season (August to October) offers optimum viewing conditions, with animals gathering at shrinking water sources and the lack of greenery allowing good visibility. After the first good rains (usually in November), the herds disperse and lush growth makes spotting harder. However this is when many mammals have their young and birdlife is at its richest. The calendar opposite indicates some seasonal wildlife highlights, but read up before visiting, so that you set out with realistic expectations. Also bear in mind your own personal comfort: summer in the bushveld can be hot and insect-ridden, some roads become impassable, and certain reserves and trails close down during the hottest months; winter in the desert and mountains gets cold. But, if you don't like crowds, remember that the 'worst' times of year attract the fewest visitors.

CHOOSING A SAFARI

Safari is the Swahili word for 'journey', now used for almost any form of ecotourism. It evokes the romanticised ideal of Africa that lures most visitors: dusty plains, spreading thorn trees, the roar of lions beyond the crackle of the campfire. Southern Africa offers all this in abundance, and there are different ways to experience it. Your choice will depend upon several factors, including destination, time, budget and whether your priority is comfort or independence.

At the upmarket end of the price spectrum, private lodges aim to combine the thrill of the wilderness with the comforts of an exclusive hotel. Guests stay in permanent camps, from where they enjoy walks or drives with trained guides who

A luxury lodge overlooking Lake Kariba, Zimbabwe: elegance in the heart of the bush. (KB)

SEASONAL WILDLIFE HIGHLIGHTS

	Land mammals	Birds	Other wildlife
January	• Most mammals bearing young.	• Seed-eating birds breeding.	• Southern right whales depart Cape waters.
February	• First rains in the Kalahari: springbok drop their young. • Fruiting marula trees draw elephants and other fruit eaters. • Roaming herds gather at Savute Marsh (zebra) and Nxai Pan (zebra and wildebeest).	• First rains fall in and west: pollen and nectar-eating species come to flowers. • Flamingos breeding at Fischer Pan (Etosha) and Sowa Pan (Makgadikgadi).	• Humpback whales start to migrate north along east coast.
March	• In arid west, pans fill with late summer rains: peak concentrations of herbivores (springbok etc) on new growth in Kalahari riverbeds.	• Summer migrants (eg: European swallow, white stork) gather for departure.	• Deciduous trees – eg: mopane – start to shed leaves.
April	• Rut starts for impala, wildebeest, warthog etc.	• Winter-flowering aloes attract sunbirds and other pollinators.	• First rains fall on the fynbos.
May	• Grazing herds gather on savannah for winter grazing (eg: Kruger Park, Makgadikgadi Pans).		• Start of crocodile breeding season.
June		• Most raptors on the nest.	• Snow falls in Drakensberg.
July	• Many predators (eg: jackals) start courtship and breeding.		• Reptiles hibernate in cooler regions.
August			• Succulent Karoo in flower, attracting insects.
September	• Bush becomes drier, pans start to shrink and wildlife is more visible.	• Most birds calling, displaying and establishing territory.	• Humpback whales migrating south along east coast and start of whale shark season off Mozambique. • Southern right whale calves born in Cape waters.
October	• Height of dry season in bushveld: herds build up at waterholes and other water sources, eg: Etosha, Okavango, Chobe and Zambezi. Hippos gather in large pods. Numbers peak just before rains. • First rains fall in most regions: large mammals disperse to breed.	• First summer migrants arrive. • Passage waders (eg: curlew sandpiper) arrive on west coast.	• Most reptiles and amphibians breed with first rains: lizard displays; frog chorus; snakes emerge to hunt frogs; crocodiles lay eggs.
November	• Many mammals – eg: impala – drop their young to take advantage of new growth.	• Insect-eating birds breeding.	• Cape fur seals breed on west coast. • Sea turtles breed on east coast.
December	• Height of summer breeding season in bushveld.		

During the dry season, as competition for water intensifies, animals are forced closer together. At this waterhole in Etosha, giraffe, zebra and black rhino all respect each other's personal space. (PP)

know the terrain inside out, often right down to the territories of individual animals. Good lodges cater to the interests of their guests, so whether your passion is snakes or seed pods, you should find it indulged by an expert. The top places guarantee a memorable wildlife experience in a spectacular setting, with the minutest attention paid to your creature comforts. However, some visitors may miss the thrill of discovering things on their own terms.

A little less exclusive are 'participation' tours, where guests travel together between camps – often between countries – pitching their own tents and mucking in with the chores. These tours can get you to relatively inaccessible destinations, such as Moremi, reasonably cheaply. Everything is planned and provided, and your driver will also act as your guide. However, you may find the itinerary congested and inflexible, and will sometimes have to compromise your own interests (eg: birding) for the sake of the group. Consult your guidebooks and choose carefully: there are many operators on the market, some better than others.

With a little planning and initiative, there are many destinations you can explore under your own steam. This is true of most national parks in South Africa, Zimbabwe and Namibia, where reasonable roads, cheap campsites or self-catering accommodation and decent facilities (fuel, food, ablutions etc) means that you need only turn up with a vehicle and, to be assured a place, a reservation. Camping gear isn't usually available in reserves, but can be hired at many major towns. Being limited by your own knowledge and resources, you may not experience everything that a professional safari outfit offers. However, as an independent traveller, you can choose your own company, set your own priorities and follow your own pace, and the rewards can be that much greater when you've done the work yourself. Adventurous types who want to rough it in the back of beyond need planning and experience for a safe and successful trip (see page 248).

WHAT TO TAKE

All good **travel guides** are stuffed with practical advice (see *Further reading* page 278), and you should plan carefully before setting out. A few basics are worth emphasising here.

Binoculars are indispensable. Much of what you see will be distant, half hidden or only spotted by methodical scanning. If you're a first-timer, practise before you set out. And bring your own pair – don't rely on borrowing other people's, who may (understandably) refuse to share them at a critical moment. When choosing binoculars, remember that small, compact ones, such as 6x25mm, are handy to carry, but have a narrow field of view and perform badly in poor light, while large binoculars, such as 10x50mm, have powerful magnification and a broad field of view, but are heavier to lug around. A mid-range specification, such as 8x40mm, is a good practical compromise. Choice of brand is really a matter of budget: the most expensive binoculars have the best quality optics and are the most durable. Get a robust strap with a rain-guard (which works for dust too). Unless you are a serious birder, a telescope is generally too cumbersome to be practical.

A good **field guide** (see *Further reading*, page 278) helps you to identify what you see, not just by appearance, but also by habitat, behaviour and, crucially, distribution. Illustrated field guides are often more useful than photographic ones – especially for birds – since they allow easier comparison between similar species by standardising their depiction on the page. Some reserves sell field guides and most private lodges have a library, but it's safer to bring your own, particularly if you want to take them into the field or scribble on them.

Clothes should be loose-fitting, lightweight and breathable, and neutral colours are important when on foot (see page 239). For hotter regions and seasons, shorts (or lightweight longs for bush walks) and T-shirts will do for the day, with long trousers and sleeves for evening when temperatures drop and insects bite. Sandals are fine around camp and in vehicles, while sturdy trainers or lightweight boots will do for most walking activities. Pockets are useful for storing bits and bobs, such as camera film, when you need something in a hurry. A hat is essential, with a brim that will protect your neck and shade your eyes but not restrict your hearing. Serious hiking demands appropriate gear, and proper advice should be taken.

Other essentials

- Sunblock: always cream up thoroughly, and beware of overcast days – you can still burn.
- Insect repellent: use in the evenings, particularly in summer; when walking, spray over clothing to repel ticks.
- Sunglasses: useful for the open road, though they can impede your vision in the bush.
- Small daypack; pack a lightweight raincoat; carry spare plastic bags to protect books or cameras from a downpour or when in a boat.
- Lightweight towel: useful for padding camera gear as well as drying yourself.
- Full waterbottle: wherever you are, always have enough water to hand.
- First-aid kit: tours will provide their own, but there's no harm in doubling up.

HEALTH AND SAFETY

Consult the travel guides and take proper medical advice when planning your trip. A few basic precautions are worth emphasising here.

- **Inoculations** Find out well before you travel whether you need any jabs.
- **Malaria** This is a serious problem in many regions, especially during the rainy season. Take prophylaxes if you are visiting a malarial area. Always complete the course, and be alert to symptoms that may appear days or even weeks after returning home. Apply insect repellent, cover up after dark, burn mosquito coils and use a mosquito net where possible.
- **Sunstroke and dehydration** Avoid the sun during the hottest hours, wear a hat, use sunscreen and drink plenty of fluids.
- **Wild animals** Most wild animals avoid people, but all are potentially dangerous and should be treated with respect – especially those around camps that have lost their fear of humans. On a walking trail, your guide will brief you thoroughly (see page 241). Only elephants can seriously threaten a vehicle (see page 238).
- **Snakebite** Snakes shun people and bites are rare. Don't panic, but take simple precautions, like wearing closed shoes and watching where you put your hands and feet – especially if gathering firewood at dusk. In the event of a bite, get urgent medical help, but meanwhile lay the victim down, keep them still and calm and reassure them. An even pressure bandage wrapped around the bitten limb – working upwards from the site of the bite – helps inhibit the spread of venom. Never apply a tourniquet, take aspirins or cut an incision. Snakebite does not necessarily mean envenomation. The shock of being bitten – even by a harmless species – can produce phantom poisoning symptoms. Envenomation only occurs when venom enters the bloodstream. Different snakes have different types of venom – cytotoxic venom (eg: vipers), causes tissue damage; neurotoxic venom (eg: cobras and mambas), causes paralysis; haemotoxic venom (eg: boomslangs and vine snakes) prevents blood clotting – so it is helpful if you can identify the snake. But don't take any risks.
- **Other bites and stings** Scorpions, centipedes and some spiders can deliver nasty bites, though few are dangerous. Reduce the risk by not going barefoot, keeping your tent zipped up, and shaking out any shoes or bags left outside overnight. Tsetse flies (see page 217) are best avoided by wearing pale colours, while swarming bees are best just avoided. After walking in long grass, especially during summer, check yourself for ticks (see page 213).
- **Driving** Southern Africa's roads have a shocking accident rate, so drive with great caution at all times – particularly on public roads outside reserves. If possible, avoid driving at night. Stray livestock, vehicles without lights or brakes, potholes, grassfires, sudden storms and loose surfaces are common hazards that visiting motorists may not have encountered elsewhere. Drive defensively, watch your speed (never stray above 80km/h on a gravel road) and keep your eyes on the road.

LOOKING FOR ANIMALS

Out in the bush, the animals do not simply queue for your viewing pleasure. The areas are often vast, your access to them is limited, and the presence and whereabouts of wildlife depends upon a host of variables, including habitat, season, time of day, weather and availability of food and water. Luck helps – you might have missed that leopard crossing the road had you rounded the bend five seconds earlier or later – but a little understanding of the environment will improve your chances.

First, time your day wisely. Start early – you can catch up on sleep later – and give yourself a few quiet moments before setting out: the hour before sunrise is a magical time to sit and listen, with the last night noises mingling with the first notes of the dawn chorus. Then hit the trail before the sun comes up. Dawn offers a chance to see nocturnal creatures returning to their roosts, and perhaps catch predators on the hunt. It is also when many birds are at their most active, and tracks and signs are still fresh from the night before. Mid-morning is a good time to stake out a waterhole, since this is when many herbivores come to drink. As the day heats up, most larger animals head for shade or cool off in wallows, and many birds wilt into silence. Find somewhere comfortable and shaded yourself, and look for basking reptiles, raptors riding the thermals or monkeys and baboons unwinding. Late afternoon often brings buffalo herds to water and is a good time to find diurnal predators such as cheetah. By sunset, night creatures are already stirring and hunters setting out. Elephants often come to drink at dusk, while the fading light triggers a final chorus of birdsong, with robins and bulbuls singing on as owls and nightjars start up.

Be alert to the habitat. On an open plain, any elevation or pocket of shade is a potential refuge for animals; perhaps dassies perched on a kopje, lions lounging beneath a lala palm or an owl roosting in a baobab. When crossing a watercourse, dry or flowing, look carefully both ways, scan the water's edge, the rocks and reedbeds, and check for tracks in the sand. Scrutinise the immediate vicinity of waterholes for predators lying up nearby. Check holes and hideaways patiently:

When the going gets hot, the hot get sleepy – so look for slumbering shapes in the shade. The generous thatch of an umbrella thorn can shelter a whole pride of lions. (MU)

a hornbill's nest, hyena den or mongoose burrow may reveal its occupants. Use any vantage point for a thorough scan with binoculars: an apparently empty landscape may contain a distant browsing elephant, baboons traversing a cliff face or vultures circling above a kill. Ecotones, where two different habitats meet, often prove productive, especially for birds, and forest dwellers such as bush pigs and red duiker are best seen in clearings and along forest margins.

Anticipating an animal's needs will help you to find it. Water, particularly in the dry season and in arid habitats, attracts everything from thirsty herds of antelope to basking terrapins and foraging waders. Look for potential food sources: a large herd of buffalo is a magnet to lions, whose kills draw scavengers such as vultures and hyenas; elephants go mad for marula trees in season, while their droppings are picked through by francolins, baboons and dung beetles. Raptors flock to termite swarms; storks and jackals follow grass fires for the exodus of rodents and reptiles; and a fruiting sycamore fig provides a real bonanza, with hornbills, monkeys and turacos flocking to the canopy by day, bushbabies and fruitbats arriving by night and bushbuck foraging for pickings on the ground.

Weather is also important. Windy conditions drive many larger animals into cover, but an advancing storm front brings a wave of swifts in pursuit of the flying insects it stirs up. The first rains bring out reptiles and amphibians *en masse*, so listen for frogs and look for snakes on roads. Rain can produce good conditions underfoot

Many animals are surprisingly unperturbed by vehicles – provided their occupants don't get over-excited. These wild dogs in Sabi Sands, South Africa, are relaxed enough to feed their litter of pups in the open. (PP)

for fresh tracks, but may obliterate older evidence. Overcast weather deprives raptors of their thermals, but it encourages nocturnal predators to remain active during the day and hippos to linger longer on land.

ON WHEELS

The standard way to view wildlife in most larger reserves is on a 'game drive', so you should get used to being in a vehicle. The higher the vehicle the better, since height makes spotting and photography easier. Remember that you may be stuck in it for long periods, so make sure that you have everything you need – map, camera, water, spare film, binoculars, biscuits, field guide, cuddly toys etc – available, not locked away in the boot. At private camps, game drives are conducted in open vehicles. These are perfectly safe, however exposed you might feel. Animals perceive you as part of the vehicle, and therefore not a threat, but they will react immediately if you disrupt its outline (and their illusions) by standing up – or even just raising an arm. If you're joining a tour in a larger truck or minibus, check in advance that everyone gets a window seat and that all windows can be fully opened. A roof that can be opened (or 'pop top') is also a big plus.

Spotting is an acquired skill. Be constantly vigilant and keep adjusting your field of view. Remember that by scanning the horizon you may miss what's under your nose, and vice versa. Look into thickets, along river beds, beneath trees and among rocks. Check the skies for raptors and the road ahead for reptiles. Even huge animals like giraffes can be well camouflaged and hard to see, so look for movement: the slightest twitch of an ear or tail tip may reveal a quietly browsing kudu or slumbering cheetah. Your ears and nose will also detect many clues – a rustle in the grass, the crack of a breaking branch , the rich aroma of fresh dung. – so keep your windows wound down; don't seal off your senses behind glass and air conditioning.

In time, you'll develop an instinct for where to look and how to interpret what you hear. Your eyes will be drawn to a telltale contour among the foliage or shadows – and your ears will pick up sounds of movement or alarm. Be alert for the behaviour of other animals: shrieking baboons or a herd of impala staring intently in the same direction (see page 238) may signal a predator; the hissing of oxpeckers flying up from a bush may mean a rhino on the other side; agitated birds flocking into a tree suggests that they've discovered an owl or snake.

Follow the gaze: you might spot what these impala have just spotted. (MU)

To make spotting easier, drive slowly, allow plenty of time and don't go too far. It is tempting, when nothing appears to be about, to keep pushing on to the next point on the map. But hours at the wheel sap energy and erode vigilance, and an overlong journey can culminate in a frustrating dash to the camp for closing time, spoiling the final, most exciting hour of the day. Professional guides tend to cover small distances, and you will find that a round trip of 25 kilometres can easily sustain a three- or four-hour drive. With no time pressure you can stop whenever and wherever you want, or change direction on a whim. Good stopping points include waterholes, raised viewpoints and riverside loop roads. Choose one with comfortable all-round visibility and turn off your engine. Once you become a part of the landscape, wildlife will adjust to your presence and, with stillness, your eyes and ears will alight on details. Soon life begins to materialise – an African monarch struggling in a golden web beside your window; a motionless steenbok staring at you from a thicket – and you'll wonder what you've been missing with all that dashing about.

If you meet animals near the road, stop slowly (not by slamming on the brakes and spewing gravel), turn off your engine and sit quietly. Observe how different animals behave. Some, such as eland, are habitually shy and unapproachable. Others, such as zebra, can seem almost oblivious to vehicles and may come very close. Elephants are the only animal likely to threaten a vehicle, so always allow yourself room for manoeuvre around these giants. Usually they will feed peacefully close by, provided you stay still and don't rev the engine or sound the horn. However, if you have inadvertently upset them – for example by separating a mother and calf – then heed the warning signs and respect their space by moving away.

Show consideration to other drivers. A vehicle stopped ahead of you is likely to be watching something, which you may scare away if you roar up or overtake quickly. If you prefer to avoid other people, then stick to the back roads. But remember that a chat can sometimes prove very worthwhile.

Most importantly, enjoy what you see and don't worry about what you miss. A choice of routes often brings an agonising dilemma. If you saw nothing on the hill road last night, might there be something this morning? Or should you take the river road instead, where a pride of lions was seen last Friday? Relax. If you spend your whole trip chasing rumours of the big five, you'll miss the excitement and sense of discovery that comes from doing your own thing at your own pace. Take it slowly, be alert to the wider spectrum of life and – who knows – you might get lucky.

Night drives

Some parks and most private reserves offer guided night drives. These are an opportunity to spot shy nocturnal creatures or predators on the prowl by picking up their reflective 'eyeshine' in the beam of a spotlight. Experienced guides can often identify an animal from the height, colour or distance between the eyes: a single red eye on the road is likely to be a nightjar (perched side-on), while two eyes bouncing about in an acacia probably belong to a bushbaby. Roosting waxbills, the pale glow of a hunched chameleon, even the glitter of spider's eyes can catch the beam.

Eyeshine is visible surprisingly deep into the bush, but can only be seen by looking directly down the beam, so try to get behind the light. Once you've spotted an animal, keep the light away from its eyes so as not to blind or disorientate it – especially larger animals such as elephants or rhinos, which may become aggressive. Also watch the road ahead for small mammals, snakes and nocturnal birds such as nightjars and dikkops.

Night drives are hit-and-miss affairs. Your vision is restricted to the beam of the spotlight, so if this turns up nothing, then there is little else to do (and nights in the bush can be very cold). However, you might just catch a big cat hunting,

Nocturnal birds, like this square-tailed nightjar, often freeze in the spotlight, allowing an excellent view. (AZ)

and this is probably your only chance to see strictly nocturnal species such as bronze-winged courser or white-tailed mongoose. You may also be surprised by the amount of activity among creatures you thought to be diurnal: kudu, for example, browse right through the night. Many smaller parks, such as the Karoo National Park, run excellent night drives, with a chance of seeing local specialities such as aardwolf, caracal or bat-eared fox. Don't forget to bring binoculars, which work surprisingly well in the dark.

ON FOOT

In most reserves with potentially dangerous animals, visitors are confined to their vehicles except at designated spots. However, if you would like to feel big game country beneath your feet, many places now offer guided day walks or – even better – all-inclusive walking safaris. These offer a completely different experience from a game drive, with a total sensory immersion in the sights, sounds, smells and textures of the bush. You will feel the heat, dryness and dust as though for the first time, and discover that the 'flat' plains are rutted and fissured, that the ground swarms with ants, and that every other tree bristles with thorns and is strung with a sticky cat's cradle of cobwebs.

On foot you are the most obvious animal around, and the bush appears to empty at your approach: impala that seemed so tame from a car melt into the scrub; a black rhino detects your scent on the breeze from a kilometre away and thunders off. But you are meeting wildlife on its own terms. Lion tracks on the trail quicken the pulse like nothing spotted from a car, and the crack of a branch takes on a new and vital resonance. With time your senses will become attuned, you will appreciate the value of silence and will learn how to stay downwind or keep to cover. In the process, you will discover the secret details of the bush: the musty odour of a waterbuck's bedding spot; the heat inside a termite mound; the sweetness of a ripe marula.

Walking safaris (or wilderness trails) are led by professional armed guides, who will ensure not only that you return to camp – and getting lost is more of a danger than getting eaten – but also that you get the most from the walk. Sometimes there are two guides, one of whom acts a tracker while the other is responsible for the group, which should never comprise more than eight trailists. Before setting out you will receive a thorough safety briefing (walk in single file, no talking, click your fingers if you want to stop etc). All clothing should be neutral-coloured – a designer khaki safari outfit is pointless if crowned with a yellow baseball cap – and artificial scents are discouraged. Lightweight longs are better protection than shorts against ticks and thorns. Walking safaris are not endurance tests and the pace is usually relaxed, though the terrain can be rough. Your guides will spot most of the wildlife (however hawk-eyed you may think you are) and will enrich the experience by interpreting what you find and explaining the complex ecological jigsaw of the

An experienced walking guide can lead you close to large animals, such as these buffalo in Zambia's Luangwa Valley. Generally they are more scared of you than you are of them. Honest. (AZ)

bush. You will learn to identify tracks, calls and seed pods, and will absorb a wealth of fascinating information – from the underlying geology of the rock you're sitting on, to the medicinal uses of the tree sprouting from it.

Close encounters

The subject of Africa's dangerous wild animals is shrouded in myth and hyperbole, and it can be difficult to keep a sense of perspective amid all the grisly stories. All animals, including the big five, generally steer well clear of people. Attacks are very rare and certainly less of a danger than sunstroke, dehydration or simply getting lost. However, wild animals are potentially dangerous (which is of course part of their appeal), and it is wise not to become blasé. Experienced guides avoid dangerous situations and will judge whether it is safe to approach an animal or more prudent to back off. Problems generally arise only if walkers inadvertently breach an animal's comfort zone and it feels threatened. Obey your guide's instructions at all times. This usually means sticking close together, and not running unless told to. Most animals will signal their displeasure in time for you to retreat, giving them space to do the same. If things get serious, then shouting or throwing rocks usually does the trick and the gun is the very last resort – though I've never seen one needed.

The thrill of a walking trail: a two-tonne white rhino can pop up from behind the weediest shrub without warning. Check your shoelaces and look for the nearest tree – just in case. (MU)

Different animals react to people in different ways. Elephants can often be approached quite close while feeding contentedly, but cows with young and bulls in 'musth' may be dangerous. An angry elephant will flap its ears and trunk and advance a few paces in a 'mock charge' before pulling up in a cloud of dust. If you stand your ground and shout or clap it will back off, and then so can you. In a rare serious attack, an elephant will roll up its trunk, fold back its ears and lead with its tusks. Buffalo in a herd are placid creatures and will back away to let you pass, but lone bulls are unpredictable and may charge if they feel threatened.

Black rhinos are also notoriously irascible and may charge if they perceive a threat, although they are just as likely to crash off in the other direction. White rhinos have a more docile reputation, though guides warn against complacency near battling bulls or females with calves. A lone hippo on land by day should be given a wide berth, since it is in an environment where it feels insecure and may charge. Never get between a hippo and the water. If charged by any of the heavy brigade, your guide may instruct you to take cover behind (or preferably up) a tree, allowing the animal to thunder on past.

Predators are less of a problem. Lions generally clear off as soon as they become aware of people, though females with young cubs, or a mating pair, may stand their ground. An unhappy lion betrays its mood with low growling, flattened ears and a twitching tail, which may herald a mock charge. Standing tall and making loud confident noises will generally stop them in their tracks (this confidence may, admittedly, come more easily to your guide), but running will only encourage their pursuit instinct. Leopards shun people, and in southern Africa attacks have only been recorded from sick or wounded animals. In the extremely unlikely event that you meet an unhappy leopard at close quarters, you should back away slowly and avoid making eye contact. Of the other predators, spotted hyenas are potentially dangerous, especially habituated individuals around camps, and should be avoided – as should any suspiciously 'tame' jackal, which may be rabid.

Many first-timers worry most about snakes, though most snakes flee from your approach – even supposedly aggressive ones such as black mambas – and bites are very rare (see *Snakebite*, page 234). If a cornered mamba or cobra rears up, you should freeze, allowing it to relax and retreat. In the case of a spitting cobra, shield your eyes. Most bites come from the sluggish puff adder, which relies on camouflage and is less inclined to flee, so just wear decent footwear, watch where you step and heed its warning hiss.

A snouted cobra getting out of the way fast. (MU)

The most dangerous reptile, and the only animal likely to see you as prey, is the crocodile. Fatal attacks occasionally happen – mostly in rural, riverbank communities – but you'll be alright if you keep away from the water's edge.

BIRDING

Birding demands particular skills, and a good ear is essential. Many species, such as cuckoos, are more often heard than seen. Once you become familiar with common calls, you will be more alert to anything unusual. Some birders play tapes to lure birds into view, though this can disrupt bird behaviour and should not be overdone. Skilled guides can achieve the same thing by imitating bird calls themselves – I have watched a virtuoso guide at Ndumu (see page 271) whistle up white-browed robin-chat, scaly-throated honeyguide and, best of all, narina trogon, without moving from one spot. A rich food source warrants extra attention: flowering proteas or aloes are excellent for sunbirds and other nectar eaters, while fruiting fig trees draw frugivores such as mousebirds, louries and barbets, and insectivores such as flycatchers, drongos and honeyguides.

Narina trogon, at Swaziland's Phophonyane Falls: a rare treat for the patient birder. (RdV)

In forest and woodland, small birds often travel in mixed feeding parties, so if you come across birds in the canopy, wait a while to see what else arrives. Keep an eye on the skies – southern Africa's are teeming with raptors and a concerted scan usually reveals something. Explore rest camps, where birds visit feeding stations and you can easily familiarise yourself with the more common species. Binoculars and a good field guide (see page 233) are, of course, pre-requisites. Serious birders may also want to bring a telescope – particularly if they are visiting wetland habitats or using hides. One note of caution: birding in the African bush can have its hazards. Don't follow the call of a mystery bush-shrike into a thicket full of lions.

BACK IN CAMP

Back in camp it is easy to switch off and imagine that the wildlife show will only resume once you hit the road again. But camps and lodges can be very productive places to spend a few spare hours. Many overlook rivers or waterholes, so if you want to settle down with a book, why not find somewhere with a view and keep one eye open for action? Or take a stroll around camp to acquaint yourself with the local trees and sort out a few bird calls. Birdbaths and picnic tables attract a procession of species at midday, and camp is often the best place for a closer look at those smaller animals, such as squirrels or agamas, that never get top-billing on a game drive.

If your camp is fenced, try taking an after-dinner stroll. You may find a hyena pacing the perimeter, lured by the scent of barbecues, or a genet foraging for campfire scraps. Owls can be tracked down with a torch, while by the light of the ablutions block a cornucopia of insects is snapped up by lurking frogs and geckos. In unfenced camps, such as most of those in Botswana and Zimbabwe, you had best stay put after dark, since almost anything may wander through, including hippos, elephants, hyenas and lions.

OTHER WAYS TO WATCH WILDLIFE

HIKING

Hiking is the best and certainly the healthiest way to explore montane, grassland and fynbos habitats, where big game is absent or scarce. Outstanding hiking can be had in all the region's major uplands, including South Africa's Drakensberg and Cederberg mountains, Namibia's Naukluft Mountains and Waterberg Plateau, Zimbabwe's Eastern Highlands, Lesotho's Maluti Mountains and Swaziland's Malolotja, where you can take gentle day hikes through gorgeous scenery or set off for days at a time with compass and bulging backpack. Taking to the hills on foot allows a ground level appreciation of flora and smaller fauna, and your exertions may be rewarded by upland specials such as berg adder (*Bitis atropos*) or bald ibis. Don't let your hat cover your ears: you'll need them to hear the alarm whistle of a mountain reedbuck, the bark of a baboon, or the clatter of mountain zebra hooves down a hidden gulley. Scan ridgetops and hillsides, watch the trail for tracks and signs, and approach water carefully – you might surprise a giant kingfisher or even an otter.

Mountains can, of course, be cold, wet and dangerous, and in southern Africa all the usual rules apply (stout boots, warm and waterproof clothing, plenty of water, good map etc). Plan carefully, always tell someone else where you're going, and never stray off the path: long grass and scree are treacherous, and a hidden aardvark hole can put you in plaster. (I speak from experience.)

TAKE A RIDE

Horse-riding is another way to get out and about in search of wildlife. Like hiking, it is often best in upland regions inaccessible to vehicles, such as the Drakensberg or Zimbabwe's Eastern Highlands. Riders travel faster and further than foot-sloggers, and the scent of the horse masks your own, allowing you to get closer to animals. For the beginner, gentle guided trails are a wonderful and novel way to experience the bush. For the more adventurous and experienced, horseback safaris in Botswana's Okavango enter big-game country, where the possibility of encountering lions requires riders

Saddle up if you want to see the best of Lesotho. (KG)

Canoeing the Zambezi brings eyeball to eyeball encounters and fantastic photographic opportunities. (AZ/FLPA)

to be fully in control of their mounts. Pony trekking is definitely the best way to explore the rugged mountain kingdom of Lesotho. Don't expect to see big game, but there is some special birdlife and the scenery is as wild and beautiful as anywhere in the region. If ponies aren't big enough for you, try a Jumbo. Elephant-back safaris are possible in the Okavango and at Victoria Falls. You will not only see plenty of wildlife but will also make an intimate acquaintance with the (supposedly untamable) African elephant.

MESSING ABOUT IN BOATS

Boats are ideal vehicles for watching wildlife. One of the most exciting ways to do this is by paddling your own canoe. On a few major rivers, including the Zambezi, Kunene and Orange, various operators offer guided trips – either for just a few hours or on longer trails lasting several days. On the Zambezi, the silent approach of a canoe allows you to drift within metres of a grazing elephant or buffalo, or beneath a sandbank colony of bee-eaters. Its small size and manoeuvrability also allows you to explore hidden backwaters, and to stop at any point to take pictures or check out a skulking waterbird. The whole experience is largely one of blissful tranquility – until you meet hippos, when your best course of action is to hug the bank, allowing them access to the deeper water where they feel safer. Crocodiles are no threat, unless you're unlucky enough to capsize, in which case make straight for the nearest shore and don't attract attention by splashing around. Always keep any valuables and your camera (when you're not using it) in sealed plastic bags.

The same precautions apply when being poled in a dugout mokoro along the hidden waterways of the Okavango – an experience even more relaxing than canoeing, since your poler makes all the effort (see page 229). Here, with the sky framed between walls of papyrus, you nose silently through waterlilies, sneaking up on jacanas and pygmy geese, spotting water snakes and reedfrogs and – if you're lucky – surprising a sitatunga. Encounters with hippo or elephant are often eyeball to eyeball, so you must trust to the experience of your poler to guide you out of harm's way.

A less intimate, but nonetheless rich wildlife experience can be had on a motorised pleasure boat. On the Chobe River for example, launches run regular sundown cruises, which – particularly in the dry season – allow comfortable viewing of the great herds that come to drink, as well as the resident hippos and crocs and a wealth of birdlife. A boat cruise is the only way to see the wildlife of St Lucia's mangroves or visit the raucous marabou breeding colony on Moremi's Gcodikwe lagoon. The downside, wildlife-wise, of some popular cruises is sharing them with other, noisier people – especially if there's a bar on board.

WATCHING WILDLIFE AT SEA

Much of southern Africa's marine wildlife can be enjoyed from shore, especially at the great seal and seabird breeding colonies of the Atlantic and Cape coasts such as Bird Island and Cape Cross. Elsewhere, spotting chances are best from elevated positions. Between July and November, when southern right whales arrive to breed, excellent land-based whale-watching may be enjoyed from the

cliffs and headlands between Cape Point and Plettenberg Bay (particularly around the seaside town of Hermanus, where a resident crier announces sightings with blasts from a kudu-horn trumpet). June to July is the best time for cetaceans along the KwaZulu-Natal coast, as dolphins congregate offshore for the 'sardine run' (see page 32), while humpback whales migrating northwards often come within sight of the beach at Cape Vidal. Whale-watching can be tricky: try to anticipate where the beast will surface next, panning ahead with your binoculars. If you have only a brief glimpse, look for key identification features, such as the position of the dorsal fin (if it has one, which southern rights don't) and the shape and angle of the blow.

Headlands such as Cape Point are also good spots to scan for pelagic birds, particularly during stormy winter weather when they may be blown closer inshore. However, taking a boat out to sea greatly increases your chances of spotting these birds, as well as a wider

Close encounters off South Africa's Cape coast: southern right whale in Walker Bay (*top* IB/FLPA); great white shark in False Bay. (*above* MS/FLPA)

Coral reefs along the Indian Ocean coast (*above*, JJ) are home to a kaleidoscopic variety of fish, including the clown triggerfish, *Bastiloides conspicillum* (*inset*, JJ).

range of cetaceans and other sea creatures, including turtles, sharks and sunfish. Many different trips are available and each region has its own attractions: pelagic birding trips from Cape Town and Durban boast thousands of seabirds, including up to eight species of albatross; Walvis Bay trips also offer pelagic birds, as well as the local fur seals and Heaviside's dolphins; Plettenberg Bay is the top spot for southern right whales and St Lucia for humpbacks (all boats follow strict guidelines to avoid harassing whales); Mossel Bay offers a rare opportunity to observe great white sharks, as these formidable predators cruise the waters around Seal Island. All boat trips are, of course, subject to the vagaries of weather, and the winter seas of the Cape are the roughest in Africa, so warm waterproof clothes and a cast-iron stomach are recommended, whatever the time of year.

DIVING AND SNORKELLING

The coral reefs of southern Africa's northeastern coastline offer some of the finest diving and snorkelling on the continent. Top spots include Sodwana Bay in KwaZulu-Natal and the Bazaruto Archipelago in Mozambique. Here, a dazzling array of fishes, corals and invertebrates are found along the reef, while turtles, eagle rays and whale sharks are among the more impressive creatures encountered by divers beyond the drop-off. In the colder waters of the Cape, the truly intrepid diver can cage-dive among great white sharks. Underwater wildlife watching is a world of its own, beyond the scope of this book, and the keen diver should read further to find out more (see *Further reading* page 278).

ROUGHING IT

This book is not the place for a crash course on outward-bound survival. If you want to look for wildlife in remote places by yourself, or are simply driven by a pioneering urge to rough it in the African bush, then you must plan carefully, consult the right guidebooks (see *Further reading* page 278) and follow the advice of those more experienced than yourself. However, a few basic considerations are worth mentioning here.

CAMPING

If you have space (ie: a vehicle), bring a comfortable tent, preferably one that allows you to stand up and is not too claustrophobic for a daytime nap. It should be waterproof, with mosquito meshing to keeps insects out and let breezes in. Practise unpacking and pitching a new tent before your trip, to avoid later chaos in the dark and rain. Choose a flat, level site, avoiding game trails (especially hippo trails near water), dry river beds (prone to flash floods) and low-lying marshy areas (cold damp mists). Keep your tent zipped up, especially at night. Nothing will bother you inside a zipped tent, but NEVER sleep outside, especially in unfenced big-game country. Store any smelly food, such as meat or citrus fruit, in a vehicle overnight. Before turning in, wash up and pack away your cooking gear and take a final pee to avoid any hair-raising excursions in the small hours. Don't wander around after dark without a torch, watch where you put your hands and feet and never go barefoot.

In known crocodile haunts, swimming anywhere is foolish – even if assured that a particular pool is safe. Some campsites have *braai* (barbecue) stands, where you can cook by charcoal or gas. If you make your own fire, use wood sparingly, and bring your own supply rather than plundering the local environment. Small fires consume less fuel and are more manageable for cooking: you can balance your pot on a couple of stones in the flames. When you leave, bury the ash and remove any rubbish to dispose of at the next town, leaving the site looking as undisturbed as possible.

Other camping essentials include a ground mat, a sleeping bag (in hot places, a sleeping sheet will do), spare tent pegs, a mallet, a good torch (preferably two) with spare batteries, candles, matches, a simple portable stove (remember, gas stoves cannot be transported on planes), cooking equipment and water containers – kept permanently topped up.

DRIVING

Many roads in southern Africa are navigable only by four-wheel drive (4WD) vehicles. This is particularly true of Botswana, most of which lies on Kalahari sand. Don't be gung-ho. Find out about your route in advance and heed the official advice. If a 4WD is required, make sure you know how to use it and don't take a chance with anything less. Driving on sand, mud or salt pans and fording rivers requires skill and experience. In some places, two vehicles are recommended, so that one can winch out the other or go for help. You will need basic spare parts and tools (and

know what to do with them), at least two spare tyres, ample water and fuel, up-to-date maps and preferably a GPS for remote areas. You will also need a failsafe contingency plan for getting stuck: help can take a long time to arrive.

In a normal vehicle, be aware that apparently good tar roads may suddenly deteriorate into bone-jarring pot-holes, and stray livestock or wildlife is a serious hazard, especially at night. On dirt or gravel roads, always take it slowly, particularly when approaching corners, and use your gears for traction on the loose surface. Slow down for oncoming vehicles, which often leave a blinding dust cloud in their wake. Punctures are a fact of life: if you hire a vehicle, first make sure that it comes with a spare wheel, jack and wheel brace, and that you know how to use them. Always plan your petrol stops carefully – you may have to travel large distances between them – and remember that 4WDs guzzle fuel.

Making camp in the wilds of Gonarezhou, Zimbabwe. Going it alone in remote locations demands proper experience and the right gear. (KB)

PHOTOGRAPHY

Safaris tend to bring out the budding photographer in everybody, and today's high-quality gear makes excellent results possible for anybody. Anybody serious about their snapping should do proper research into equipment and techniques. Meanwhile, the following tips may be helpful for a first-timer.

EQUIPMENT

- **Camera** Make sure you know how yours works. If you buy a new camera, get in some practice before your trip; you don't want to be struggling with mysterious dials and displays at a critical moment.

- **Lenses** For a film or digital SLR camera, you will need a long lens – at least 230mm. A zoom is more versatile, though a fixed length may give sharper results. A wide-angle lens (eg: 28mm) allows panoramic shots, while a macro lens (or filter) gets you in close to small stuff. Remember that a digital camera will increase your lens magnification by about 50%, thus a 200mm lens becomes 300mm.

- **Image storage** A memory card of at least 4–5GB is best, plus at least two spares – you'll take more shots than you think. If using film, take plenty of it. Bear in mind that fast film is better for fast-moving subjects while slower film gives sharper definition, so a medium range (200–400ASA) is a good compromise.

- **Other equipment** A tripod (if you're serious) – or a beanbag as a less awkward alternative (you can improvise with a packet of rice); a flashgun is useful at night and for fill-in illumination by day; a polarising filter brings colour to bleached skies.

- **Protect your gear** Always use lens caps; change lenses in sheltered places and with the open camera body facing downwards, to avoid dust; use lens cleaning tissue, not spit or paraffin; bring a handy, portable camera bag that holds everything at once.

- **Don't forget** Instruction booklet; spare batteries; power supplies (for recharging your digital camera); spare memory cards / film.

TAKING PICTURES

Light conditions will determine your photographic options: it's difficult to use a long lens and fast shutter speed in poor light, while a bright midday glare may overexpose the subject. A digital SLR allows you to capture images in low light by raising the ISO value. An ideal time to photograph wildlife is often early morning or late afternoon, when rich colours and long slanting shadows add depth.

If your aim is simply to take a clear, well-lit portrait of your subject, make sure that there's nothing in the way and that the image is not lost against its background. A lilac-breasted roller photographed against the sky will appear silhouetted, but a little greenery behind the bird will reveal all its glorious colours (see page 160). Think about composition. You can often tell a more interesting story by capturing context, so try panning out a little to shrink your subject, or moving it off-centre. Shoot the same subject from different angles and distances. Elements of the background – a curve of shoreline, a diagonal branch or a reflected cloud – can all

A winning composition, beautifully lit, with the perfect exposure and depth of field. A shot of this quality requires skill, experience and – as ever with a leopard – a slice of luck. (AZ)

balance and enhance the image. Look for behaviour that brings life to a picture – the tense distance between predator and prey or the comedy of oxpeckers on the snout of a submerging hippo – and don't be afraid to experiment.

In order to anticipate good photo opportunities, observe the way animals use their habitat. Your vehicle is a movable hide. Find a good spot, such as a game trail leading to water or a favourite perch, get in position early, with the light behind you, and be patient. Keep all your windows down – you may want to swivel and photograph something behind you without moving the vehicle. And don't be afraid of the shutter: in a brief moment of action you may not have time to compose the perfect image, but one winner is worth 20 duds. Don't always aim to get as close as possible; watch how the animal behaves – it may move into a better position if allowed to relax. Avoid sudden movements. If you want to get closer to an animal, move when it looks away and freeze when it looks up. For small animals such as birds, reptiles or squirrels, keep a low profile, stay still and allow them to accept you as part of the environment.

One final warning (from bitter personal experience): unless you're a serious photographer, don't allow your camera to dominate the trip. Untimely equipment crises and frantic lens changing can ruin a magic moment, while lugging round an awkward and expensive pile of gear can prove more trouble than it's worth. Accept that you may miss a few shots and stock up on some decent memories instead.

MINIMUM-IMPACT CODE

All national parks have their own rules and regulations to protect the environment and safeguard visitors. You should aim to have a minimal impact on the environment wherever you are. Always follow these few simple guidelines:

- **Don't feed animals** All wild animals are potentially dangerous. Feeding them breaks down their fear of humans, distorts their natural diet and behaviour and encourages a dependency on handouts. When this happens, problem animals – from monkeys to elephants – have to be destroyed.
- **Stay on the road** It may be tempting to get closer to a slumbering lion by driving off road, or simply to test out your 4WD credentials. Don't. All tracks damage the environment by contributing to soil erosion and retarding vegetation growth. Also, you may well get stuck – or worse.
- **Hygiene** When camping rough, dig your pit toilet deep and fill it in when you move on. Burn used toilet paper. If you wash in a river or lake, soap up and wash it off on land to avoid polluting the water. Use biodegradable soap.
- **Rubbish** Remove all your waste, and if you find rubbish dropped by other people then grit your teeth and remove that too. Litter bins in campsites often overflow, so if possible bag up your rubbish and take it to the next town. Keep a supply of bin bags. Biodegradable waste can be burnt and buried along with ash from the fire.
- **Firewood** Bring your own, if possible, or buy wood supplied by the camps. Never chop branches from living trees.
- **Host communities** If you stay in an area inhabited by a local community, be respectful and sensitive. Ask permission to camp, pay appropriate fees where required (don't haggle), and don't take intrusive photographs without consent. Consult guidebooks for appropriate advice for different regions. Remember that you are a highly privileged intruder.
- **TAKE ONLY PICTURES; LEAVE ONLY FOOTPRINTS** It's a cliché, but a good one.

BACK HOME

Once you return from your trip, there are many ways to extend and develop your interest. Read up on what you have seen and experienced: there is a wealth of information on the subject, from websites and travel guides to coffee-table books and game-rangers' diaries (see *Further reading* page 278). Join clubs and societies to keep updated and informed, and to meet other people who share your interest. If you would like to help the conservation effort, there are many organisations who would welcome your contribution, either by campaigning or fund-raising at home, or by returning to the region to do volunteer work in the field.

WHERE TO GO

Female bushbuck at Victoria Falls (RT)

There are over 500 reserves or protected areas in which to look for southern Africa's wildlife, ranging from vast national parks, spanning thousands of square kilometres, to municipal botanical gardens. Each of the seven countries in the region has a different combination of habitats, with distinct wildlife attractions. The following account offers a broad overview of their basic wildlife and geography. Visitors planning a trip should consult the relevant travel guides for details.

BOTSWANA

Although Botswana has a surface area of over 580,000km², a little larger than France, its population density (or scarcity) is only about two people per square kilometre – one of the world's lowest. Most of the 1.7 million people live in the narrow 'Eastern Corridor'; elsewhere there lies a genuine and largely unspoilt wilderness. The country and its natural history are dominated by the dry, empty expanses of the Kalahari 'desert' (see page 14), yet, in the northwest, it also boasts one of the world's most important wetlands, the lush Okavango Delta (see page 27) and adjoining Linyanti Swamps. The rest of northern Botswana consists largely of mopane woodland, with moist savannah along the Chobe floodplain. Along the northern fringe of the Kalahari lie the sweeping grasslands of the Nxai Pan complex and the parched wastes of the Makgadikgadi Pans, while in the far northwest, the remote and beautiful Tsodilo Hills and Gcwihaba Hills (within which are Drotsky's Caves) relieve the general flatness. The rocky, undulating landscape of far southeast Botswana is more typical of neighbouring Zimbabwe and South Africa.

With neither sea, forest nor mountains, Botswana lacks the natural diversity offered by other countries in the region. But for sheer scale of wilderness and abundance of wildlife, it is hard to beat. Over 17% of the country is protected within national parks and reserves, and these include some of Africa's finest. For most visitors, Botswana means big game, and the dusty frontier town of Maun is now the hub of a prolific safari industry. Alhough there are government campsites in most reserves, roads are rough, facilities are minimal and exploring the wilderness can present serious challenges to the independent traveller. Most tour operators and private lodges target the more upmarket visitor, reflecting a government policy of low-impact, high-revenue tourism in order to fund conservation whilst preserving the environment. In Botswana, all parks, lodges and campsites are unfenced, so visitors should be prepared for some close encounters with the wild.

The **Okavango** region comprises a number of distinct areas. In the far northwest is the **Panhandle**, where the Okavango River flows southeast towards the delta. This is a birder's paradise, with Pel's fishing owl and African skimmer among the well-known residents. Further east, the **Delta** itself comprises a myriad islands and hippo-dredged papyrus channels, where a mokoro – or dugout – is the best way to get around. Here, wildlife includes hippos, crocodiles and the rare sitatunga, as well as numerous waterbirds. Herds of red lechwe splash through the shallows, while elephant and other large mammals occur on the larger islands. **Moremi Game Reserve**, abutting the northeast corner of the Delta, offers game viewing as rich as anywhere in Africa. This beautiful reserve is administered by the local community, and comprises 3,000km² of floodplain, waterways and mopane woodland, extending from **Chief's Island** in the west to the **Khwai River** in the northeast. Wildlife includes seasonal herds of elephant and buffalo, with abundant giraffe, zebra, waterbuck, kudu, red lechwe, tsessebe and impala. Roan and sable often venture out of the mopane to drink and white rhino have been reintroduced to the **Mombo** area of Chief's Island. Large predators include lion, spotted hyena, leopard and cheetah, and Moremi is the wild dog capital of Africa. Serval, bat-eared fox and side-striped jackal are all common. Bird highlights include wattled crane and slaty egret (*Egretta vinaceigula*) on the floodplains, Arnot's chat (*Myrmecocichla arnoti*) and barred owlet (*Glaucidium capense*) in the mopane, and a breeding colony of marabous on **Gcodikwe Lagoon**. North of the Okavango, extending into Namibia's Caprivi Strip, lie the **Linyanti Swamps** – sometimes linked to the Okavango via the seasonal Selinda spillway. This remote region harbours similar wildlife, and in the dry season it can be a magnet for game. There are a number of private fly-in lodges. Alternatively the region is more easily accessible from Namibia (see page 265).

Chobe National Park covers 11,700km² in the north of Botswana and is the country's premier national park, contiguous with the greater Okavango region to

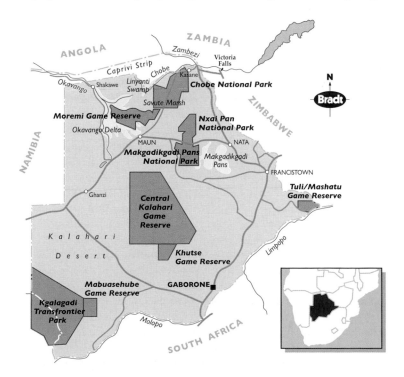

the west. It is justly famous for the huge elephant herds that congregate in the dry season along the **Chobe waterfront**, and this is the most popular part of the reserve – easily accessible from Victoria Falls or Livingstone, just across the nearby borders with Zimbabwe and Zambia respectively. Among the usual large herbivores are a few less common antelope, including red lechwe, Chobe bushbuck (a local, more boldly marked race) and puku – found nowhere else south of Zambia. Enormous herds of buffalo, sometimes thousands strong, draw lions on to the floodplains, while other predators include leopard, spotted hyena and wild dog. Baboons raid the campsites, while hippo, crocodiles and, with luck, Cape clawless otters, can be seen in the river. The riverfront is a waterbird paradise, with skimmers, fish eagles, bee-eaters and local highlights such as western banded snake eagle (*Circaetus cinerascens*). Chobe's elephant population is contiguous with that of Zimbabwe's Hwange National Park, and peak numbers can reach 60,000. In the rainy season most move

Double-banded courser (MU)

deeper into the park, congregating in the mopane woodland around **Ngwezumba Pans**, 100km south of the river. This area is also home to sable and roan, and is Botswana's only site for the rare oribi.

In the southwest of Chobe, across the notorious Magwikhwe sand ridge, lies **Savute** – a quite distinct area of dry marsh. In recent years the Savute Channel has resumed its flow, after drying up inexplicably in the early 1980s, and is once more attracting the abundant wildlife for which it is famous, including large lion prides, boisterous hyena clans and resident bull elephants that wander disarmingly through campsites. To the south, the grasslands of **Savute Marsh** are prime cheetah habitat, with bat-eared foxes, kori bustards and secretary birds among other conspicuous residents. This area, and the **Mababe Depression** further east, offer summer grazing for masses of zebra, along with wildebeest, tsessebe and their attendant predators.

East of the Okavango, deep in the northern Kalahari, lie the **Makgadikgadi Pans**. The two huge adjacent salt pans of **Sowa** and **Ntwetwe** are all that remain of a prehistoric 'superlake' that once covered central Botswana. Today these flat, lifeless crusts of silt briefly flood again after good rains, when flamingos and other waterbirds flock to breed. The surrounding palm-studded grasslands support typical Kalahari species such as springbok, springhare, ostrich, northern black korhaan and double-banded courser. The **Makgadikgadi Pans National Park** extends west from Ntwetwe Pan to the Boteti waterfront. Here, peak season (August–November) gatherings of zebra and other grazers attract lion and spotted hyena, while brown hyena and bat-eared fox can be seen around the pan margins. **Nxai Pan National Park** comprises a separate complex of more vegetated pans to the north, and includes the famous Baines' Baobabs of **Kudiakam Pan**. Here the wildlife follows a different seasonal pattern to that of Makgadikgadi. The arid grasslands are transformed by lush green summer growth (December–April), bringing huge

Red lechwe bounding through the shallows is a quintessential Okavango sight. (FL/FLPA)

breeding herds of zebra and other grazers to join the resident springbok. Herds of giraffe prune the acacia thickets, while the fringing mopane woodland shelters browsers such as impala, kudu and a few elephant. Predators include lion and spotted hyena, and this is good cheetah country. Grassland birds, such as kori bustard, are joined by summer migrants such as storks, bee-eaters and kites, while red-necked falcons nest in the stands of fan palms.

The **Kalahari** (see page 14) dominates the southern three-quarters of Botswana, comprising endless miles of arid savannah, with sandy, tree-lined watercourses and occasional exposed dunes. Summer rains fill scattered seasonal pans and bring growth to the grasslands, drawing nomadic herds of springbok, gemsbok, red hartebeest and other grazers – food for predators including lion, leopard, cheetah and spotted hyena. Key permanent residents include brown hyena, bat-eared fox, meerkat, ground squirrel, yellow mongoose and springhare, with birds such as ostrich, coursers, korhaans and sandgrouse. Barking geckos fill summer nights with their territorial calls and giant bullfrogs emerge with the rains to take over pans. However, wildlife in the Kalahari – particularly large mammals – is nomadic and shy, and though peak season can bring spectacular rewards, a trip into any of its remote reserves should be seen as a wilderness experience rather than a big-game safari. The vast **Central Kalahari Game Reserve**, right at the centre of Botswana, was established to protect the few indigenous San people who still pursue a traditional life there. Today there are a few public campsites, particularly in the **Deception Valley** area where huge herds of grazers gather after the rains. Adjoining this reserve to the south is the much smaller **Khutse Game Reserve**, where wildlife clusters around the pans. In the far southwest lies the **Kgalagadi Transfrontier Park**, a cross-border project that combines Botswana's undeveloped Gemsbok Park with South Africa's better known Kalahari Gemsbok Park to form the biggest conservation area in southern Africa, totalling 36,000km^2. This park is best explored from the South African side (see page 268) where a network of roads and waterholes makes life easier for visitors.

The **Eastern Corridor** is the most fertile and best watered area of Botswana, and is heavily farmed and populated. Its undulating landscape of mixed bushveld includes valleys, rocky outcrops and seasonal watercourses that drain into the perennial Limpopo and Shashe rivers (forming the borders with South Africa and Zimbabwe respectively). Much of this region is protected within the privately owned reserves of the **Tuli Block** – including **Mashatu Game Reserve**, which has southern Africa's largest elephant herd on private land. Wildlife includes animals of rocky terrain otherwise rare in Botswana, such as klipspringer, rock hyrax and Verreaux's eagle.

LESOTHO

Lesotho, with an area of 30,345km², is only about the size of Belgium, and is dwarfed by surrounding South Africa. However, the 'mountain kingdom' perched on top of the lofty Drakensberg has a rugged grandeur that belies its modest size. Dominated by the Maluti Mountains, it is the only country in the world where the entire surface area lies above one thousand metres, and in Thabana Ntlenyana (3,841m) it has Africa's highest peak south of Kilimanjaro. The bulk of Lesotho's two million people live in the western 'lowlands', an extension of the rolling grasslands of South Africa's Free State. Here, population pressures have severely degraded the environment, leaving little room for wildlife. By contrast, the eastern highlands is a wilderness of bare basalt peaks, thundering streams, deep gorges and barren alpine pastures where the scattered population subsists in isolated villages. Here the sturdy Basotho pony provides a lifeline of communication, and heavy winter snows leave many areas cut off for months at a time. From these peaks, some of South Africa's great rivers, including the Orange, the Caledon and the Tugela, carve their way down into the lowlands, and it is a land of dramatic waterfalls, including southern Africa's highest – the 192-metre **Maletsunyane Falls**.

Hiking or pony-trekking (the latter for those with buttocks of steel) are the best ways to explore Lesotho's wildlife and wilderness. Although dinosaur footprints are

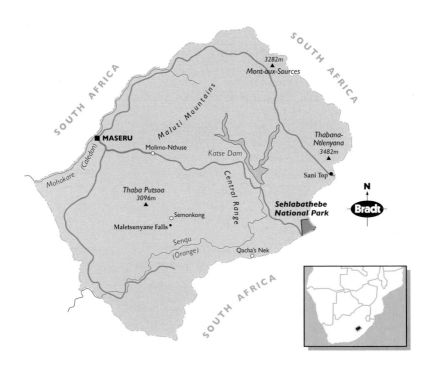

embedded in the rock along the Subeng River, large animals today are thin on the ground – partly because of the terrain and partly due to a history of hunting. In remote areas, antelope including grey rhebuck (supposedly unpalatable and so passed over by hunters), mountain reedbuck and a few shy eland can all be found. There are also baboon in the gorges, caracal, black-backed jackal and occasional rumours of leopard. Birding is more rewarding, and mountain specials include lammergeier, orange-breasted rockjumper (*Chaetops aurantius*) and Gurney's sugarbird (*Promerops gurneyi*).

Other plant and animal species include the threatened spiral aloe (*Aloe polyphylla*) which is virtually endemic to Lesotho, and the Maloti minnow (*pseudobarbus quathlambae*), once thought to be extinct, which has been rediscovered in the Tsoelikana River. A good selection of upland wildlife, including the rare oribi, can be seen in the **Sehlabathebe National Park**, a small, rugged reserve of 6,500 hectares in the remote eastern Qacha's Nek district.

The spiral aloe is confined to the remote uplands of Lesotho, where its survival is threatened by illegal plant collectors. (MU)

MOZAMBIQUE

Mozambique's coastline extends 2,500km from South Africa to Tanzania, and only the southern half of the country, as far north as the Zambezi River delta, falls within the southern African region. This half is dominated by the hot, low-lying savannah of the Mozambican plain, transected – from south to north – by the broad Inkomati, Limpopo and Save rivers. To the north and west, the land rises towards the central Mozambican plateau, and Mozambique's highest peak, Mt Binga (2,436m) stands on the western border with Zimbabwe. However it is the coast, flanked by coral reefs with their kaleidoscopic marine life, that remains the biggest lure for most visitors.

Of all countries in the region, Mozambique has seen the bloodiest human conflict. The civil war, which lasted much of the 1970s and '80s, left an impoverished and traumatised population and a devastated natural environment, with national parks plundered and wildlife widely eradicated (ivory was heavily poached to fund the conflict). Today, an ambitious process of rebuilding is restoring some of Mozambique's conservation areas to their former glory.

In the very south, the **Maputaland** region shares a coastal, dune-forest habitat with neighbouring KwaZulu Natal (see page 271). Here, a few elephant still survive in the **Maputo Elephant Reserve**, along with small antelope such as

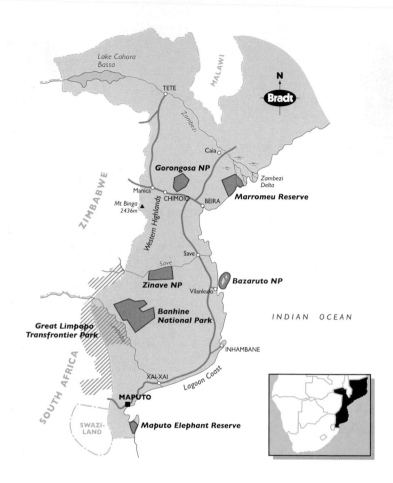

red duiker and suni, while the rich birdlife includes dune forest specials such as Neergaard's sunbird (*Cinnyris neergaardi*). North of the capital Maputo, the '**Lagoon Coast**' comprises a string of lakes trapped behind the dunes, where the shallow waters and marshy wetlands draw flamingos and many other waterbirds. Further north, the idyllic islands of the **Bazaruto Archipelago** are now protected within a national park, where three species of turtle breed, rare dugong graze the seagrass beds and crocodile hunt the island lakes. The coral reefs here offer some of the world's richest diving and snorkelling, while, offshore, whale sharks, manta rays and migrating humpback whales cruise the warm waters of the **Mozambique Channel**. Further north still, beyond Beira, the coast is lined with mangroves, extending as far as the **Zambezi Delta –** an inaccessible 1,500km² labyrinth of channels and islands, where good numbers of elephant, buffalo and hippo escaped the years of slaughter. The Zambezi River itself enters Mozambique in the far west through the enormous **Lake Cahora Bassa**, created in the 1970s to provide hydro-

Much of Mozambique's most interesting wildlife is found along its tropical coastline. The beaches aren't bad either. (CM)

electric power. South of the river, and inland of Beira, lies the famous **Gorongoza National Park**. Once devastated by the war, an impressive rehabilitation programme has seen the recovery of antelope populations, including sable, impala and oribi, the return of lion and elephant, and the reintroduction of zebra and buffalo. Among over 500 bird species in the region is the rare greenheaded oriole (*Oriolus chlorocephalus*). Southwest of Gorongoza are the **Chimanimani Mountains**, shared with Zimbabwe and home to a few shy eland, leopard and baboon. Further south still, **Banhine National Park** protects a mixed savannah and mopane woodland habitat, similar to the neighbouring Kruger Park and now forming part of the **Great Limpopo Transfrontier Park** (see page 8), which aims to link these regions in one vast 35,000km² conservation area.

Whale sharks are regular visitors to the Mozambique coast, providing spectacular encounters for snorkellers. (RD/FLPA)

NAMIBIA

Like its eastern neighbour Botswana, Namibia is a largely arid country dominated by great tracts of wilderness. With an area of 824,000km² – over twice that of its former coloniser Germany – and a population of two million, it shares Botswana's population density of about two people per square kilometre, making it one of the world's emptiest countries. However, Namibia's terrain is more varied than Botswana's, and its extremes seem that much more extreme. The country can be crudely divided from west to east into three sections: the Namib Desert runs for 1,600km down the Atlantic coast; the central escarpment rises from the desert on to a plateau that forms the spine of the country; the Kalahari slopes east from this plateau down to the border with Botswana. Rain falls largely from December to March, though some areas see none for years. The Caprivi Strip in the northeast hardly seems part of Namibia, with several major rivers feeding its lush, green landscape. Outside Caprivi however, Namibia's only permanent rivers are the Orange, along the southern border, and the Kunene, along the northern one.

Despite its forbidding landscapes, Namibia has a good transport network and is surprisingly easy to explore. The rewards are breathtaking scenery and abundant wildlife. Roughly 15% of the country (a staggering 99,000km²) is protected within reserves, and the healthy tourist infrastructure ranges from simple national park accommodation to upmarket lodges. Camping rough is a delight, but the hostile terrain should never be underestimated.

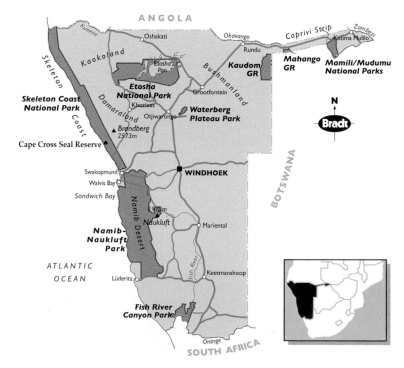

A hundred kilometres inland, the sand dunes of the Namib Desert give way to barren, gravel plains. Beyond lie the rugged hills of the Naukluft Plateau. (MU)

The **Namib Desert** comprises a variety of arid landscapes, including some of the driest on Earth. A field of enormous, shifting sand dunes extends inland from the coast, dominating the western reaches of the immense **Namib-Naukluft National Park**, with the most impressive arrayed in a much-photographed panorama around the dried pans of **Sossusvlei**. Here, even in the deepest desert, linear oases of greenery snake along subterranean watercourses, providing sustenance for hardy gemsbok, while a fascinating microcosm of lizards, scorpions and insects has evolved an armoury of tricks to survive the life-sapping conditions.

North and east of the dune fields lie apparently barren gravel flats, where tenacious flora includes the bizarre *Welwitschia mirabilis* (see page 21), minuscule lichens and various hardy *Commiphora* and *Euphorbia* species. After the rains, mountain zebra pick their way down from the escarpment to crop the new grasses, while bat-eared foxes, meerkats and other small predators scratch a living from the ground. Inland, the mountainous **Naukluft** section of the park straddles the edge of the escarpment, where mountain zebra thrive among the verdant ravines alongside baboon, leopard, kudu and klipspringer.

Along the **Atlantic coast**, the meeting of cold ocean and hot continent generates a regular fog that shrouds the coastline and rolls in across the Namib, bringing life-sustaining moisture to a range of plants and animals. Offshore, the nutrient-laden Benguela Current, welling up from the Antarctic, feeds a wealth of marine life. Seabirds, including flamingos, pelicans and migrant waders, flock to protected harbours such as **Sandwich Bay**, while cormorants, penguins, Cape fur seals and Heaviside's dolphins ply the waves for fish. Further north, the barren shore merges seamlessly with the desert to form the ominously named **Skeleton Coast**. Here, thousands of Cape fur seals breed at the huge **Cape Cross** colony,

A herd of desert elephants roams the wastes of Damaraland. (AZ/FLPA)

drawing scavenging black-backed jackals from the desert. Inland, **Damaraland** is a panoramic region of gravel plains, granite inselbergs and striking dolomite formations, where hillsides are daubed with cave paintings and the fauna includes endemic birds such as Ruppell's korhaan and Herero chat (*Namibornis herero*). Further north lies the remote **Kaokoveld**. This wasteland of rock, sand and gravel is transected by ancient, tree-lined watercourses that offer a lifeline to some remarkable desert populations of large mammals, including elephant, giraffe and Africa's only black rhinos to thrive outside a national park.

East of the Kaokoveld, a swathe of arid thorn and mopane scrub extends across the shallow soils of northern Namibia. **Etosha National Park**, the country's best-known nature reserve, dominates this region and centres upon the huge 6,000km² Etosha Pan – a blinding white expanse of dry clay. As the dry season wears on, animals gather at the waterholes and springs that fringe the pan. Peak-season game-viewing can be spectacular, and continues into the night at floodlit waterholes beside the camps. Most of southern Africa's large mammals occur here. Burchell's zebra, springbok, blue wildebeest, giraffe, kudu and elephant are particularly plentiful, along with eland, red hartebeest, roan, mountain zebra (to the west) and abundant predators such as lion, leopard, cheetah and spotted and brown hyena. Etosha specials include Damara dik-dik and black-faced impala, and it is probably the easiest place in Africa to observe black rhino at close quarters. In summer the game disperses, much of it trekking west into the hills, but flooded pans draw breeding flamingos and other waterbirds. Among over 350 bird species are blue crane, and the near-endemic violet woodhoopoe (*Phoeniculus damarensis*), Carp's tit (*Parus carpi*) and bare-cheeked babbler (*Turdoides gymnogenys*).

East of Etosha lies **Bushmanland**. This remote thornveld region of the northern Kalahari boasts the little-known **Kaudom Game Reserve**, where reedbuck, roan, tsessebe and wild dog all occur alongside more common bushveld species. Beyond Bushmanland, in the far northeast corner of Namibia, the improbable **Caprivi Strip** perches like a cap on top of Botswana, offering a rich mosaic of moist woodland and wetland that links this region with the Okavango and Chobe regions of Botswana. In western Caprivi, **Mahango Game Reserve** lies on the banks of the Okavango River. Here, elephant and buffalo (the latter rare in Namibia) gather during the dry season, and antelope include wildebeest, reedbuck, red lechwe, impala, roan and plentiful sable. Further east, **Mamili National Park** is situated in the **Linyanti Swamps** – a wetland region best explored by boat, with wildlife similar to that of the Okavango. Caprivi is an outstanding bird habitat, with nearly 400 species, including Dickinson's kestrel (*Falco dickinsoni*) and African finfoot.

South of Etosha, the **Waterberg Plateau Park** protects a rugged plateau ringed with imposing dolomite teeth. Hikers may meet klipspringer, Damara dik-dik and baboons, and birds include black eagles and Namibia's only colony of Cape vultures. A number of rare larger mammals have been reintroduced to their former habitat on the plateau, including white rhino, roan and sable. Further south, the **Central Plateau** is dominated by rough cattle-ranching country, on which a large proportion of Namibia's 2,000-strong cheetah population, the largest in Africa, still survives. To the east lies a scrubby Kalahari landscape of sand and gravel plains, relieved by scattered clay pans, rock outcrops and stands of the distinctive *kokerboom*, or quiver tree (*Aloe dichotoma*). In the far south, **Fish River Canyon**, the world's second largest canyon, cuts a 400m-deep rift through the plain and runs 65km south to the border with South Africa. The river seldom flows, but the canyon walls and permanent pools provide a refuge for wildlife, including klipspringer, baboon, rock hyrax and caracal.

Quiver trees sprout from the rocky hillsides of southern Namibia, creating weird, unearthly landscapes. Waxy leaves and fibrous branches allow them to conserve water in relentlessly arid conditions. (MU)

SOUTH AFRICA

South Africa is much the largest country in the region, with an area of nearly 1.2 million km². Its diversity of landscapes is matched by few others in the world, and includes arid semi-desert, moist tropical savannah, rolling grasslands, mountains capped with winter snows, deep primeval forests and over 2,000km of coastline. The land can be divided into three basic regions: the interior plateau, the eastern coastal plain and the Kalahari basin, each subdivided into a mosaic of more localised habitats. A tapestry of ecosystems ranges from the classic African bushveld of the northeast to the endemic floral wonders of the Cape. In short, South Africa is a wildlife paradise, and the 'world in one country' claims of the brochures are spot on.

Unfortunately, South Africa has also felt a heavy human hand, and centuries of agriculture and industry have irretrievably modified much of the land. Many precious habitats are reduced to protected pockets or marginal strips and, with a population approaching 45 million, the demand for land is not likely to abate. Gone are the great hardwood forests that blanketed much of the eastern Cape – felled for furniture and farmland; gone are the million-strong springbok herds that once trekked across the Karoo – ousted by fences and sheep farmers; gone is the precious indigenous flora of the highveld grasslands – ploughed up for wheat fields and blue-gum plantations. Today, however, South Africa shows an enlightened approach to conservation and the wherewithal to put it into action. An impressive

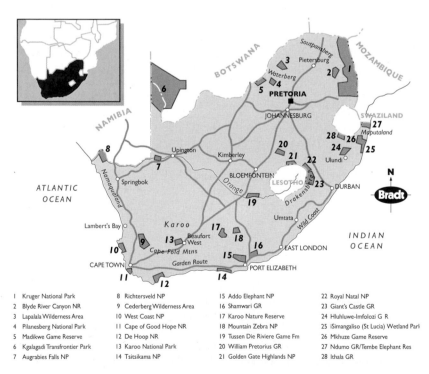

1 Kruger National Park	8 Richtersveld NP	15 Addo Elephant NP	22 Royal Natal NP
2 Blyde River Canyon NR	9 Cederberg Wilderness Area	16 Shamwari GR	23 Giant's Castle GR
3 Lapalala Wilderness Area	10 West Coast NP	17 Karoo Nature Reserve	24 Hluhluwe-Imfolozi G R
4 Pilanesberg National Park	11 Cape of Good Hope NR	18 Mountain Zebra NP	25 iSimangaliso (St Lucia) Wetland Park
5 Madikwe Game Reserve	12 De Hoop NR	19 Tussen Die Riviere Game Fm	26 Mkhuze Game Reserve
6 Kgalagadi Transfrontier Park	13 Karoo National Park	20 William Pretorius GR	27 Ndumo GR/Tembe Elephant Res
7 Augrabies Falls NP	14 Tsitsikama NP	21 Golden Gate Highlands NP	28 Ithala GR

network of national parks is supported by numerous private schemes to restore land and reintroduce indigenous wildlife. For the visitor, South Africa's development means an efficient infrastructure and a sophisticated tourist industry. Everything is on offer: from 'big five' safari lodges, to whale-watching cruises, mountain-hiking trails and spring-flower tours.

The **Kruger Park** is South Africa's conservation flagship, and protects roughly 22,000km² of bushveld in the country's northeastern corner along the border with Mozambique. Its diverse habitats include granite hills, knobthorn-marula savannah, mopane woodland and lush riverine forest, and with at least seven major rivers, it can guarantee a year-round water supply. The

Why struggle through irritating grass? Lions, like tourists, make good use of the Kruger Park's excellent road network. (MU)

Kruger claims to protect a greater biodiversity than any other park in southern Africa, and certainly there is little that isn't found here. Elephant number over 10,000, white rhino have proliferated since their reintroduction from KwaZulu-Natal and the small black rhino population is expanding. Other major herbivores include abundant buffalo, hippo, zebra, giraffe, wildebeest and impala, as well as kudu, waterbuck and many other antelope. The Kruger has southern Africa's largest lion population, along with plentiful leopard and spotted hyena, and stable cheetah and wild dog populations. Many smaller nocturnal mammals can be seen on night drives, while over 500 species of bird have been recorded, with the complete bushveld spectrum being supplemented by more tropical species in the northern Pafuri district. The park also boasts 117 species of reptile and more species of tree than the whole of Europe.

The trouble with the Kruger, some argue, is that it's too developed, too regulated and too popular; not a 'true wilderness' by comparison with parks elsewhere. Certainly it is intensively managed, and has a network of roads and camps large enough to handle an annual quota of over 900,000 visitors. However, it is still easy to lose yourself in the remote back routes and byways of the Kruger, and the heavily oversubscribed three-day wilderness trails offer an outstanding wildlife experience on foot. For a more exclusive safari, several private concession areas along the western border of the Kruger, including **Timbavati** and **Sabi Sands**, share the same habitat and offer fantastic wildlife viewing, with expert guides, from the comfort of luxurious upmarket lodges. Here, for those with the dosh, the 'big five' – and much more – are virtually guaranteed.

West of the Kruger, the land climbs vertiginously over the **Eastern Escarpment** on to the plateau. Mists, ravines and waterfalls characterise the escarpment, while pockets of indigenous forest harbour rare cycads and forest birds. Though much of this habitat has disappeared beneath plantations, reserves such as the spectacular **Blyde River Canyon** protect the best of what's left. On the **highveld plateau**, the grassland has been ravaged by cultivation, but rarities such as oribi, bald ibis and blue swallow cling on in wilder corners, while private game farms have led the way in reintroducing indigenous wildlife, such as blesbok and black wildebeest. To the north, the plateau slopes down towards the **Limpopo lowveld**, where arid thorn bush, with scattered baobabs and aloe-studded kopjes, extends into adjacent Botswana and Zimbabwe. The dusty plain is corrugated with mountain ranges, including the **Soutpansberg**, where baboon, leopard and numerous raptors haunt the cliffs and ravines, and the **Waterberg**, where rhino and sable are among the large mammals reintroduced into the **Lapalala Wilderness Area**. The northwest lowveld also has a number of impressive reintroduction projects, where indigenous ecosystems have been rebuilt on former ranchland. These include the **Pilanesberg National Park**, a 500km² bowl of thorn bush surrounded by extinct volcanoes, and **Madikwe Reserve**, South Africa's third-largest conservation area. Both have the 'big five' and virtually everything else you would hope to find in the Kruger, plus western species such as red hartebeest and brown hyena. Madikwe is also home to a rare successful wild dog introduction scheme.

Further west, the dense bushveld gives way to the arid fringes of the southern Kalahari. Here, the enormous **Kgalagadi Transfrontier Park**, shared with neighbouring Botswana (see page 257), is the best place to see Kalahari wildlife, particularly after the rains, when big herds of blue wildebeest, and smaller numbers of red hartebeest and eland, join resident gemsbok and springbok to crop the seasonal growth along the Auob and Nossob river valleys. This is an excellent park for viewing predators, from the big (lion, leopard, cheetah, spotted and brown hyena) to the not-so-big (bat-eared fox, Cape fox, African wildcat, meerkat and yellow mongoose), while a wealth of raptors includes martial, bateleur and tawny eagles, rednecked and pygmy falcons and secretary birds. In camp, ground squirrels and Brandt's whistling rats burrow among the chalets, while camelthorns harbour owls, black-tailed tree-rats and the huge haystack nests of sociable weavers. Some 150km south of the park, the Orange River plunges 56m over **Augrabies Falls** as it carves a rocky course through an arid volcanic landscape. Here, fauna and flora such as rosy-faced lovebird and quiver tree give an indication of what lies over the nearby Namibian border.

South of the Kalahari and the Orange River lies the **Karoo**; the great bowl of semi-desert scrub and flat-topped sandstone hills that dominates the western third of South Africa. Centuries of sheep farming have denuded this region and evicted its wildlife. Today, dense thickets and rugged outcrops still harbour a few kudu

Permanent waterholes in the Kgalagadi Transfrontier Park sustain a healthy resident population of springbok. After the rains, fresh growth draws migrating herds from the deeper Kalahari – sometimes thousands strong. (PP)

and klipspringer, while smaller predators such as caracal, aardwolf and bat-eared fox may sometimes be glimpsed in the headlights, but this is also a place to seek out the fascinating smaller fauna, from tortoises to toad grasshoppers. The best of the Karoo's wildlife is protected in the beautiful **Karoo National Park**, where mammals such as Cape mountain zebra and springbok have been reintroduced, and the **Karoo Nature Reserve**, with its grand rock formations and aptly named Valley of Desolation. The western Karoo, known as **Namaqualand** (see page 23), is a distinct region of winter rainfall, characterised by its succulent flora and famed for its early spring displays of wild flowers. Its coastline stretches from the northern wastes of the **Richtersveld**, along the Namibian border, down to the tidal mudflats and seabird colonies of the **West Coast National Park**.

Lying at the very tip of Africa, **the Cape** is a unique biogeographical area, with its indigenous fynbos habitat (see page 25) rich in endemic plants. Wildlife highlights include the annual calving of southern right whales in the sheltered bays of the south coast, breeding African penguins on the Cape Peninsula, endangered bontebok saved from extinction in **Bontebok National Park**, and several endemic birds, including Cape sugarbird and Cape rockjumper. Although fertile soil and a Mediterranean climate has seen much of the indigenous habitat lost to orchards and vineyards, a number of excellent small reserves include the **Cape of Good Hope Nature Reserve**, easily accessible from Cape Town, and the larger **De Hoop National Park**, with its endangered blue cranes and Cape vultures. Inland, the **Cape fold mountains** divide the temperate Cape from the hot African interior.

Here a relic population of leopard hunts baboon, rock hyrax and klipspringer, and the mountain fynbos harbours many endemic reptile and plant species.

Heading east, the **Garden Route** is a coastal strip of farmland and lush river valleys, where precious fragments of indigenous forest harbour giant yellowwoods and retiring birds such as Knysna turaco. In **Tsitsikama National Park**, where the forest meets the sea, Cape clawless otters forage for marine invertebrates along the shore. Further east still, dolphins fish the secluded bays of the **Wild Coast**, where tree hyraxes scream at night from hidden tangles of forest. Inland lies the **Addo Elephant Park**, where the Cape's last surviving elephants holed up in dense thorn bush during the 19th century, after a concerted drive to exterminate them. Today the reserve protects over 250 elephants, along with reintroduced buffalo and black rhino and the endemic flightless dung beetle (*Circellium bacchus*). North of Addo, the **Mountain Zebra National Park** was proclaimed in 1937 to protect the last of this rare species. East of Addo at **Shamwari** an ambitious re-introduction project has seen the Big Five restored to their original habitat.

At the centre of South Africa, between the Karoo and the Drakensberg, lie the rolling grasslands and sandstone hills of the **Free State**. Here, despite heavy cultivation, reintroduced antelope such as blesbok and black wildebeest thrive on game farms, and grassland birds such as widows, larks, longclaws and chats abound. Important reserves include the **William Pretorius Game Reserve** and **Tussen-die-Riviere Game Farm**, both of which have seen extensive reintroductions. **Golden Gate Highlands National Park**, in the shadow of the Drakensberg, is famous for its looming sandstone buttresses. Here eland, mountain reedbuck and grey rhebok graze the slopes, while breeding raptors include a few pairs of rare lammergeier.

In eastern South Africa, **KwaZulu-Natal**, its smallest province, offers the greatest diversity of landscape and wildlife. To the west, the **Drakensberg Mountains** raise an imposing barrier of towering crags and montane grasslands. Wildlife is more abundant here than in neighbouring Lesotho (see page 258),

The montane grasslands of the Drakensberg harbour many endemic species. Hiking is the best way to find them. (AZ)

and includes mammals such as grey rhebok, eland and baboon, and birds such as bald ibis and ground woodpecker. Reserves include the postcard-perfect **Royal Natal National Park**, and the wild **Giant's Castle Game Reserve**, where a raptor hide, baited with carcasses, allows close-up viewing of Verreaux's eagle, lammergeier and others.

Northeast of the Drakensberg lies the hot, rugged bushveld of **Zululand**, where the **Hluhluwe-Imfolozi Game Reserve**, proclaimed in 1897, is one of Africa's oldest. This is the rhino heart of Africa: the final retreat of the white rhino after near extermination in the 1930s and now an equally important refuge for the even more threatened black rhino. It also has a broad selection of other large mammals, including the rest of the 'big five' and most major herbivores.

Rare everywhere else, nyala are two-a-penny in the parks of northern KwaZulu-Natal. The hornless female has a sleek chestnut coat, unlike the shaggy male. (MU)

The reserve's varied topography spans grassy hillsides and wooded valleys in the eastern Hluhluwe section, and dry thornveld in the western Imfolozi section – best explored on foot, on one of the celebrated wilderness trails.

Development has claimed much of the southern KwaZulu-Natal coast, but north of Durban, the **isimangaliso (St Lucia) Wetland Park** protects one of southern Africa's most important wetlands. Hippos, crocodiles and waterbirds thrive in the lake system, while mangroves lining the estuary are the haunt of mudskippers and fiddler crabs and a vital breeding ground for reef fish. The dune forest behind the beach supports subtropical species rare elsewhere in southern Africa, including samango monkey, African broadbill (*Smithornis capensis*) and gaboon viper, while reedbuck graze the adjoining marshlands. A mosaic of lake, sandveld and coastal forest, known as **Maputaland**, extends to the Mozambique border and includes the separate ecosystems of **Lake Sibaya** and **Kosi Bay**. The birdlife here is the richest in South Africa, while the beaches are home to breeding turtles. Offshore, an unbroken coral reef harbours countless reef fish, corals and invertebrates, while dolphins surf the breakers and, in early spring, humpback whales breach close inshore *en route* to their Antarctic feeding grounds. Inland, in the shadow of the Lebombo Mountains, **Mkhuze Game Reserve** is a real gem – its lush savannah, towering fig forest, dense sandveld and swampy pans support over 400 species of bird, while large mammals include elephant, black and white rhino, leopard, and a dense population of nyala, the region's most common antelope. Nearby, the luxurious **Phinda Resource Centre**, Mkuzi's upmarket neighbour, has also reintroduced lion, cheetah and elephant. Further north, **Ndumu Game Reserve** has abundant crocodiles, rare suni and an even more impressive bird list than Mkhuze, while the neighbouring **Tembe Elephant Park** has a shy and irascible population of elephants – one-time refugees from the former war in Mozambique.

SWAZILAND

Rocky kopjes punctuate the grasslands of Swaziland's highveld. (KG)

Swaziland is the smallest country in the southern hemisphere. It lies sandwiched between South Africa on three sides and Mozambique to the east, and its total area of 17,365km^2 is substantially smaller than the Kruger Park to the north. However, size isn't everything, and this tiny kingdom embraces a diversity of habitats and wildlife all too often overlooked by visitors to the region.

Perched on the edge of the eastern escarpment, where the central plateau of South Africa falls away eastwards towards the Mozambique floodplain, Swaziland can be divided from west to east into four regions: the western **highveld** is a land of hills, valleys, mists and waterfalls, buttressed by massive granite extrusions; the **middleveld** is a fertile, lower-altitude region of undulating bush and moist savannah, transected by several broad rivers; the eastern **lowveld** is a land of hot, dry savannah – a different world from the well-watered highlands less than 150km away; the **Lebombos** are the chain of rhyolite hills that rise from the lowveld to straddle the eastern border with Mozambique, and continue southwards into Zululand.

With nearly 1.2 million people, Swaziland is relatively populous, and much of its indigenous habitat has disappeared under agriculture – notably forestry plantations in the highveld and sugar estates in the lowveld. But the country still abounds in flora and fauna, including more than 500 species of bird, all of which can be seen in

Malolotja Nature Reserve protects a breeding colony of the rare southern bald ibis. (RH)

a number of delightful and accessible nature reserves. **Malolotja Nature Reserve** in the highveld is a hiker's heaven, with a network of rugged trails that descend from protea-covered hillsides down deep forested ravines, where rare cycads flourish and otters hunt the rivers. Blesbok and black wildebeest are among large mammals reintroduced to the grasslands, alongside indigenous species such as oribi, grey rhebok, mountain reedbuck, aardwolf, serval and baboon. Birds include highveld specials such as bald ibis, blue swallow and ground woodpecker. North of Malolotja, the gorgeous **Phophonyane Falls Nature Reserve** protects a pocket of lush middleveld forest below the sculptured rock contours of the Phophonyane Falls, and is an excellent spot for the elusive Narina trogon (*Apaloderma narina*).

In the populous middleveld, beneath the imposing summit of Nyonyane, the popular **Mlilwane Nature Reserve** has reintroduced antelope, zebra and hippo. Black and crowned eagles overfly this area, while vervet monkeys and greater bushbabies are common residents of the adjacent **Mantenga Falls Nature Reserve.**

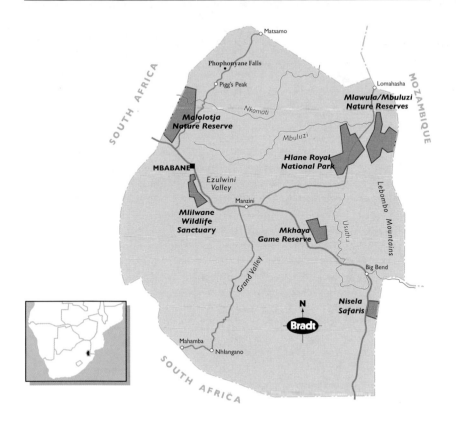

The hot, dry lowveld harbours several reserves that have gone some way to restoring the great game herds of yesteryear. **Hlane Royal National Park**, in the northeast, was proclaimed to protect Swaziland's last free-ranging wildebeest and impala. It now also has white rhino, elephant, hippo, giraffe, numerous antelope and – reintroduced into an enclosed area – the country's only lions. Hlane forms part of the **Lebombo Conservancy**, which extends into the Lebombo Mountains along the Mozambique border. This wild and scenic region also includes **Mlawula Nature Reserve**, where rugged trails offer sightings of wildebeest, zebra, impala, nyala and baboons, and the beautiful little **Mbuluzi Game Reserve**, which has all these, plus giraffe and a small population of hippos in the Mbuluzi River. A few shy leopard and spotted hyena roam throughout the area, though generally only their tracks are seen. Crocodile, python and black mamba are all common, while the prolific birdlife includes martial eagle, African finfoot and Africa's most southerly marabou storks.

Further south, near the Usuthu River, the upmarket **Mkhaya Nature Reserve** has restocked extensively and counts black rhino among its star attractions, alongside white rhino, elephant, giraffe, buffalo, numerous antelope and rich birdlife. **Nisela Safaris**, in the southwest, also has giraffe, zebra and various other herbivores.

ZIMBABWE

Zimbabwe is a landlocked country of great scenic beauty, with impressive wildlife to match. At 390,000km², it is smaller than its neighbours, but its landscapes are hewn on a grand scale, from the roaring abyss of Victoria Falls to the misty peaks of Nyanga. Plum in the centre of the subcontinent, Zimbabwe lies on a high central plateau, the highveld, that falls away north and south to the hot, dry river valleys of the Zambezi and Limpopo lowveld. To the west, Kalahari sands encroach from Botswana, while to the east, the Eastern Highlands form a natural border with Mozambique, rising along the fault line that scars Africa from Rift Valley to Drakensberg. A good communications network and tourist infrastructure means that Zimbabwe's wildlife is readily accessible to the visitor, and there is a host of national parks and private reserves with an excellent conservation record. The widely reported political and economic problems at the start of the 21st century led to a crash in tourism and placed many conservation areas under pressure. Problems remain, but there are signs of recovery and an excellent wildlife experience still awaits the visitor.

The **highveld** is a relatively well-watered, fertile and populous region. In good times it serves as the bread basket of southern Africa, and most major towns are located here, including the capital city Harare. The natural highveld habitat is moist savannah or *miombo* woodland (see page 16), dominated by *Brachystegia* species and punctuated with elaborate granite kopjes. However, most of the country's major conservation areas are down in the lowveld. **Hwange National Park**, in the northwest corner of the country, is Zimbabwe's best-known reserve – on a par with Kruger or Etosha – and comprises 14,650km² of teak forest, thornveld and mopane woodland, with scattered dolomite hills in the northwest. This hot, dry land forms part of the broader Zambezi basin and is contiguous with the Chobe area of neighbouring Botswana, much of whose wildlife it shares. Game is seasonal and the bush very dense in places, but the dry season draws enormous herds of elephant and buffalo to permanent waterholes, while giraffe, zebra, kudu, blue wildebeest and – especially – impala are abundant throughout the year. Despite a history of poaching, both rhino species retain a precarious foothold, and all the major predators occur, including wild dog. Sable are a Hwange speciality, while brown hyena, bat-eared fox and occasional gemsbok all reflect the Kalahari influence. All of this, along with over 365 species of bird, may be encountered on decent tourist roads within the park, or from upmarket lodges in nearby private concession areas.

North of Hwange, the **Zambezi River** flows rapidly eastwards towards the **Victoria Falls**, finally plunging over the 1.7km-wide precipice in a cloud of spray. Despite the tourist circus, the Falls is a rich wildlife area, with baboon, warthog, vervet monkey and banded mongoose roaming hotel grounds, numerous hippo and crocodile in the river, and buffalo, elephant, lion and sable all regularly seen in the neighbouring **Zambezi National Park**. A 'rainforest' created by the spray provides cover for bushbuck, while a walk along the Zambezi may reveal local bird specialities such as trumpeter hornbill, Livingstone's turaco, rock pratincole and African finfoot. Verreaux's eagles hunt dassies in the gorges downstream, where

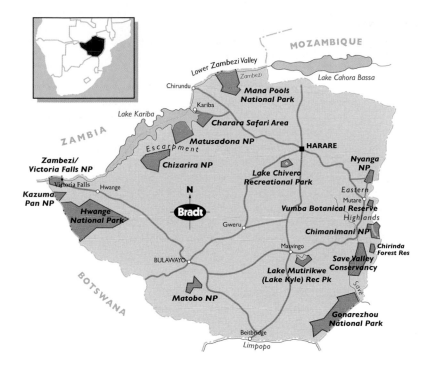

the rare taita falcon (*Falco fasciinucha*) also sometimes breeds. East of Victoria Falls, the Zambezi reaches **Lake Kariba**, an enormous manmade lake created by the damming of the Kariba gorge in 1957 to supply hydro-electric power to Zimbabwe and Zambia. The lake teems with crocodile and hippo and is a haven for waterbirds. Inland lies the dramatic Zambezi escarpment, where **Chizarira National Park** offers wild hiking and impressive views. Big game occurs throughout the area, but congregates towards the east, particularly in **Matusadona National Park** and the neighbouring **Matetsi Safari Area**. Here, large numbers of elephant, buffalo and zebra graze the lake shore, while lion are numerous and the last of the Zambezi Valley's beleaguered black rhino find refuge in the foothills.

Downstream from Kariba lies some of the wildest and most beautiful country in southern Africa, and **Mana Pools National Park** is the jewel in the crown of the **Lower Zambezi Valley**. Between towering escarpment walls – on both the Zimbabwean and Zambian sides – lies a broad floodplain of riverine forest and trapped meander loops, where game masses during the dry season beneath the statuesque ana trees (*Faidherbia albida*). Over 12,000 elephant and 16,000 buffalo invade this area, along with zebra, kudu, eland, sable, bushbuck and the rare nyala. All major predators occur and wildlife in general – from elephants to hyenas and honey badgers – shows no qualms about rooting through the unfenced campsites. Unusual birds include Pel's fishing owl, white-backed night heron (*Gorsachius*

Mana's 'pools' are a chain of oxbow lakes in the open parkland of the Zambezi floodplain. Elephants come here to slake their thirst, while waterbirds – including yellow-billed storks, saddlebills and spoonbills – trawl the shallows for fish. (KB)

leuconotus), Lilian's lovebird (*Agapornis lilianae*) and the elusive Angola pitta (*Pitta angolensis*), while storks, egrets, kingfishers, fish eagles and bee-eaters abound. Visitors can explore the riverfront on foot, though very much at their own risk. Roads are rough, and are closed during the rainy season, but canoe trails are an excellent alternative means of exploring this magical area.

Southern Zimbabwe is dominated by extensive cattle-ranching country, where some free-roaming wildlife – including impala, wildebeest, kudu, giraffe and even cheetah – retains a foothold outside protected areas. South of Bulawayo, Zimbabwe's second city, the **Matobo Hills National Park** protects a remarkable moonscape of granite rock formations, riddled with caves and rock paintings. This provides perfect habitat for Verreaux's eagle, rock hyrax, klipspringer, baboon and an unusually high concentration of leopard. A separate fenced reserve also has rhino, both black and white, and other plains game. In the far southeast **lowveld**, beyond the sugar estates, lies the panoramic **Gonarezhou National Park**, home to wary elephant herds now recovering from years of poaching. Gonarhezhou is a remote and challenging destination, but on its western boundary, the **Save Valley Conservancy Project** has restocked a huge tract of former ranchland to create the largest private reserve in southern Africa (320,000 hectares), which offers an easier big-game experience, with all the trimmings. Since December 2002 Gonarezhou has been linked – via a game corridor – with the Kruger Park in neighbouring South Africa. This ambitious project, known as the Great Limpopo Transfrontier Park (see page 8), aims to re-establish ancient migration routes between the two regions.

By startling contrast with the rest of the country, the **Eastern Highlands** is a region of cool, moist grasslands, mountain streams and deeply forested valleys.

Zimbabwe's highest peak, at 2,790m, is Inyangani, in **Nyanga National Park**. This is hiking country, where sunbirds dart between flowering aloes – including the rare local *Aloe inyangensis* – and Verreaux's eagle hunt the hillsides for dassies. Further south, eland roam the craggy uplands of **Chimanimani National Park**, accessible only on foot. Much of the region's indigenous forest has been cleared for tea estates, but precious pockets remain in such localities as **Vumba Botanical Gardens** and, further south, **Chirinda Forest Reserve**. Here, moss festoons the giant ironwoods, gaboon vipers hunt the leaf litter and samango monkeys crash through the canopy. A wealth of forest birds includes many found nowhere else in southern Africa, such as Swynnerton's robin (*Swynnertonia swynnertoni*) and red-faced crimsonwing (*Cryptospiza reichenovii*).

The lush climate and fertile soils of Zimbabwe's Eastern Highlands have produced a landscape dominated by agriculture, where commercial plantations vie for space with traditional subsistence farming (*above*, RH). Pockets of forest support a rich birdlife, including sub-tropical species such as the silvery-cheeked hornbill (*right*, AZ) – a noisy and ungainly resident of the canopy.

FURTHER INFORMATION

There is a wealth of excellent literature and websites to help you find, identify and enjoy Southern African wildlife. The following brief selection is for both information and inspiration. Many were invaluable in the writing of this book.

FIELD GUIDES

Mammals

Mammals of Southern Africa
Chris and Tilde Stuart, Struik/New Holland

Kingdon Field Guide to African Mammals
Jonathan Kingdon, Academic Press

The Safari Companion
Richard Estes, Russel Friedman Books
(animal behaviour)

Birds

Newman's Birds of Southern Africa
Kenneth Newman, Struik/New Holland

Roberts' Birds of Southern Africa
Maclean, Struik/New Holland
(bulky, but the birder's bible)

SASOL Birds of Southern Africa
Sinclair, Hockey & Tarboton, Struik/New Holland

Other wildlife

Butterflies of Southern Africa
Ivor Migdoll, Struik/New Holland

Snakes and Other Reptiles of Southern Africa
Bill Branch, Struik/New Holland

Southern African Insects and their World
Alan Weaving, Struik/New Holland

Tracks and Tracking in Southern Africa
(a photographic guide)
Louis Liebenberg, Struik/New Holland

Trees of Southern Africa
B & P Van Wyk, Struik/New Holland

The Wildlife of Southern Africa
Vincent Carruthers, Southern Books
(everything from mammals to molluscs)

TRAVEL GUIDES

Bradt Travel Guides

Botswana: The Bradt Travel Guide Chris McIntyre

East and Southern Africa: The Backpacker's Manual
Philip Briggs

Mozambique: The Bradt Travel Guide Philip Briggs

Namibia: The Bradt Travel Guide Chris McIntyre

Swaziland: The Bradt Travel Guide Mike Unwin

Zimbabwe: The Bradt Travel Guide Paul Murray

Other travel guides

Southern African Game and Nature Reserves
Chris & Tilde Stuart, Struik/New Holland

Top Birding Spots in Southern Africa
Hugh Chittenden, Southern Books

BACKGROUND READING

The Complete Book of Southern African Birds compiled Ginn, McIlleron, Milstein, Struik/New Holland

The Complete Book of Southern African Mammals
compiled Gus Mills & Lex Hes;
Struik/New Holland

Desert Adventure Paul Augustinus, Swan Hill Press
(an artist's travels in Botswana and Namibia)

The Kalahari: Survival in a Thirstland Wilderness
Michael Knight & Nigel Dennis,
Struik/New Holland

Kruger: Images of a Great African Park Michael Brett & Nigel Dennis, Struik/New Holland

Okavango: Sea of Land, Land of Water Peter Johnson & Anthony Bannister, Struik/New Holland

Zambezi: River of Africa Mike Coppinger & Jumbo Williams, Struik/New Holland

Cry of the Kalahari Mark and Delia Owens, HarperCollins (hyena researchers in the central Kalahari)

The Sheltering Desert Henno Martin, *Jonathan Ball Publishers* (wartime fugitives surviving the Namib desert)

WEBSITES

www.botswanatourism.co.bw
information and bookings for Botswana

www.namibiatourism.com.na
information and bookings for Namibia

www.kznwildlife.com information and bookings for
KwaZulu-Natal (South Africa) parks

www.sanparks.org information and bookings for
South African National Parks

www.welcometoswaziland.com
information and bookings for Swaziland

www.ecotravel.co.za information for visitors to the
entire region, including wildlife checklists

www.alloutafrica.com
volunteering opportunities and wildlife tours

White rhino, Hlane, Swaziland (MU)

Duelling dung beetles. (MU)